Counselling for
Anxiety Problems

Second Edition

Diana Sanders and Frank Wills

SAGE Publications
London • Thousand Oaks • New Delhi

First published 1992
This edition first published 2003

 SAGE Publications Ltd
6 Bonhill Street
London EC2A 4PU

SAGE Publications Inc
2455 Teller Road
Thousand Oaks, California 91320

SAGE Publications India Pvt Ltd
32, M-Block Market
Greater Kailash – I
New Delhi 110 048

British Library Cataloguing in Publication data

A catalogue record for this book is available
from the British Library

ISBN 0 7619 6574 2
ISBN 0 7619 6575 0 (pbk)

Library of Congress Control Number: 2002108287

Typeset by Mayhew Typesetting, Rhayader, Powys
Printed in Great Britain by TJ International Ltd, Padstow,
Cornwall

Contents

List of figures and tables

List of Figures

List of Tables

Preface

We were both very pleased to be invited to write a revised edition of Richard Hallam's original book, *Counselling for Anxiety Problems*, first published in 1992. We have worked together on a number of projects, including writing *Cognitive Therapy: Transforming the Image*, published by Sage in 1997, which aims to present counsellors with the developments in cognitive therapy which, we believe, make it more attractive for counsellors to use or to integrate with their practice. The opportunity to work on *Counselling for Anxiety Problems* follows on from our theme and interests: to promote the successful developments in cognitive therapy for anxiety problems in a way which is accessible and attractive to the counselling world. We are convinced by the strong evidence that cognitive therapy offers a realistic and effective therapy for our many clients burdened by anxiety problems, while at the same time being aware of the criticisms and dangers inherent in adopting one approach too rigidly. We hope to present the balance of our thinking in this book.

As Richard Hallam states in the preface to the first edition: 'All of us can empathize with what it might be like to suffer from an "anxiety problem".' Anxiety is second to depression as one of the most common psychological problems for which people seek help, from their GPs, counsellors, psychologists, psychotherapists and psychiatrists, and can be pervasive and disabling. Anxiety is an experience of many dimensions, affecting our physiology, feelings, behaviour and patterns of thinking, and is both triggered and maintained by environmental factors. There are many different manifestations of anxiety, the main ones being panic disorder, agoraphobia, specific or social phobias, obsessive compulsive disorder, post traumatic stress disorder, acute stress disorder, generalised anxiety disorder and anxiety problems related to medical conditions or substance abuse. Whatever our feelings and beliefs about the value of diagnosis and diagnostic categories, understanding the kinds of problems our clients are experiencing is vital to being able to offer appropriate solutions. The approach in therapy and counselling for anxiety problems varies for different types of anxiety, and what works for one problem may well be counterproductive for another. This book therefore separates different types of anxiety problems, and describes specific counselling approaches for the different problems, rather than considering anxiety as a single problem.

Why Cognitive Therapy for Anxiety?

In this book, we aim to offer an overview of anxiety problems, to look at how cognitive therapy seeks to understand and conceptualise anxiety, and to offer practical guidelines for working with anxious clients generally, and with different forms of anxiety. The reader may stop at this point and ask whether they wish to subscribe to a cognitive approach to anxiety problems. We would urge that the approach is fully understood and evaluated, for both its strengths and weaknesses, before the reader makes up his or her mind. Why cognitive therapy for anxiety? Firstly, cognitive therapy for anxiety problems has improved in leaps and bounds over the past decade, enabling psychological therapists* to have greater understanding of the problems and offer more targeted therapeutic interventions. This is particularly true for some of the most difficult and complex types of anxiety, such as obsessive compulsive disorder and severe agoraphobia. The essence of cognitive therapy is to understand the meanings that thoughts, events, ideas, physical symptoms or behaviours hold for clients. A careful and detailed understanding of meanings, and specific work targeting meanings that are unhelpful, outdated or out of proportion, is central to cognitive therapy, and we have many ideas and tools at our disposal to help us, and our clients, to do this work. Secondly, good research shows that cognitive therapy is effective in helping people recover from anxiety disorders (Clark, 1999a) and cognitive approaches emerge as the treatment of choice for anxiety (Roth and Fonagy, 1996; DeRubeis and Crits-Christoph, 1998; Department of Health, 2001). Thirdly, it is a parsimonious form of therapy, and clients can feel much better, as well as addressing underlying problems, in relatively few sessions. Fourthly, cognitive therapy is not simply a short-term fix for symptoms (Wills and Sanders, 1997), but can offer clients a real understanding of why they are anxious, what is important to

* We use the term 'psychological therapist' as a generic term to encompass counsellors, psychotherapists, psychologists and others offering psychological therapies.

them, and what keeps the anxiety going, in terms of both present and past experience.

Having extolled the virtues of cognitive therapy for anxiety, we are by no means underestimating the potential for other therapies to significantly help anxious clients. Therapists from different disciplines, be they humanistic, psychodynamic, interpersonal, integrative or cognitive analytic, have their various understandings of anxiety disorders, and can help clients to understand and work with anxiety in different ways. All therapies, we believe, aim to encourage understanding of meanings, but within different conceptual models. In non-cognitive therapies, there is less 'benchmark' research evidence to demonstrate effectiveness. We suspect that this is mainly because the outcome variables, often of symptom reduction, running through randomised controlled trials of anxiety treatments, are different to the outcome variables of non-cognitive therapy. The recent publication in the *British Medical Journal* of studies looking at the effectiveness of counselling for depression is a welcome addition to the research on counselling (Bower et al., 2000; Ward et al., 2000). We hope to offer, in this book, both a 'purist' cognitive understanding of anxiety disorders, based on both clinical and empirical evidence, and ideas and focus from other disciplines. However, we also believe that if cognitive therapy is practised well, it automatically includes many of the active ingredients of other forms of psychotherapy, particularly the qualities of the therapeutic relationship necessary for any therapy to succeed. Cognitive therapy has been called 'the integrative psychotherapy', integrating ideas and approaches from many other therapies, within a cognitive framework or conceptualisation (Alford and Beck, 1997).

Counselling and Cognitive Therapy

How do cognitive methods fit within the counselling world? Demands are growing for counselling to be more accountable and to 'prove itself', particularly in one of the main settings in which British counselling takes place, the National Health Service, where evidence-based practice and accountability are required. As cognitive therapy was formed within the research-minded orbit of Beck and his colleagues (Wills and Sanders, 1997), it has benefited by being able to claim much evidence for effectiveness (Department of Health, 2001). In some cases, the strong evidence for cognitive therapy has been used as evidence against other therapies, and we have watched with increasing alarm as otherwise rational people have spoken of counselling and cognitive behavioural therapy (CBT) in oppositional terms. The writing partnership between the two authors (and hence the approach of this book) is based on the concept that counselling and CBT are complementary skills which empower each other. Diana is a counselling psychologist who finds that cognitive therapy is a powerful aid to her practice. Frank is a counsellor who has found that the psychological dimension of cognitive therapy has sharpened and amplified his counselling practice. Both authors have considerable experience in training and have found that good counselling skills greatly enhance the quality of cognitive therapy practice (Wills and Sanders, 1997).

In operating in the middle ground between counselling and cognitive therapy, there is always the danger of succeeding only in offending both parties. Our basic position is that if counselling is to become truly 'post-tribal' then the focus should be on what different models can learn from each other (Inskipp and Proctor, 1999). While this position will be exemplified throughout the book, a few tasters here might persuade the doubtful reader to read on. Counselling can learn from cognitive therapy the use of structure, the concentration on generalising the gains of therapy outside the sessions and building ongoing evaluation into sessions. Cognitive therapy can learn from counselling that psychological theory can only take you so far, that clients are essentially individuals who often do not react in textbook fashion, and that self-awareness and good skills add immensely to the interpersonal reality of sessions.

Overview of Counselling for Anxiety Problems

This second edition of *Counselling for Anxiety Problems* has a number of key themes, which are different from the first edition, based on thinking and research in the field over the past decade. We focus on developments in describing and conceptualising individual anxiety problems, enabling counselling to be more targeted on the specifics of the problems. We describe counselling protocols for different anxiety disorders, and look at the pros and cons of protocol-based counselling. We bring new thinking in cognitive therapy, including the specifics of thinking in anxiety, the anxiety equation, concepts of safety behaviours where people's attempts to cope with anxiety become part of the problem, and developments in using 'behavioural experiments' as ways of helping people test out their fears and develop new ways of seeing that are less laden with anxiety.

The book is divided into two parts. Part I describes general issues and themes relevant to counselling clients with anxiety. We start with an overview of anxiety problems, what causes them, how they keep going, and how to distinguish the different forms. We outline the cognitive approach to anxiety disorders, and describe how different problems can be conceptualised. The book goes on to look at the therapeutic relationship when working with anxious clients, highlighting particular issues in developing a working alliance. The following chapters describe in detail how to assess anxiety problems, and the tools and techniques that can be used with anxious clients.

Part II is devoted to the nuts and bolts of counselling with different types of anxiety, with separate chapters describing different anxiety disorders and how to adapt counselling accordingly. We cover problems of panic, agoraphobia, worry and general anxiety, specific phobias, social anxiety, health anxiety and obsessive compulsive disorder.* The book aims to provide an overview of working with clients with these problems, giving information about relevant research and further reading. The book concludes with an appendix of resources, self-help organisations, publications and web sites, with information for both counsellors and clients.

The client studies throughout this book are ficticious characters, but are based on examples from our clinical experience, chosen to illustrate specific problems, issues and ways of working.

---

* The problems of post traumatic stress disorder and general stress are well covered in Palmer and Dryden (1995) and Scott and Stradling (2000).

Acknowledgements

We have learned much of what we know about anxiety through our work with colleagues in Oxford and Newport, Wales, and through our clients, and we are very grateful to all concerned. We thank the kind souls who spent time reading and tactfully commenting on drafts: Jacqueline Tonin, Ann Perry, Brian Hunter, Kathy Baines, June Parkinson, Barbara Sanders and Norma Morrison, and thanks to Helen Jenkins for her help with references. We are, as always, supremely appreciative and grateful to our respective spouses – Diana to her husband, Mo Chandler, and Frank to Annie Wills – who have put up with us changing into preoccupied beasts during intensive writing phases, and helped us in all sorts of ways. We are of course appreciative of each other for negotiating and working collaboratively in this joint project. Alison Poyner and Louse Wise at Sage have been supportive and helpful throughout.

Every effort has been made to trace all the copyright holders, but if any have been inadvertently overlooked the publishers will be pleased to make the necessary arrangement at the first opportunity.

Figure 1.1   C.A. Padesky and K.A. Mooney (1990), 'Clinical tip. Presenting the cognitive model to clients', *International Cognitive Therapy Newsletter*, 6: 13–14. Huntington Beach, CA: Center for Cognitive Therapy. © 1986 Center for Cognitive Therapy. Reproduced with permission.

Table 2.1   S. Palmer and W. Dryden (1995), *Counselling for Stress Problems*. London Sage.
A.T. Beck, G. Emery with R.L. Greenberg (1985), *Anxiety Disorders and Phobias. A Cognitive Perspective*. New York: Basic Books.

Figure 2.3   © 1995 Center for Cognitive Therapy.

Figure 2.4   C.A. Padesky and K.A. Mooney (1998), 'Between two minds: the transformational power of underlying assumptions', workshop given at 28th Congress of the European Association for Behavioural and Cognitive Therapies. © 1995 Center for Cognitive Therapy. Reproduced with permission.

Figure 2.5   M. Fennell (1989), 'Depression', in K. Hawton et al. (eds), *Cognitive Behaviour Therapy for Psychiatric Problems: A Practical Guide*, p. 171. Oxford: Oxford University Press. Reprinted by permission of Oxford University Press.

Figure 6.3   A. Wells and A. Hackman (1993), 'Imagery and core beliefs in health anxiety: content and origins', *Behavioural and Cognitive Psychotherapy*, 21 (3): 265–74. Cambridge: Cambridge University Press.

Figure 6.5   A.T. Beck, A.J. Rush, B.F. Shaw and G. Emery (1979), *Cognitive Therapy of Depression*. New York: Guildford Press.
A.T. Beck, G. Emery with R.L. Greenberg (1985) *Anxiety Disorders and Phobias. A Cognitive Perspective*. New York: Basic Books.
D. Burns (1999), *The Feeling Good Handbook*, rev. edn. London: Penguin.

Table 7.1   APA (2000), *Diagnostic and Statistical Manual of Mental Disorders: 4th edition text revision*. Washington, DC: American Psychiatric Association.

Figure 7.1   D.M. Clark (1986), 'A cognitive approach to panic', *Behaviour Research and Therapy*, 24: 461–70. Oxford: Elsevier Science. Reprinted with permission from Elsevier Science.
A. Wells (1997), *Cognitive Therapy of Anxiety Disorders. A Practice Manual and Conceptual Guide*. Chichester: John Wiley & Sons Limited.

Table 7.3   APA (2000), *Diagnostic and Statistical Manual of Mental Disorders: 4th edition text revision*. Washington, DC: American Psychiatric Association.

Table 7.4   A. Wells (1997), *Cognitive Therapy of Anxiety Disorders. A Practice Manual and Conceptual Guide*, pp. 113–18. Chichester: John Wiley & Sons Limited.

Table 8.1   APA (2000), *Diagnostic and Statistical Manual of Mental Disorders: 4th edition text revision*. Washington, DC: American Psychiatric Association.

Figure 8.1   T. Ricketts and G. Donohoe (2000), adapted from A. Wells (1997), *Cognitive Therapy of Anxiety Disorders*, p. 204. Chichester: John Wiley & Sons Limited.

Figure 9.1   APA (2000), *Diagnostic and Statistical Manual of Mental Disorders: 4th edition text revision*. Washington, DC: American Psychiatric Association.

Table 10.1   APA (2000), *Diagnostic and Statistical Manual of Mental Disorders: 4th edition text revision*. Washington, DC: American Psychiatric Association.

Figure 10.1   D.M.Clark and A. Wells (1995), 'A cognitive model of social phobia', in R.G. Heimberg et al. (eds), *Social Phobia: Diagnosis, Assessment and Treatment*, pp. 69–93. New York: Guildford Publications.

Table 11.1   APA (2000), *Diagnostic and Statistical Manual of Mental Disorders: 4th edition text revision*. Washington, DC: American Psychiatric Association.

Figure 11.1   D. Sanders (1996), *Counselling for Psychosomatic Problems*. London: Sage.
P. Salkovskis and C. Bass (1997), 'Hypochondriasis', in D.M. Clark and C. Fairburn (eds), *Science and Practice of Cognitive Behaviour Therapy*. Oxford: Oxford University Press.

Table 12.1   APA (2000), *Diagnostic and Statistical Manual of Mental Disorders: 4th edition text revision*. Washington, DC: American Psychiatric Association.

Table 12.2   Obsessive Compulsive Cognitions Working Group (1997), 'Cognitive assessment of obsessive-compulsive disorder', *Behaviour Research and Therapy*, 35: 667–81. Oxford: Elsevier Science.

Figure 12.2   P. Salkovskis, E. Forrester, H.C. Richards and N. Morrison (1998), 'The devil is in the detail: conceptualizing and treating obsessional problems', in N. Tarrier, A. Wells and G. Haddock (eds), *Treating Complex Cases*, p. 56. Chichester: John Wiley & Sons Limited.

PART I

THEORY AND PRACTICE OF COUNSELLING FOR ANXIETY

1

Introduction

Imagine a world without fear or anxiety. A new-born baby, entering such a world, would not survive long. Without innate fears, such as fear of strangers, the unknown, the unexpected, the dark, creeping insects, or heights, the curious child would soon be unprotected from danger, not knowing that the fear response leads them to safety. The fear response enables us to survive: being rightly fearful of actual dangers leads us all to take care, to seek help, to fight the dangers or run away. Bowlby (1969) described how animals of all species are genetically biased to respond with anxiety to any stimuli that are cues to potential danger to that species. Such threats include not only obvious threats to life, but also anything that endangers our relationships with other people. We are social beings: our need to relate and be close to other humans plays such an important role in the survival of humans as a species that it is not surprising that anxiety can be aroused by anything perceived as potentially disrupting or damaging to our interpersonal relationships, often a central theme in counselling.

The fear response can be overcome in extreme situations, such as bungee jumping, tightrope walking across two hot air balloons, getting friendly with tigers. The authors cannot speak with personal experience about overcoming such extreme dangers, but many of us are familiar with the experience of fear and anxiety, and have been both saved from danger and limited by our individual fears.

Anxiety is the experience of fear which has overtaken the sense of 'objective' danger. The line between, on the one hand, normal, sensible levels of fear, and anxiety on the other is a fine one. Most of us are familiar with the experience of anxiety: anxiety about failing exams, about being thought well of by friends, about travelling to new places and so on. We may feel anxious meeting a new client, giving a talk, writing a book. All these might seem entirely normal and understandable. For an infant to be nervous of strangers and start crying, is normal; for an adult to be so scared of other people's evaluation that the individual is unable to speak to others without being overwhelmed by fear, is classified as anxiety. To be vigilant when crossing the road helps us to avoid stepping in front of traffic; to be so scared of something awful happening that the individual cannot leave the house, is anxiety. In these cases the fear response has spiralled out of control, bringing into play a host of other ways of being: we start behaving differently, avoiding things that make us anxious, trying to cope with the anxiety, or worrying excessively. We are beginning to enter the realm of anxiety disorders.

In this chapter we describe the experience of anxiety, and look at how it can be understood in terms of a network of different interacting elements: cognition, emotion, biology, behaviour and environment. We describe how these elements are dominant to different degrees in different problems: for example, the cognitive activity of worry predominates in generalised anxiety problems; panic attacks may be primarily a physical experience; agoraphobia is characterised by the behaviour of avoidance, such as not leaving the house. We describe the different forms of anxiety our clients may experience and present with, and suggest how diagnostic categories can be useful in helping both to understand our clients' difficulties and to plan our counselling. We look at the evolutionary origins of anxiety, enabling us and our clients to gain a more sympathetic understanding of problems which result from over-effective evolutionary adaptation. We end by looking at how clients with anxiety problems present to counsellors.

Understanding Anxiety

Early psychotherapeutic formulations of anxiety centred on the psychodynamic concept of repression developed by Freud. This was founded on the idea that many anxieties took on the function of helping to repress much deeper worries, often associated with the sexual content of the unconscious. Although these ideas are no longer so influential, they contain several features which have proved of enduring value. Most modern concepts of anxiety, for example, give 'avoidance' a central place in the maintenance of anxiety problems and this involves a type of repression, yet not that of the strictly Freudian mode. Additionally, more recent approaches to anxiety have returned to the concept of trait anxiety, the view that certain people have enduring personality traits which make them more predisposed to developing anxiety disorders. Thus, as Freud proposed, there might be much deeper, personality-based aspects to anxiety than has sometimes been suggested by others who have focused on 'state' anxiety. The behaviourists have been particularly keen to challenge the psychodynamic view of anxiety. Watson and Rayner (1920) in their famous 'Little Albert' experiment, conditioned a little boy to be fearful of white rats, and wrote rather gloatingly that some psychoanalysts would later attribute the boy's fears to a deep-seated anxiety in the unconscious. As will be seen later, while learning does undoubtedly play a role in the development of anxiety disorders, it is far from a complete explanation of the phenomenon.

In more recent models, anxiety is understood to arise when the individual has certain beliefs about the dangerousness of situations which hold important individual meaning for that person. Once situations, events, sensations and mental events are seen as dangerous, a complex web of emotions, actions, physiological reactions and thoughts is formed. This leads to the cycles of anxiety which cognitive therapy has aimed to describe, understand and change (Clark, 1999a). The central theme of anxiety problems, in contrast to other difficulties, is that anxiety is based on anticipating problems in the *future*: 'I will die'; 'I will lose my job'; 'My partner will leave me'; 'I will make a fool of myself.' In this respect, it differs from depression, which tends to be more associated with the *past* – 'I failed'; 'I've been abandoned' – and with hopeless rather than threatening predictions about the future: 'There's no point, nothing will change.' While loss is the key cognitive theme of depression, for anxiety it is the theme of impending threat and danger (Beck et al., 1985).

Elements of Anxiety

Anxiety is a complex, multifaceted experience, a feeling which comes flooding into our whole selves, affecting many different aspects of our being. It was eloquently described by one of our clients as 'a sudden visitor who has a habit of calling unexpectedly and penetrating into every nook and cranny of my house all at once – and who won't take any hints to leave'. Anxiety is a

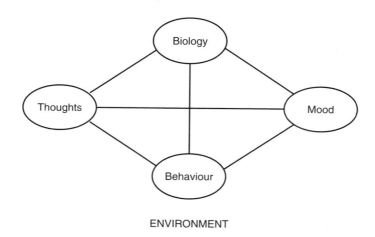

ENVIRONMENT

Figure 1.1   *Generic cognitive models for understanding anxiety*

Source: Padesky and Mooney (1990) (reproduced with permission)
© 1986 Centre for Cognitive Therapy

combination of different elements – cognition, emotion, biology, behaviour and environment – which are linked and trigger one another off. A generic model for understanding anxiety is shown in Figure 1.1, and illustrated by the following short examples:

Anxiety affects us **physically**, with a large number of somatic symptoms:

> An explosive tight feeling in my chest.
> I worried to the point where I began to feel dizzy and sick.
> My heart was racing and seemed to be missing beats.

Anxiety affects the way we **think** and use our mental powers:

> I think to myself 'I'm going trippy again . . . I'm going mad . . . You must think I'm a loony.'
> I thought to myself 'I can't go to work like this, I'd screw up for sure.'
> I thought that if I just keep trying to work this out, I'll work out the answer but my attention kept wandering, I never did work it out.

Anxiety is itself an **emotion** and is strongly related to other emotions. Anxiety can result from other emotions, such as low mood or depression, and can produce many other emotions:

> I felt really happy that Sue wanted to see me but then I began to really worry – perhaps she is just going to hurt me again.

> I used to be really worried and work myself into huge anxiety states about my job but just lately I seem to have given up and I've been feeling so down.

Anxiety affects what we do and how we lead our lives: our **behaviour**:

> I used to worry so much about my business presentations that I started turning up early so I could plan every single aspect of it. One time I got there before the office even opened and the cleaner called security, I was terrified that it would be reported and I'd be seen as an emotional wreck.
> I felt so awful I knew I had to leave the restaurant— I mumbled something and rushed out to the loo, I was in there for ages and then asked my husband to get me home as soon as possible.

There are also enormous **social and environmental** factors in anxiety that both trigger and maintain problems, as Chris's situation demonstrates. Chris was originally in a public sector job which had very little to do with selling services. During the 1990s, when introducing the business ethic to public services was seen as a way of making them more efficient, his job changed so that he had to sell the services of his agency.

> You have to go out and sell the research services we have. I have never had to do things like that. I have had no training for it and, looking back, it wasn't me at all. The other thing is that you kind of came to feel that being a public service person was a bad thing to be, like you were inefficient by definition almost – so this isn't the best frame of mind to go out and sell yourself and the agency. . . . Now it is hinted that your job depends on generating income. There are constant reorganisations and threats of redundancy. There haven't been any yet but several people have gone on early retirement or through ill health.

Anxiety is a complex network of all these elements, all of which are linked by cause and effect to each other. Thoughts, feelings, physiology, behaviour and environment interact with each other in many different ways, each playing varying roles in the different anxiety problems. The elements of anxiety and their interactions are described in more detail in Chapter 2.

Anxiety can be very disruptive, weaving its way into the individual's personal relationships, social life and work. It may begin subtly – beginning to prepare slightly more than usual for giving lectures – but then roller-coasting towards spending hours preparing, lying awake at night worrying about whether the teaching is good enough, and eventually having to give up teaching, because of anxiety.

Types of Anxiety Problems

The thorny issue of diagnosis

Diagnosis is a medical task which creates a simple dichotomy between the sick and the well. (Pilgrim, 2000: 304)

One of the many fascinating aspects of anxiety is its wide and varied expression and the range of problems categorised as 'anxiety disorders'. The panic-prone individual and the worrier may be easier to stereotype than the apparently accomplished socialite who engages in a multitude of hidden 'safety' behaviours to prevent other people's negative evaluation, or the individual with obsessive compulsive disorder who internally tries to control his or her thoughts.

In this book, we divide anxiety problems into the different disorders as described by the diagnostic systems of *DSM–IV* and *ICD 10* (*International Classification of Diseases*, 10th edn.). Since 1952, the American Psychiatric Association has published a *Diagnostic and Statistical Manual* (*DSM*) on a periodic basis, the latest being the revised edition in 2000 (*DSM–IV-TR*). The value and use of *DSM* criteria to understand, categorise or offer therapy to our clients is a rich source of reference and also a minefield, full of debate and lack of resolution, and is a controversial topic in the therapeutic world. We summarise some of the debate and present our rationale for using diagnostic categories in a parsimonious and thoughtful way to guide our counselling practice for anxiety.

Diagnostic categories are much used in psychotherapy research, particularly in cognitive therapy, where researchers attempt to define a uniform population in order to generalise results to other uniform populations. They are also used in psychiatry, where matching the right pharmacological therapy to the problem is vital. However, in the world of counselling and psychotherapy we are aware of the pitfalls. Strawbridge and James (2001) and Sequeira and van Scoyoc (2001) summarise a debate on the issue held by the British Psychological Society Division of Counselling Psychology, listing concerns such as the questionable nature of categories, the power of labelling clients, pathologising distress, the risk of using psychiatric and research categories outside these contexts, and competence of practitioners to diagnose, given limited training in using diagnostic tools.

For a number of reasons, we believe that using some system to classify and categorise the different forms of anxiety our clients are experiencing is important. We would take a pragmatic approach, and look for what may be helpful in using 'labels' and try not to get sucked into being absolute or obsessional. A pragmatic view of diagnostic categories is to see them as useful guidelines for practitioners to help us to understand and help our clients, but also as guidelines to be reviewed critically. We need to avoid reifying diagnostic categories, that is, treating them as more discrete and 'real' phenomena than they actually are. In particular, being clear about clients' problems can help us to gear up our therapy to be more effective. Much of the work on cognitive therapy for anxiety has shown how specific approaches work well for specific anxiety problems, as described in later chapters. Methods of formulation and specific techniques to use have been shown to work differently with different problems: for example, some of the methods to identify and challenge thoughts that are useful for managing panic attacks may become counterproductive and unhelpful for problems such as general anxiety and worry. The importance of clarifying what the problem is in order to find solutions is illustrated in the case of Stan:

Stan was a young man who came for employee counselling for help with excessive anxiety and panic. Initial counselling focused on helping him to deal with his panic attacks. As counselling proceeded, it became clear that feelings of panic mainly happened when he had to meet a new client at work and in other unknown social situations. Stan imagined that other people, especially potential clients, were negatively judging him from the word go. It became clear that his problems lay mainly in the arena of social anxiety, which needed addressing directly in counselling. After realising this, it made more sense to help Stan learn to check the evidence more closely on whether people were judging him, rather than try to help him to stay calm in the face of supposed judgement.

Categories of anxiety problems

DSM–IV (APA, 2000) describes seven main 'anxiety disorders': panic, agoraphobia, specific phobia, social phobia or anxiety, obsessive compulsive disorder (OCD), post traumatic stress (PTSD) and generalised anxiety disorder (GAD). An eighth type of anxiety is health anxiety, classified as hypochondriasis in the somatoform disorders, despite sharing many of the salient characteristics of anxiety problems. Many have characteristics in common, but differ according to whether there are specific triggers for the anxiety, or whether the anxiety appears to accompany the person all the time. All the problems are disabling, distressing and have a significant impact on the person's life; often such problems are misunderstood by others, who cannot understand the level of fear experienced. We describe the different disorders in more detail in the chapters on individual problems, but briefly outline the differences below.

Panic disorder is characterised by episodes of intense physical symptoms of anxiety, arising out of the blue, and that feel frightening and uncontrollable. Often people experience panic and fear in situations in which they have experienced previous attacks. Panic attacks are a 'fear of fear': the individual interprets a range of sensations from the body, including those arising from anxiety itself, as evidence that something catastrophic is about to happen, such as fainting, sudden death, loss of control, or negative social evaluation. The person may develop a range of ways of coping with real or possible attacks, such as keeping control, being extra vigilant for bodily signs and avoiding trigger situations.

Agoraphobia can be understood as a variant of panic disorder: the individual may well suffer from panic attacks, and learns to cope by avoiding situations completely, or by engaging in a wide range of more subtle ways of avoiding facing their fears, such as only going out with someone else, or restricting the range of places visited. People with agoraphobia can appear free of anxiety, but would be stricken with fear if they had to go to feared places.

The main feature of **specific phobias** is strong and persistent fear that is 'excessive or unreasonable', triggered by specific objects or situations: animals, aspects of nature, vomit or blood, for example. The fear leads the person to take lengthy and complex steps to avoid coming into contact with their fears, which interferes with their normal activities. People with specific phobias can be misunderstood, mocked or teased for their fears, but this is to belittle the impact phobias can have on the individual and his or her life.

In **social phobia**, the person fears negative evaluation or judgement from others, and lacks confidence in their own abilities as social beings. This may well ring true for many of us, particularly when put before a critical audience, but for the socially fearful individual any kind of social interaction, including standing next to a stranger at a bus stop or taking shopping through the checkout at the supermarket, can be a huge ordeal. Socially phobic

people engage in many subtle techniques tha
themselves as socially incompetent, by focusin_
than the social situation. They use their bad feeli.
that they are coming across badly, and believe th.
judged because they are judging themselves. Man_
phobic clients are skilled at avoidance.

Generalised anxiety disorder is characterised by worry: t.
individual worries about many everyday events and possibilities,
the worry feeling out of control, persistent and severe. Generalised anxiety is also characterised by many of the physical and
emotional symptoms of anxiety – the individual may feel anxious,
on edge and tense most of the time. The themes of their worries
may be of inability to cope, and of personal vulnerability.

The central theme of **health anxiety** concerns interpreting bodily
signs, past and present, as indicators of serious illness, leading the
individual to check for illness and seek reassurance. Both panic
and health anxiety may be seen as a fear of the consequences of
physical changes, but in panic disorder the threat is seen as
imminent, whereas in health anxiety the danger may be no less,
but round the corner. The individual with health anxiety worries
excessively about their own health, the possibility of disease and
any bodily symptom, and tries to allay such anxiety by repeatedly
checking, going to doctors, reading up on their problems, and
discussing them with others.

Obsessive compulsive disorder can be complex and difficult to
understand. It is marked by a range of obsessions and/or compulsions, which take up a large proportion of the individual's
time and energy, and cause distress to themselves and others.
Most people with OCD can recognise that their obsessions
and compulsions are unnecessary or out of proportion, but feel
unable to stop. Some people 'ritualise', engaging in repeated ritual
behaviours; others 'ruminate', worrying about their thoughts and
engaging in mental ways of controlling their thoughts or behaviours, to stop the thinking. The central themes involve a sense of
over-responsibility for self or others. The individual fears that their
actions or thoughts themselves can have untoward consequences,
and this leads to a variety of ways to stop, control or neutralise
them. For example, they feel responsible for others' health, which
may result in excessive rituals of washing and cleaning to avoid
harm; or they feel responsible for controlling the bad thoughts that
they have about others.

Anxiety and Evolution: a Necessary Part of the Human Experience

is a mistake to see the anxiety response to threat as necessarily a pathological process. Anxiety has a strong evolutionary survival value and is therefore likely to be 'hard-wired'. All the different components of anxiety – somatic, cognitive, emotional and behavioural – are, in essence, primitive reactions to danger, which serve to keep us safe and thereby promote our survival (Beck et al., 1985; Beck, 1991).

> When we consider the common fears of childhood – falling, being injured, drowning, suffocating, the dark, deep water, and so on – we can see that some of these at least may serve to deter the child from venturing into unfamiliar or dangerous places before he has the requisite abilities and skills . . . the interpersonal fears, such as fear of strangers or of separation from a caretaker, may be conceived of in similar terms . . . the fear of negative evaluation seems to serve as a deterrent to behaviour that will alienate other people. (Beck et al., 1985: 13)

We may all be born with innate fears, such as fears of the dark, of strangers, creeping insects, strange noises, or of blood or vomit, which later on in life can be evaluated more rationally in order to overcome the innate fear response. Specific phobias may represent such innate fears which the individual has not grown out of.

Beck et al. (1985) describe many of the protective mechanisms to deal with specific dangers, all of which prompt the individual to engage in behaviours that will lead to safety. These include:

- autonomic responses designed to repel an attack, such as a pronounced drop in blood pressure and fainting for those with a fear response to needles or blood injury – a mechanism designed to prevent further blood loss after injury;
- responses designed to stop the individual going further into a 'danger zone', such as automatically grabbing at a stationary object if the person feels he or she is falling (such as the individual with panic attacks who clings on the supermarket trolley to prevent 'passing out' in public);
- gastrointestinal responses to the fear of having eaten something noxious;
- reflexes which stop us falling, such as the so-called 'visual cliff' reflex, discovered by research conducted in the 1960s (Walk and Gibson, 1961) that showed that babies and young children, as well as a host of other infants including turtles and kittens, immobilise when they come to the edge of a

ledge, thereby avoiding falling off (although not all parents of young children or kittens would agree with or trust such a reflex).

The way in which we think when anxious also has evolutionary advantage. Take, for example, our ancestors growing up on the plains of Africa during the Stone Age. It would make more sense for the hunter, hearing a loud noise in the background and prepared only with a club, to appraise the situation by overestimating the danger and underestimating their ability to cope, than vice versa. The thought, 'Oh no, a huge mammoth is coming my way at speed. I'm going to be trampled and eaten. I need to run or hide or get ready . . .' is likely to lead the intrepid hunter to prepare for effective action, and a hot dinner and is safer than a more relaxed approach: 'Maybe it's a mammoth, probably just a baby one, I can handle it, no problem' (apologies for anthropological inaccuracies).

Overall, anxiety is necessary to all animals and adaptive for humans in their evolution. This may be of no comfort at all to those in the throes of severe panic attacks or disabling worry, but its hard-wired and important function can enable clients to normalise their experiences. It may be of comfort to know that anxious genes have survival value. Whereas worrying insufficiently about your personal safety can lead to death, worrying too much mostly leads to a lot of inconvenience – although not, unfortunately, for the boy who cried wolf. A false negative (dismissing a real danger as an unreal one) is potentially much more dangerous than a false positive (identifying a false danger as a real one). An analogy may be found in setting the sensitivity of a burglar alarm. If the alarm is too sensitive, then you will get many false alarms and may often have to get up in the middle of the night. If, however, you go too far the other way and adjust the alarm so that it is not sensitive enough, then you may end up being burgled. We offer these analogies as ways for our clients to see that the solutions for anxiety problems lie in making adjustments to a normal response, to make it more appropriate to the situation, rather than to eliminate totally a 'pathological' response.

Anxiety: Facts and Figures

Anxiety problems are extremely common, but may go unrecognised as such both by the individual and by others, including general practitioners and other doctors: the range of disorders, and the fact that people often present with physical or social problems as the first sign, may mask the true nature of their difficulties. As we discuss below, anxiety often goes hand in hand with other problems, including depression, and it can be unclear which is the major problem for which the individual is seeking help.

Around one-quarter to one-third of people consulting in general health care have some form of psychological difficulty, anxiety disorders and depression being the most common (Brown and Barlow, 1992). Research summarised by Jim White (2000) shows that 28 per cent of the American population will suffer from anxiety at some stage in their lives; in the UK, around one in six adults will experience anxiety problems, with mixed anxiety and depression making up 50 per cent of this figure, and generalised anxiety, 20 per cent. The four most common symptoms of anxiety are tiredness, sleep problems, irritability and worry (Jenkins et al., 1998). From our experience in counselling practice, both in primary care and private, we have found that the earlier a client seeks and receives help for one anxiety problem, particularly panic attacks or simple phobia, the less likely the client is to experience a range of other problems. We see many clients with panic attacks, for example, where the first attack may have occurred in relative isolation, but the resulting anxiety and avoidance lead to a host of other problems, including low mood and difficulties with work and relationships. Someone may have a very specific phobia, such as a fear of vomit, which can begin to permeate into so many other areas that these problems also need addressing early in counselling.

Research on gender and prevalence of anxiety disorders and the rate at which men and women seek help raises interesting issues. If one looks at statistics on those seeking help for anxiety problems, it seems that most anxiety problems are more prevalent in women than in men. For example, twice as many women as men seek help for panic problems or other phobias. This is not the same as saying that anxiety is more frequently suffered by women than by men, but it may be more socially acceptable for women than for men. Although such views may be changing in line with other gender stereotypes, men are still expected to function without anxiety and thereby to show their supposed 'emotional toughness'. The exception to this finding is social phobia, where equal numbers of men and women seek help. It may, therefore, be more acceptable for men to admit to being socially phobic than to being anxious about other aspects of life: perhaps the stereotype of women being good with people and men good with everything else, permeates our help-seeking. There are also cultural differ-ences. Kendall and Hammen (1998) report that agoraphobia in Japan and India is much more of a male problem, because of cultural beliefs that 'a woman who is homebound is not con-sidered abnormal'.

Anxiety problems very often co-exist with other psychological difficulties. If we use diagnostic categories, 70 per cent of those meeting *DSM* criteria for one anxiety disorder also met criteria for another, with 90 per cent of those with generalised anxiety dis-order also meeting criteria for other disorders (summarised by White, 2000). Anxiety also comes hand in hand with depression, and with other difficulties such as abuse of alcohol. The fact that one anxiety problem often co-exists with another anxiety problem presents challenges both for the use of strict diagnostic categories and for the development of individual client formulations, which we discuss in later chapters. Suffice to say at this point, the complexity of difficulties with which our clients present makes it necessary not only to try and understand the key elements, both common and unique, to the different 'diagnostic' problems, but also to be cautious in trying to rigidly categorise our clients.

Anxiety and Counselling

For counsellors, around 40 per cent of their caseload can be for problems with anxiety (Harvey et al., 1998). The journey towards counselling may well start with GP consultations. Clients present to their GPs with a variety of physical symptoms: the initial call for help may be with difficulty sleeping, weight loss, irregular heart beats, skin rashes or headaches, or many physical symptoms characterising panic attacks. Clients may also present with more overt behavioural problems, such as extreme avoidance of parti-cular situations or events, agoraphobia, or the complex beha-viours seen in obsessive compulsive disorder. Within the context of an independent practice, clients may not arrive with the label 'anxiety' attached to their referral, which is frequently a self-referral. The anxious client often conveys anxiety in the way they make their referral. There is frequently an urgency for an initial meeting to take place. The client is greatly primed for action and getting an appointment can be the focus for this action. Referral details may include fears about the consequences of the anxiety: 'I'm going mad', 'I'll get ill if I go on like this', 'I'm breaking down'.

Many clients come directly to us for help with anxiety prob-lems. Others come for help because of difficult life events, which they see as their main problems. They may describe themselves as stressed, burned out or unable to cope.

> John came for counselling because his marriage was breaking down. He showed many of the symptoms of anxiety but attributed these to his stressful situation. He responded well to crisis counselling and significantly improved after the six sessions allowed by his employee counselling scheme. He returned for further counselling three years later, when he was about to re-marry and had started to experience unexplained panic attacks. He and his counsellor concluded that he had had a degree of panic disorder for many years but it was only precipitated into an acute state by big life changes. He then addressed the panic directly and made long-term gains.

John's case shows us that it may take some time before it becomes clear that general life stresses may be concealing specific anxiety problems. Clients may also come with a combination of anxiety and depression, both triggering off and maintaining the other. Having more complete knowledge of anxiety disorders and problems helps the counsellor to make distinctions between environmental stresses and underlying anxiety problems and to select appropriate interventions.

Anxiety is a common, normal response to danger, taken to extremes, and depends on the individual's appraisals of the threat in different situations. Anxiety as an appropriate response to danger may have significant evolutionary advantage, enabling us to survive in a hostile world, but being able to distinguish different types of danger is central to reacting with appropriate 'fight or flight' rather than being paralysed with anxiety in daily life. There are many different forms of anxiety, and understanding these types enables us to offer more targeted forms of help. While using diagnostic categories can help us to tailor therapy to the individual, we need, also, to be aware of some of the pitfalls of over-using diagnostic categories at the expense of fully understanding the individual. How to conceptualise or formulate the individual client's difficulties, based both on our knowledge of the anxiety problem in general and on our understanding of the client, is covered in the next chapter.

2

Conceptualising Anxiety

'That's a great deal to make one word mean,' said Alice in a thoughtful
tone.
'When I make a word do a lot of work like that,' said Humpty Dumpty, 'I
always pay it extra.'
'Oh!' said Alice. She was much too puzzled to make any other remark.
'Ah, you should see 'em come round me of a Saturday night,' Humpty
Dumpty went on, wagging his head gravely from side to side: 'for to get
their wages, you know.' (Lewis Carroll, *Through the Looking Glass*)

Central to our understanding of anxiety is the theme of danger,
whereby the individual appraises a range of situations or symptoms as dangerous, setting up a maintenance cycle of anxiety.
Understanding how anxiety fits together is the aim of conceptualisation or formulation: providing a working map of the client's
difficulties to guide our understanding and counselling. We focus
throughout the book on the maintenance of anxiety, rather than
on the search for the client's early experiences which may underlie the anxiety problem. The conceptual model for anxiety starts
with the day-to-day aspects of anxiety and what keeps it going,
and then moves upward to consider background beliefs and
assumptions which may underlie the problems, and where such
beliefs and assumptions may have come from. In this sense it is a
'bottom-up' model. Much of the effective work in dealing with
anxiety problems starts with the day to day aspects, and much
evidence shows that this work is both effective and sufficient to
make long-term changes. Some of the clients with longer-term
problems may need work focusing on early experience and their
background beliefs and assumptions, but even for these clients we
start with the maintenance cycles.

   In this chapter, we look in greater detail at the key elements of
the conceptualisation of anxiety: physical aspects, thoughts, emotion and behaviour and how these interact with each other. We
describe some of the more recent understandings of cognitive
processes in anxiety, including concepts of metacognition, and
describe recent thinking on how behaviours can keep anxiety

going. We discuss how to build up the elements of conceptualisation into a general working model for the individual client, integrating what we know generally about the particular anxiety problem, and what we learn about our specific client as an individual. In later chapters, we describe varying conceptualisations for different anxiety problems.

Understanding What Keeps Anxiety Going

A general model of anxiety is shown in Figure 2.1. The model consists of several elements: central appraisals of danger and anxious thoughts, anxious feelings and the physiological response of anxiety, and behaviours to try to cope with danger. The cycle of anxiety is located within an *environment* where certain events may be connected with provoking anxiety. Environmental features such as work performance and work relationships can in turn be affected by the client's anxiety. The main elements of anxiety, anxious feelings and physiology, anxious thoughts and anxious behaviours, interact with each other, creating the vicious cycles of anxiety which keep it going. During assessment of anxiety problems, described in Chapter 5, client and counsellor aim to build up a unique picture of the client's difficulties, bearing in mind the likely interactions of different key elements.

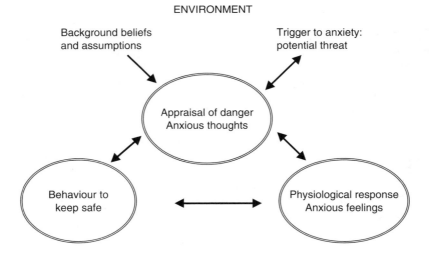

Figure 2.1 *Model of anxiety*

Table 2.1   *Physical sypmptoms of anxiety*

Palpitations, increased heart rate	Irregular heart beat and pulse	Breathlessness, increased breathing rate
Shortness of breath	Lump in throat	Choking
Gasping	Chest pains	Feeling faint, dizzy
Numbness or tingling in hands and feet	Numb legs and arms	Stomach pains, cramps
Increased bowel frequency	Need to urinate	Dry mouth
Sweating hands	Jumpiness	Startled response
Hot and cold	Sweating	Shaking
Muscular twitches	Aches and pains	Tiredness
Sleep disturbance	Exhaustion	Headaches
Twitchiness, tics	Loss of appetite	Increased appetite
Vomiting	Weakness	Skin rashes
Feeling unreal, derealisation, depersonalisation	Inability to concentrate	Feeling 'weird'

Sources: Palmer and Dryden (1995), Beck and Emery (1985) and our life experience

The prominence of different elements varies according to the characteristics of different anxiety problems: in panic, for example, physical symptoms and emotions of anxiety and fear predominate; people are not always aware of the cognitive component without careful examination of what is going on. In general anxiety, in contrast, people can feel many physical and emotional symptoms of anxiety, but also be acutely aware of, and more distressed by, the never-ending cognitive component, in the form of relentless worries. In agoraphobia, and social phobia, the behaviour of avoidance may predominate; obsessive compulsive disorder involves many behavioural rituals and compulsions.

The feelings of anxiety: physiology and emotion

Anxiety is characterised very much by the physical component of fear, the 'fight or flight' adrenaline response going into overdrive in the apparent absence of appropriate triggers. For many anxiety problems, clients initially describe their difficulties in terms of a range of physical symptoms. The list can seem endless, and incorporate all the various bodily structures and functions altered by the 'fight or flight' adrenaline response. Some of the possible symptoms are summarized in Table 2.1.

Whatever the particular symptoms of anxiety or stress the individual experiences, the role within vicious cycles of anxiety will vary depending on the particular interpretation and response to the symptoms. For example, some people who experience palpitations, muscle tension, tiredness and sleeping difficulties will conclude that they are getting over-stressed and tired out by life. They will see the triggers to their problems as external and to some extent soluble, and take measures to reduce their stress. For another client, the same set of symptoms, such as experiencing changes in heart rate, could be interpreted as meaning that something is seriously wrong, leading to cycles of panic or health anxiety: thus, the path to anxiety depends on the interpretation.

Cognitive processes in anxiety

The central themes of anxiety result from preoccupation or 'fixation' with the concept of danger, along with an underestimation of the personal ability to cope (Beck et al., 1985). The theme of danger pervades all levels of cognition, thinking and belief – moment-to-moment thoughts, negative automatic thoughts, but also the individual's assumptions and schema. The theme of danger in anxiety contrasts markedly with themes of loss, hopelessness, self-deprecation and worthlessness which characterise depression, or themes of emptiness, pointlessness and sorrow that characterise loss and grief. When we meet an individual client, we may meet several of these themes at once. For example, it is not unusual for people to start off anxious and fearful, and later to experience depression, perhaps as a result of a long period of feeling fear with no respite. Or, loss and grief can lead to anxiety about coping, about the future and how the individual will survive alone.

The way of thinking when anxious is characteristic of a range of what have been called 'cognitive distortions' or 'thinking errors', and which have been linked to the development of psychological problems since the beginning of cognitive therapy (Beck, 1976; Padesky, 1994; Wills & Sanders, 1997; Burns, 1999). While the terms 'errors' or 'distortions' may seem judgemental, the way of thinking can, when analysed rationally, be seen to be far from objective reality: in the cool light of day, we are able to see that our thoughts were overestimations, over-generalisations, black and white, or overly negative, although at the time they seemed highly congruent and likely. The thoughts that come to mind when we are anxious or distressed seem to occur of their own volition, hence the descriptive term 'negative automatic thoughts'. We also think in images, which occur spontaneously and uncontrollably and increase the individual's sense of danger (Hackmann, 1997, 1998; Hackmann et al., 1998, 2000).

The content of negative automatic thoughts and images in anxiety arises from a balance between different ways of thinking:

- overestimating the likelihood of occurrence of an event
- overestimating the cost of an event
- underestimating how the person may cope with the situation
- underestimating rescue factors – how others may help, for example.

These four can be put into an equation (Salkovskis, 1996a), which will be unique to each client:

$$\text{anxiety} = \frac{\text{perceived likelihood that threat will happen} \times \text{perceived cost/awfulness}}{\text{perceived ability to cope} + \text{perceived rescue factors}}$$

We can see that the greater the likelihood and cost of an event, and the less the individual sees himself as able to cope, or the fewer 'rescue factors' around (such as the less others are seen as helpful), then the greater the anxiety. It is important to under- stand which part of the equation is most important to the individual. For example, a risk may be seen as highly unlikely, but hold a very big cost, such as fears of disease in health anxiety; or situations may be seen as highly likely, and very costly, such as fainting and making a fool of oneself when panicking – many people when anxious totally ignore or 'forget' that other people are likely to help, or that the person has a wealth of internal resources with which to cope. Two vignettes illustrate different appraisals overestimating the likelihood of unlikely events and underestimating rescue factors.

- **Over-estimating the likelihood that threatening events will occur**

  Zoe had been unable to drive or to get to work following involve- ment in a severe traffic accident on the motorway. Unfortunately, she lived in a place where reaching work without using a motorway was extremely difficult. It became apparent that she was suffering from PTSD and she began to feel extreme panic and 'relived' the accident whenever she was near a car. In her first therapy session, she estimated that the chances she would have an accident were 80 per cent, whereas realistically the chances of being involved in a motorway accident are much less even than 1:100,000.

- **Overestimating costs and underestimating rescue factors in tricky situations**

  Ron suffered from a debilitating form of social anxiety, which meant that he often gave up on things he would like to do, such as going to parties. He thought that he would make a fool of himself by making mistakes and gaffes and that when he did, people would be horrible to him: that is, no one would be there to help, or be on his side. He was quite sure that he would die from embarrassment, and lose all his friends. After much encouragement from his therapist, he invited a friend to go for coffee with him and deliberately spilled his coffee in front of her. He was immensely relieved to realise that his friend was very helpful and sympathetic to his plight, and indeed shared experiences of dropping various foods and beverages in embarrassing situations, while nevertheless managing to live and retain friends.

We need to understand which of these factors are the most significant for the individual client: the fact that an event is highly unlikely does not reassure some people because of its high cost – for example, the health-anxious individual who has led an unblemished life but is worried about HIV infection. A highly likely event is not anxiety-provoking for some individuals because of its perceived low cost or high benefits – for example skiing off piste in avalanche areas. Interestingly clients' way of evaluating costs and probabilities can be erratic, an example being the health-anxious individual who smokes.

Types of cognitive activity

Wells (1997) suggests that it is valuable to distinguish between different cognitive processes such as negative automatic thoughts, worry and obsessions. Although to the client these may initially all seem like one thing, each may be generated and maintained by different processes. As we will consider throughout the book, the solution to each is very different. It is valuable, for example, to reflect on our negative automatic thoughts, and try and come up with a more realistic and helpful way of thinking ('I know I feel like I'm about to die, but I know really that I'm just anxious'), but trying to record and answer all our worrying thoughts or obsessional ruminations can make things much worse. Instead our task is to look at the process, not the content. If we do not distinguish our client's negative thoughts from the process of worry, we can find ourselves in the familiar position of enabling a client to find an alternative to one thought, only to be swamped with the torrent of other worries sweeping aside all attempts at rationality.

Further, the mode in which worries, thoughts or obsessions are experienced may vary: Wells and Morrison (1994) found that in 'normal' populations, worries are rated as more verbal, and obsessions are seen more as part of the imagination; worries lasted longer than obsessions, were less involuntary and more realistic than obsessions. Obsessional thoughts are often alien to people's view of themselves, and seem senseless – for example, a parent holding a young baby may get a sudden fleeting thought about harming the baby, in the complete absence of any desire to do harm; a driver may get a sudden thought about running over a pedestrian. Understandably, such thoughts and images can cause a great deal of distress, as described in more detail in Chapter 12 on obsessive compulsive disorder. Worries, on the other hand, may have a 'what if . . .' quality: 'What if I'm not a good enough parent and do harm to my children . . .?' 'Driving is so dangerous, I might run someone over and that would be terrible . . . .' These are discussed further in our chapter on worry (Chapter 8). The main point of relevance here is that the way of working with clients differs according to whether their main difficulties in the cognitive realm are negative automatic thoughts, worries or obsessions. We need therefore to be clear about the different cognitive processes that may be going on for the individual client.

Links between thoughts and feelings

Once we start thinking in an anxious way, our methods of taking in information and processing it are altered. For example, when very anxious the individual is on the lookout for any signs of danger, and likely to see danger in situations which others may ignore completely or see as benign. The conclusions drawn about information will also be biased by the style of thinking. Other moods affect the way we think and process information: for example, in depression, thinking is globally negative, affecting how people see themselves, the world, the past and future. Cognitively based therapy has been interpreted, we think wrongly, as saying that we feel how we feel because of how we think. In fact, from our understanding of cognitive theory, our own experience and that of our clients, the link works both ways. The causal argument may be a red herring, because for the low, upset or anxious individual, what is causing what may be less important than understanding how things can change. When we are depressed our low mood creates a low, negative pattern of thinking, which in turn makes us feel bad. The links between our feelings of fear and anxiety, and our thoughts, work both ways. We feel anxious and therefore think anxious thoughts; our anxious thoughts make us feel anxious (Wells and Matthews, 1994).

Theories of metacognition

One of the exciting new developments in cognitive therapy is the work on metacognition, and how this influences emotional distress. The work has arisen from cognitive and developmental psychology, with a consequent stream of theories, complex flow-charts and research. However, the basic ideas are, we think, reasonably common-sensical. Wells summarises metacognition as 'thinking about thinking: any knowledge or cognitive process that is involved in the appraisal, monitoring, or control of cognition' (Wells, 2000: 6).

Metacognition has three components:

- metacognitive knowledge, the individual beliefs people hold about their own thoughts (worrying is uncontrollable and dangerous; worry is a useful way of solving problems);
- metacognitive experiences, the meaning people give to think-ing processes ('An unpleasant thought just popped into my head, it must mean I'm a bad person or going mad');
- metacognitive control strategies, attempts to control thinking, such as trying to stop thoughts.

Thus, we need to take into account not only what people think, the content of thoughts such as may be collected in thought diaries (p. 85), but what people think, believe or feel about the thinking itself. 'In exploring thinking styles, we will need to focus on beliefs about thinking and the individual's strategies for controlling attention and thinking that arise from metacognitive beliefs' (Wells, 2000: 15).

The information that arises from metacognition is often experienced as subjective feeling: a feeling of knowing, a sense that something 'feels right'. For example, a sense of 'certainty' that something bad is going to happen will lead to anxiety; and people with obsessive checking rituals may need to repeat them until it 'feels right'. People often use their feelings as a basis for their thinking and action: 'I feel afraid, therefore there must be some-thing wrong.' For many, feelings have far more impact on beliefs and behaviour than thoughts. Metacognitive theory enables us to understand the common human phenomenon of feelings leading to thoughts as well as thoughts leading to feelings. Recent research has backed up the idea that changes in our feelings lead to changes in thinking and the way that we think (Wells and Matthews, 1994; Wells, 2000). Metacognition gives us a way of understanding and working with this common phenomenon when working with clients, that they understand something is incorrect on an intellectual level, but it still feels right ('I know I am not really a worthless worm, but I feel like one all the time'). In this case, metacognitive theories allow us to understand that the individual's thinking style is to interpret feelings as evidence for accuracy of a thought or belief. We are able then to work both on an experiential and rational level (Epstein, 1994).

Behaviour and Anxiety

A man was sitting on a train, carefully folding pieces of paper and then throwing them out of the window. A fellow passenger asked him why he was doing this. 'It keeps the elephants off the line', was his reply. 'But there aren't any elephants on the line', the passenger responded. The man responded, 'See, it works.' (Personal communication, Oxford Psychology Department)

Once we perceive danger, by deeming a situation, event, bodily change, thought or image as evidence of some kind of threat, it makes sense that we will take evasive action to protect ourselves. Many of our responses to threat, in terms of our thought processes and behaviour, are active strategies and plans to protect ourselves from danger (Beck et al., 1985; Wells and Matthews, 1994). If we saw a runaway bus careering towards us on the pavement, we would find ourselves running away very quickly, without even thinking about it.

The problem in anxiety is that our appraisals are often out of proportion to the 'true' danger of the event, and therefore the evasive actions may be unnecessary and unhelpful. When anxious, people will avoid situations, get out of the situation at the first sign of anxiety, breathe heavily in order to calm down, sit down or clutch on to something to avoid passing out, gain reassurance from another person, focus entirely on the self in order to keep in control and avoid being seen in a negative light. The individual may always perform tasks in a certain way in order to cope and avoid change. The specific behaviour varies according to the specific anxiety. While avoiding things that scare us or make us feel uncomfortable, inadequate or ill, makes perfect sense on one level, such behaviours are very unhelpful and can serve to maintain the anxiety.

The notion of 'safety behaviours' was introduced by Paul Salkovskis (Salkovskis, 1991, 1996a, b) to explain why the individual can experience repeated situations in which they 'survive' such fears as dying of a heart attack when feeling anxious, and yet not 'learn' that their body sensations are simply benign anxious feelings rather than signs of imminent danger and death. The safety behaviours that individuals use protect them against danger as they see it, but prevent them learning that the situation was not dangerous after all. Safety behaviours also serve to keep the individual focused on themselves, their anxious feelings and fears, and so increase the sense of anxiety and danger. In earlier models of anxiety, behaviours such as trying to relax, breathing deeply, trying to calm down or removing oneself from the anxiety-provoking situation may have been seen as helpful coping strategies; in more recent models, these may at times be unhelpful in the long term. We discuss the thorny issue of when a behaviour is a safety behaviour rather than a useful way of coping with life, in Chapter 5.

> Maureen had suffered panic attacks for many years, when she would feel light headed, shaky, sweaty, with a sense of being disconnected from everything around her. She believed that these symptoms were a sign that she was going to pass out, an event which represented an extreme personal danger to her: as a child, she had been bullied at school and one day when she was going down with flu she fainted in the class. The school bullies used this as further ammunition against her, doing mock faints when she walked by. The fear of fainting and 'making a fool of myself' persisted into Maureen's adult life; during a period of stress, she suffered a panic attack apparently 'out of the blue' when she felt very faint and unwell. As a result, Maureen developed strategies to stop herself from fainting; when she felt panicky, she quickly sat down, clutched on to something, and tightened up her legs muscles to stop herself keeling over. She would also breathe deeply and slowly to try and calm down. Although such responses make sense in terms of Maureen's belief that she was going to faint, they stopped her learning that it is nearly impossible to faint in a panic attack, that her strategies in themselves made her feel more uncomfortable (breathing deeply made her hyperventilate and feel more dizzy), and that even if she were to faint, as an adult she could cope much better with the event, and that most other people would be sympathetic and offer her help.

During the chapters on specific problems, we describe a range of safety behaviours that people use to try and control their anxiety which may be unhelpful, such as trying to suppress worrying thoughts or obsessions, avoiding problems or trying to control themselves in social interactions.

The notion of safety behaviours has to a large extent revolutionised the way we understand and work with anxiety problems in cognitive therapy, indicating why and how strategies to keep ourselves safe are unhelpful and keep anxiety going (Wells, 1997):

- The behaviours themselves may exacerbate physical symptoms, which then may be taken as evidence that something bad is happening: for example, when flying, the individual may clutch on to the seat, tense up, stare fixedly at a point in the aircraft, all of which serve to make the person more tense and anxious, and be hypervigilant for any signs that the plane is about to crash; people may try to control their breathing, which leads inadvertently to symptoms of hyperventilation, which can then be interpreted as signs that the person is about to collapse; people worried about their health may repeatedly check and prod a small area of skin which then becomes irritated and swollen, which is then interpreted as a symptom of cancer. People's safety behaviours can be overt or subtle, and need to be carefully assessed and brought into awareness for both client and counsellor.

- When something bad does not happen – the individual does not collapse in the middle of a panic attack, for example – they put this down to the fact that they engaged in the behaviour that saved them, such as sitting down, getting a grip, moving out of the situation, rather than to the fact that anxiety itself is not dangerous. Behaviour stops us from disconfirming our fears: the client never learns that situations are not as dangerous or terrible as expected if he constantly one way or another removes himself from the situation or tries to control the 'danger'. Such learning may go on at an emotional level, so that the safety behaviour then 'feels right' as a way of coping. Emotional learning occurs: 'It makes me feel safe so I must be safe.'

- Keeping an eye out for danger, or hypervigilance (the spider phobic scanning every corner of a room to spot any sinister shapes or cobwebs) increases the likelihood that we will notice it.

- Certain behaviours, such as trying to control one's thoughts, can increase the likelihood of those feared events happening. Social phobics do all sorts of apparently odd things to keep control, which can confirm their worst fears:

Steve had learned that in order to appear socially skilled, he must come across as Mr Nice Guy all the time. He smiled a great deal, maintained eye contact, and tried to be terribly interested in what people were saying, down to hearing and remembering all details of them. He was so acutely conscious of coming across well, and not forgetting anything, that he missed much of what others were saying, and appeared to smile regardless of the seriousness of what was being talked about. People would feel discomfort at his fixed stare. Afterwards, Steve could remember little of what was spoken about, and felt like a complete fool, vowing to try even harder next time.

The Central Role of Avoidance in Maintaining Anxiety

When some situation or thing makes us anxious or uncomfortable, we naturally want to avoid it. People with anxiety problems often use avoidance as a main strategy for coping with anxiety, which both maintains their anxiety and causes further problems. The main problem is that fear and anxiety can grow out of proportion if the individual does not risk entering a situation where they can make realistic appraisals of the threat: either it is worse than predicted, in which case the person needs to find ways to cope, or it is much less frightening – the more likely scenario with anxiety problems.

One of the mechanisms whereby avoidance keeps anxiety going is that the client is unable to learn that anxiety goes down of its own accord, and taking evasive action only prolongs the process. Following a trigger, anxiety levels shoot up. The individual predicts that, unless they do something or get out of the situation, their anxiety would go off the scale and terrible things would happen. They then avoid, which reduces the anxiety somewhat, but next time they think about or come into contact with a potential trigger, the same mechanism happens. In reality, once anxiety has shot up, it gradually comes down over time, regardless of the presence of the trigger, allowing time for learning about the true extent of danger. This is shown graphically in Figures 2.2 and 2.3. The attempts the client makes to reduce anxiety or avoid mean that the anxiety reduces in the short term, but is kept high in the long term.

Underlying Assumptions and Beliefs in Anxiety

The cognitive model specifies three levels of meaning: the level of thoughts, specific thoughts or images connected to particular situations or triggers; the level of assumptions, conditional beliefs

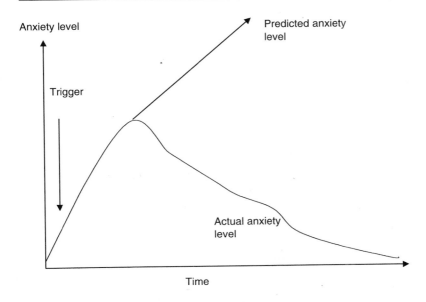

Figure 2.2   *Changes in anxiety levels over time if client does not try to avoid or reduce anxiety*

and rules which determine how we respond in the world; and core beliefs, underlying schema about ourselves, the world and other people (Figure 2.4). Much of the work we do with anxiety problems occurs at the level of thought and assumptions.

Cognitive models have explicitly separated underlying core beliefs, or schema, from underlying assumptions, although in practice we are often looking at general rules or ways of being. Core beliefs or schema, so called 'early maladaptive schema', relate to central feelings of badness or worthlessness, unlovability, lack of trust of self or others, and lack of control of life (Beck et al., 1990; Layden et al., 1993; Young and Klosko, 1993; Young and Behary, 1998). Core beliefs are learned early on in life, and are enduring and slow to change. Core beliefs tend to be absolute, unconditional statements about the self, others and the world: 'I'm a bad person'; 'Everyone else copes'; 'Everyone is out to harm me'; 'People are dangerous'; 'The world is a dangerous place.' Although these sound like oversimplifications of the complexity of humans, we often come down to very bland, short statements of how the client views herself, others and the world.

Assumptions, in contrast, are a set of rules that we learn early on in order to structure and lead our lives. Rules are conditional

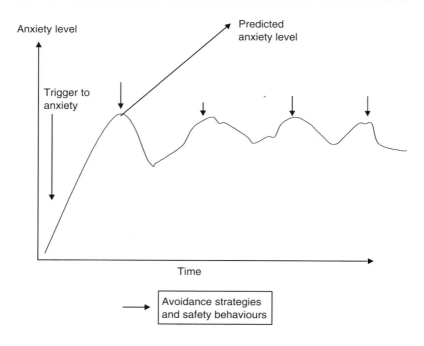

Figure 2.3   *Changes in anxiety levels over time if client avoids or reduces anxiety*

© 1995 Centre for Cognitive Therapy

statements determining what makes us and our actions worthwhile and acceptable to others. 'If I trust other people, then they'll let me down'; 'If I show that I cannot cope, people will think badly of me'; 'I must never show that I am anxious or afraid.' Many of the rules are indeed helpful, but some may be so rigid that they pose problems. For example, the rule 'If I work hard and do my best all the time, I'll get on well in life and be more acceptable' can enable the individual to succeed in ways that are personally important; however, trying too hard at everything may have a cost in high levels of stress and exhaustion should circumstances change. Life being what it is, there will be occasions when the person does work hard but does not get recognition or acceptance for their work. Rigidly holding the belief that relates acceptance to hard work makes the individual vulnerable to setbacks at these times. Ellis's early work described how our 'irrational beliefs' lead to disturbed appraisals and emotional consequences. Beck et al (1985) describe a pervasive sense of vulnerability underlying

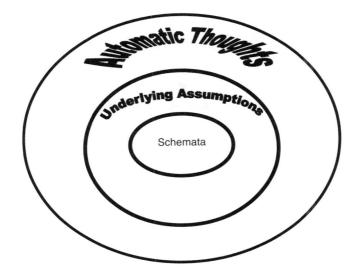

Figure 2.4   *Levels of thoughts and beliefs*

Source: Padesky and Mooney (1998) (reproduced with permission)
© 1995 Centre for Cognitive Therapy

anxiety problems, making the individual tend to overestimate threat and underestimate individual coping resources.

Various assumptions may underlie anxiety problems: assumptions and rules to do with control, perfectionism, feeling vulnerable, not trusting others, seeing problems as insoluble, lacking self esteem, or feeling ineffective (Beck et al., 1985; Wells, 1997). Beck et al. (1985) label assumptions as 'major concerns', as beliefs underlying anxiety problems. For example, the thought 'I can't go out alone' may relate to different major concerns for different individuals: not trusting oneself to be able to cope if difficulties arise, believing that difficulties and danger are around the corner, or not trusting other people to help should problems arise.

A longitudinal conceptualisation, such as shown in Figure 2.5, enables us to understand the background to anxiety, and what makes the individual vulnerable. It offers an understanding of why the individual might be vulnerable to anxiety in terms of their schema and assumptions, developed from experiences throughout life.

Assumptions and beliefs represent the higher layers of the cognitive model, or bottom line, depending on which way up

Early Experience

Information about the client's early and other significant experiences
which may have shaped core beliefs and assumptions.

Development of Beliefs about the Self, Others and the World

Unconditional, core beliefs developing from early experience, such as
'I am bad', 'I am weak and vulnerable', 'Others will always look after me'
or 'The world is a dangerous place.'

Assumptions or Rules for Living

Conditional statements, often phrased as 'If . . . then . . .' rules, to enable the
individual to function despite core beliefs: e.g. 'If I am vigilant about my health
at all times, then I'll be safe, despite being vulnerable'; 'If I work hard all the time,
I'll be OK, despite being a bad person.'

Critical Incidents which Trigger Problems

Situations or events in which the rules are broken or assumptions are activated.

Problems and Factors Maintaining the Problem

Physical symptoms, thoughts, emotions, behaviour interacting in a 'vicious circle'.

Figure 2.5   *Longitudinal conceptualisation*

Source: Melanie Fennell in Keith Hawton, Paul Salkovskis, Joan Kirk and
David M. Clark (1989). Reprinted from *Cognitive Behaviour Therapy for
Psychiatric Problems: A Practical Guide* by K. Hawton et al. (1989) by
permission of Oxford University Press.

the model is drawn. They can be seen as the umbrella under the
shade of which the individual leads their life; or the roots of
the problem. We discuss particular individual assumptions and
beliefs that underlie different anxiety problems in Part II. We
stress also that building up a conceptualisation for our individual
client takes time, and is a stage-by-stage process. We do not aim to
have a fully fledged longitudinal model of the clients' problems
until we are well into therapy, if at all: for many clients working at
the level of maintenance cycles and maintaining cognitive processes is sufficient for effective therapy.

Anxiety is, in summary, a fear response, based on our appraisals of danger. When a perceived danger activates our beliefs or assumptions related to danger (I'm vulnerable, something bad is around the corner, spiders will kill me), we have a stream of danger-related thoughts (this is terrible, I cannot cope, people terrify me), and we engage in a whole range of behaviours designed to keep us safe. Unfortunately, although we may feel safe, such thoughts and behaviours prevent us from disconfirming our beliefs, and prevent us being able to re-evaluate and learn. Our task in counselling is to look at how the general model of anxiety presented in this chapter applies to our individual clients and the complexities of problems they bring to counselling. How to juggle working with general models and working with the individual client is covered in the next chapter.

3

Cognitive Approaches to Counselling for Anxiety

> There is nothing either good nor bad, but thinking makes it so. (*Hamlet*, II.ii. 259)

Cognitive therapy began as a treatment of depression in the 1960s and since then has increasingly moved into many other areas. Researching both the causes and treatment of anxiety problems has been a major part of this expansion. While it is probably the case that the cognitive model for depression stays much the same for the different varieties of depression, the developments in cognitive therapy have been highly specific within the varieties of anxiety. Cognitive conceptualisation and therapy methods vary markedly depending on the variety of anxiety experienced by the client, as illustrated in later chapters on the specific problems. However, there are many common principles for working with clients with anxiety.

In this chapter, we cover a broad introduction to cognitive therapy and anxiety. We start by summarising the key elements of the cognitive counselling model, including its search for meanings, emphasis on collaboration, and structure and focus. We look at general principles across counselling for anxiety problems, focusing on newer developments in cognitive understanding of the origins and maintenance of anxiety. We discuss the effectiveness of cognitive therapy for anxiety, and what such evidence may and may not mean. We finish by looking at the debate about using protocols for working with clients with anxiety problems, and at how to balance these with individual client conceptualisations.

Key Elements of the Cognitive Counselling Model

We outline below the heart of cognitive therapy: collaboration, conceptualisation, structure and focus, use of a wide range of methods, and its educational and empowering philosophy.

Cognitive therapy is the search for meanings

At the heart of cognitive therapy is its search for the meanings our clients give to symptoms, thoughts, feelings, behaviour, and the meanings of situations and events in their lives. At a simplistic level, we talk about 'cognitive distortions' or 'thinking errors', where people's thinking is not necessarily helpful or in touch with reality. However, this is an oversimplification of the cognitive model, where we aim to understand clients' reality in terms of their past and present, and work with them to re-frame and come up with more helpful and realistic interpretations. This work occurs at many levels: identifying and working with streams of negative thinking; identifying rules that underlie the way the client interprets and acts in the world; and identifying and working with more pervasive schemata, which determine the sense of self, others and the world.

Within the cognitive model of anxiety, the central meanings are to do with threat and danger. Anxiety is related to the over-estimation of danger in certain situations. It is also related to people underestimating their ability to cope. People are anxious about what is important to them, whether it is health, social approval and acceptance, being responsible for the self and others, or a basic sense of existential security. We cannot presume to understand why people feel anxious without really understanding the individual meanings.

The key aims of counselling for anxiety are to gain a clear, empathic understanding of what are the important issues and fears for our individual clients, and work with them to find more realistic interpretations of the threats and danger. This involves a process of identifying specific fears and using a spirit of 'guided discovery' and 'behavioural experiments' to test alternative explanations. This way, clients are able to take on board different appraisals of themselves, others and the world and use these new ways of interpretation as a basis for living their lives, solving problems, or appraising situations.

Cognitive therapy focuses on problem maintenance

Anxiety is kept going by many factors: changing what maintains the anxiety is often more the focus of therapy, than is understanding why the person became anxious. Both, however, are rich sources of meaning. How people have tried to cope with or manage anxiety in the past is now thought to be counterproductive. Understandably, we do anything to reduce our bad feelings, such as avoiding anxiety-provoking situations and developing ways, often subtle, of controlling anxiety. Methods of control and management formed the backbone of much of therapy for anxiety over the past 20 years: however, anxiety management techniques such as controlled breathing and relaxation, may all serve inadvertently to make the problems worse. Trying not to worry, or not to be anxious, does not work, for reasons that are now better understood within cognitive processing models. The focus in therapy now is more on decatastrophising the natural processes of anxiety rather than getting rid of the feelings. This work has involved identifying the unhelpful 'safety behaviours' clients use as an aid to coping, and learning to try out life without such potentially unhelpful strategies.

Cognitive therapy is based on a collaborative therapeutic relationship

Collaboration is a central aspect of the therapeutic relationship within cognitive ways of working. Client and therapist ideally form a team, which then jointly works on the client's main problems. As in many teams, members do different but parallel jobs. The therapist's role is to provide conceptual and methodological expertise about the nature of psychological problems and how such problems are resolved. There is a teaching element to this but, like all skilled teaching, it is most effectively achieved when geared to the individual client and his frame of reference. The client's job is to provide honest information about his situation, about which he may be regarded as an expert. It is the putting together of these two forms of expertise – the general and the specific – which maximises the chances of coming up with creative and lasting changes to the client's situation. No matter how hard or how well they work, these separate sources of expertise usually cannot by themselves crack the client's key problems. They must work together.

Cognitive therapy is based on conceptualising both the problem and the individual

As described in the previous chapter, at the heart of cognitive therapy lies case conceptualisation (Persons, 1989; Wills and Sanders, 1997; Butler, 1998; Tarrier and Calam, 2002), which acts as a map to understand the layout of the client's difficulties and to guide the therapy process. At its most simple, conceptualisation enables us to see links between clients' thoughts, feelings, behaviour and physiology, and the links with environmental influences; it also aims to build up a unique understanding of the individual in terms of cognitive schema and assumptions arising from the person's history and experience. Conceptualisation provides a bridge between our general understanding of the client's difficulties, and an understanding of the client as an individual.

Cognitive approaches are generally backed up by considerable amounts of research by both general psychologists and researcher/practitioners, particularly in providing working models or conceptualisations of anxiety problems. For example, research by Wells (1997) painted a vivid picture of the functioning of clients experiencing social anxiety. Such accounts not only provide a clear clinical picture of the client's problems but also give a convincing explanatory model of how the different aspects of the picture relate to each other. While this kind of 'off the peg' conceptualisation gives the therapist a head-start in knowing what to look for with a client, it also gives powerful ideas of how the client's symptoms may be interacting with each other. This strong clinical picture helps the therapist to go into sessions with rationales for treatment and relevant techniques readily at hand.

Yet the art of therapy always lies in the fact that our models must be applied to an individual client, who will be in some respects different from any client the therapist has met before. Assuming that a general model allows one to know what is going on with the client is a foolhardy and fatal arrogance. The conceptual model must be shaped by the client's actual reports and experiences and, even then, it should always be regarded as provisional and open to revision according to new information. A good conceptualisation needs to be compassionate, describing the client's experiences and leading to understanding of the problems, without in any way judging their coping strategies as other than human and understandable.

Mary suffered from severe anxiety, especially at work. On the first occasion that she met the therapist, she asked him many questions about where he had trained, whether he liked the work and so on. So many such questions are really quite unusual for a first session of therapy. As Mary soon revealed an unhappy childhood, the therapist initially assumed that she might have problems in trusting people and saw her questions in that light. It soon emerged, however, that she suffered agonies about what negative evaluations people might be making of her. One of her friends had, however, told her that if you wanted people to be interested in you, then you had to be interested in them first. By showing her interest in me, Mary had hoped to make me interested in her. This tendency drove her colleagues at work to distraction, and it frequently backfired. The fact that it was revealed in therapy, however, allowed valuable new learning to emerge – for both client and therapist. It also allowed Mary to consider whether there might be better ways of winning interest from others, and to go on to try these as behavioural experiments.

Therapy is a structured and focused process and begins with an assumption that it will be short-term

It is recommended that cognitively based counselling sessions should begin by setting an agenda and should finish by taking feedback from the client to evaluate the usefulness of the session. In between these two steps, there is an additional set of steps to ensure that the session is well focused on the client's key problems and issues. The rationale for a structured approach is that it provides good boundaries for clients at a time in their lives when they may be confused and disorientated, maximising the chances that what has been gained in the session will be taken out into the client's life. A structured and focused approach may be useful in helping clients to look at areas which they would want to avoid, since avoidance is often a central feature of anxiety: certain ways of bringing up material can be subconsciously or consciously linked to the desire to avoid other material.

There is as yet little solid evidence on whether this rationale for structure and focus works for all clients, though many of our clients have expressed satisfaction with it. Like all things, however, structure suits some people more than others. Therapists should be ready to adapt the structure to the individual needs of their clients and even sometimes to their own needs, acknowledging that structure can be very difficult for some. There are times when it is necessary to stray from the agenda to pick up an emergent issue or to respond to client need. Many times in therapy the client needs to 'just talk', to have their stories heard and witnessed. In focused therapy, however, this should be done in an intentional way and in a way that can be justified in the overall counselling approach, for example using summaries and reflections to see how the elements fit together.

A similarly pragmatic approach is taken to the length of therapy. Cognitive interventions have been designed predominantly as short-term interventions: Beck originally developed cognitive therapy for depression to be conducted over 12–20 sessions, with comparable lengths of therapy for anxiety (Beck et al., 1985). Much useful work can be done within this time frame, not only working at the issues that trigger and maintain anxiety for the client, but also beginning to look at clients' underlying rules which may predispose them to anxiety. It is also possible to work within a much shorter framework, as may be required where there are policy and resource constraints. In the NHS, for example, there is pressure to offer the shortest intervention which can be effective. Cognitive therapy was developed to be a parsimonious type of therapy, working efficiently to meet clients' goals using the most direct and useful methods of change. We are seeing more evidence that, for many of our clients, short-term work, which targets specific problems and enables clients to become their own therapists, is as effective as longer-term work. This appears to be especially true for working with anxiety problems. For example, the original therapy for panic was 12 sessions (Beck et al., 1992; Clark et al., 1994), whereas there is evidence that working within a limit of 7 sessions is as effective (Clark et al., 1999). This is not to argue that long-term therapy is never appropriate – the circumstances where cognitive therapy might be conducted in a longer-term version are described in Chapter 4. However, especially where the client's time and/or money are concerned, and resource limitations dictate length of therapy, shorter-term interventions as a first assumption are generally the rule of thumb.

Cognitive therapy, based on cognitive conceptualisation for individual clients, uses many techniques, methods and concepts – some unique to cognitive therapy and some from other therapies
Cognitive therapy is characterised as a technocratic therapy with many techniques in its toolbox (Wills and Sanders, 1997). We describe many of these techniques and methods throughout the book. Some have been developed within cognitive therapy, such as thought monitoring and challenging, and key methods of behavioural experiments. Other methods are based on those developed in other forms of psychotherapy and counselling. While many good methods and interventions have been generated and described within cognitive therapy, it is important that the therapy should not be driven by the need to use these techniques. Overall, the conceptualisation should drive the therapy. Any intervention, whether it comes from the casebook of cognitive therapy or from that of some other therapy, can be used quite happily – provided that it hits home on the issues for intervention identified in the conceptualisation.

We have argued elsewhere (Wills and Sanders, 1997) that cognitive approaches can be implemented in several different ways or at several different levels. In brief, cognitive interventions can be used to augment the use of counselling skills to give extra focus, especially when the client has problems, such as anxiety, which are known to respond to cognitive therapy. Cognitive interventions can also be used in a fuller implementation of the therapy. Finally, cognitive approaches can also be used as elements of an integrated approach which seeks to maximise the impact of different therapy approaches, which might be most efficacious to individual clients (Alford and Beck, 1997; Bateman, 2000; O'Brien and Houston, 2000).

Cognitive therapy teaches skills which clients can use after therapy

In counselling and therapy, there appears to be a considerable problem of 'washout': gains made during therapy may be lost quite quickly afterwards (Ivey et al., 1987). Therapists should therefore be seeking actively to promote generalisation of therapy, seeking to ensure that whatever works in the therapy is transferred into the client's everyday life. Cognitive therapy has a good track record in this respect: for example, clients who have overcome depression using cognitive therapy are less likely to relapse than those treated with anti-depressant medication (Hollon et al., 1996). The overall philosophy is that learning goes on apart from and after the sessions. As stated by Judith Beck, 'A therapist who views himself as responsible for helping the patient with every problem risks engendering or reinforcing dependence and deprives the patient of the opportunity to test and strengthen her skills' (J. Beck, 1995: 269).

Cognitive therapy has promoted the idea of homework, tasks which the client works on between sessions. This maximises the chances of clients learning skills that they will be able to use during and, crucially, after the therapy. Much therapy should be going on between sessions, as well as within sessions. The word and concept of 'homework' can have difficult connotations for clients and counsellors alike, as discussed further in Chapter 6. We need, when introducing and working on homework, to negotiate carefully what is possible, and to aim for 'no-lose' tasks. The true aim of cognitive therapy is to have the client become his or her own therapist.

Cognitive therapy aims for both rational and emotional change

Cognitive therapy has a reputation for being a therapy working mainly at the level of the rational mind: enabling clients to think more rationally about themselves and their difficulties, and thereby to feel or behave differently (Wills and Sanders, 1997). However, lasting change has to occur at an emotional as well as a cognitive and a behavioural level; recently cognitive therapy has been addressing this issue more directly, and learning about the process of change from other therapeutic models. Our minds are both experiential and rational (Epstein, 1994, 1998; Padesky and Mooney, 2000). The experiential mind is based on emotion and intuition, reacts and learns quickly, learns from experience rather than 'facts', and is associated with the realm of images, metaphors and memories. The experiential mind tends to dominate when emotion is high: the mind that leads the person to react regardless of the logic: 'I just knew I had to get out, I had to run, I felt like something bad was going to happen.' The 'ah-ha' experience, when things fall into place and make sense on an emotional level, may be learning at the experiential level. The rational mind, in comparison, is more slow, deliberate, works on cause and effect, and is active and conscious. The rational mind is swayed by sense and logic. In order to produce change, we need to work with and integrate both minds. Many cognitive methods can be seen as helping to give the client more access to their rational mind at a time when they are driven by negative feelings. This does not imply that the rational mind should over-rule the experiential mind, but rather that they can work alongside each other to achieve more balanced and functional responses.

Cognitive therapy at its most basic has been seen to appeal to logic and the rational mind, and classical techniques such as monitoring and challenging thoughts and beliefs rely strongly on working with this mind. This is very effective many times and for many people. But true change needs to occur by bringing together both mind-sets. With its experimental approach, cognitive therapy has evolved ways of helping clients try out something different in order to experience differences and thereby make changes to thinking and beliefs – so-called 'behavioural experiments'. These aim to help the client to try out what makes sense, to have a new experience, and learn from this, thereby integrating both minds and enabling them to work together. Cognitive therapy also uses approaches such as working with imagery, or techniques used in Gestalt therapy, to produce understanding and change.

Protocols for Anxiety: the Pros and Cons

Beck's very beginnings of cognitive therapy involved developing and testing out highly specific, manualised* therapeutic methods

---

* 'Manualisation' usually refers to the preparation of detailed treatment protocols, often in a step-by-step fashion, for clinical trials. Such manuals are subsequently often available as treatment guidelines.

and stages, applied to the treatment of depression. The rationale was against a background of analytic therapy, where the techniques and methods were hard to put into operation. Beck started the quest to know what might work and why, so the results could have more general applicability. The development and research in cognitive therapy has followed this tradition of a degree of manualisation and operationalising of the stages and methods of therapy. In research, it is usually necessary to produce therapist protocols for research trials so that therapists in the trial can make sure that they are giving the same treatment as each other. Without this uniformity, the trial is not a fair test of a therapy model. This means that after successful trials, protocols can be published so that other therapists can work to guidelines which have been shown to be successful in the treatment of specific problems. There now exists a variety of protocols which allow therapists to apply the cognitive model to specific problems in a systematic way. Leahy & Holland (2000), for example, describe up-to-date protocols and pro formas for all the main anxiety disorders mentioned in the previous section. Steketee (1999a, b) provides a specific protocol for the cognitive-behavioural treatment of OCD, and accompanying therapist and client handbooks.

As readers examine the cognitive-behavioural protocols and approaches to the different problems of anxiety, they will notice that certain core features of the approach are common to many problems. Just as there are subtle differences in the cognitive explanatory models between problems as described earlier, so readers will also notice differences in the treatment approaches. These distinctive concepts and techniques will be described in later chapters on counselling for distinct anxiety problems.

At the very heart of cognitive therapy is the development of individual client conceptualisations which guide our understanding of the client and the direction of counselling; against this, we have the development of specific protocols for specific problems which are shown to be effective. How do we, as counsellors and therapists, balance these two apparently contradictory ways of working? Overall, when working with clients with anxiety problems, the art of therapy is to be able to balance our knowledge and consideration of protocols with the individual client conceptualisation, as we discuss in the following section.

Protocols versus individual conceptualisation

Some, if not many, counsellors will start to feel rather alarmed by the ideas of protocols and manuals for conducting therapy, given that counselling and psychotherapy philosophy and training is geared to treating each client as an individual with individual problems. There is currently a debate within cognitive ways of working (such as the debate being conducted on the British Association for Behavioural and Cognitive Psychotherapy website at the time of writing) about the relative values of, on the one hand, sticking to individual formulations and using whatever approaches are suggested by the formulations, and in contrast, using specific therapy protocols matched to the category of problem the client is facing, with diagnostic categories as a guide. We suggest that the debate is worth listening to and joining in with, just as the debate about using diagnostic categories is rumbling on throughout the psychotherapies.

The argument for using protocols goes along these lines. For clients with specific phobias, following a standard, manualised approach, focused on exposing the client to their fears, shows better results in terms of getting rid of the phobias than using specifically tailored programmes which may allow for too much flexibility and tailoring. The latter may allow the therapy to wander away from the specific ingredients shown in research to be helpful (Schulte et al., 1992; Schulte, 1997). The superiority of protocol-based versus individual tailoring has also been reported for working with clients with obsessive compulsive disorder (Emmelkamp et al., 1994). The protocol debate centres around the finding that there are certain active ingredients which have been shown to be effective for clients with anxiety problems and without which the therapy may be less effective. Exposing phobic clients to their feared situations or objects is definitely an active ingredient. Giving counsellors and therapists free rein to design their own therapy for the individual may mean that such active ingredients are left out. For example, people with specific phobias are by definition scared of the thing that they are phobic about and do not want to be exposed to their fears. They may predict 'I couldn't do it', or 'I'll be overwhelmed with anxiety.' As therapists it is difficult to go against our compassion and encourage clients to do something which they fear will make them worse – but challenging these fears, both for ourselves and our clients, may be necessary to helping the client overcome specific fears and phobias.

Nicola was 34 when I first saw her and had been phobic of spiders most of her life. The phobia was having an increasing impact on her life. Going to strange places was difficult, she had to check out any rooms she went in and felt uncomfortable being at home on her own in case a spider should appear and she would not be able to deal with it. Nicola was also troubled with periods of low mood during which her phobia would get much worse. She had been for counselling and help many times, often focused on her mood, building self-esteem, understanding how her fears might be important to her relationships, and looking at the origins – work which she found had given her valuable insights but did not tackle the phobia. Nicola simply refused to do any exposure work to spiders. We spent several sessions in preparation, formulating her difficulties and fears, attempting to decatastrophise her predictions about herself and spiders. However, Nicola would not do the exposure work and remained very phobic. She asked for her GP to refer her several times, each time really wanting to make a fresh start and to really try: but each time I had collected spiders for the exposure work and lovingly kept them alive and happy for their important work in therapy, Nicola would cancel or not turn up. The unemployed spiders were returned to their webs. Nicola reported that counselling and therapy had been helpful for many things, but no progress was made on her phobia without the exposure work. Therefore, if we take symptom reduction as a successful outcome, the therapy could not work without the active ingredient of contact with spiders.

Research on protocol-based therapy has mostly been conducted within research trials, often at the more behavioural end of cognitive behavioural therapy (Wilson, 1996). Research trials are usually based on a fairly homogeneous population and use symptom reduction as the outcome resource. Clients with complex and multifaceted difficulties more common in clinical practice would not be included in such research. Nicola may have felt better, been more proactive in her life and developed greater self-esteem, but not following the therapy protocol means that she would have been in the 'treatment failure' group. So, the protocol versus individual therapy debate needs to take into account what 'good outcome' means.

We would say that the debate needs to continue and be widened out to include all varieties of clients and a variety of therapeutic methods. If, for example, a client who is increasingly disabled by panic attacks, can really experience a marked reduction in attacks from a manualised, six-session approach to treatment designed for panic disorder, then it would make far more sense for the therapy to proceed along standard lines than to spend many sessions building up a detailed formulation. At the other extreme, rigidly going along the same lines for all our clients without individual tailoring, might be aversive for all concerned. The big questions are what exactly works, and why, questions which might never be answered in a simple way.

The conceptualisation approach to cognitive therapy is based on the idea that, although ideas can helpfully be gleaned from general models and protocols, in the end the treatment of the individual client will be best formulated according to an individual assessment of that client. This is built into the rationale of cognitive therapy theory which emphasises the fact that people will react to events, including the experience of having Cognitive Therapy, according to their idiosyncratic cognitive frameworks. Given that clients often present with complicated issues, it can feel good for a therapist to go into the session with a framework for understanding and working with the client. This framework can act both as a map to locate where we are and as a rudder to guide us forward. The framework, however, should never lead us to impose ideas or activities on the client. It should help us to negotiate an individual approach to the client based on general principles. The art and skill in cognitive therapy may well lie in being able to develop models and counselling plans which are unique to the individual in all their idiosyncrasies, and yet follow methods and approaches that have been found to be helpful for specific problems. This combination of the general and particular is the science and art of therapy.

The Effectiveness of Cognitive Therapy for Anxiety

There is substantial research evidence showing that cognitive therapy helps a significant number of people with anxiety problems, with varying degrees of effectiveness depending on the type of problem (Salkovskis, 1996a; Clark and Fairburn, 1997; Clark, 1999a). Although much of this evidence is based on strictly controlled studies with carefully selected clients, more naturalistic studies have also shown good results (e.g. White, 2000). We summarise the evidence in the chapters on different anxiety problems.

It is important to be clear about what this evidence does and does not mean. Evidence showing that cognitive approaches work well does not imply that other therapies do not work. Cognitive therapy has followed a scientific tradition since its earliest days: much of the evidence favouring cognitive therapy comes from the many randomised controlled trials that abound. Other therapies have been slow to get involved in research evaluations and randomised controlled trials, partly because some of their concepts are harder to operationalise than are those of cognitive behavioural therapy. While therapies such as interpersonal psychotherapy (Weissman et al., 2000) have also been shown to be highly effective in the treatment of depression, as yet cognitive therapy really does stand ahead in the evaluation of psychological treatments for anxiety problems. As other therapies get more geared up to research, it is quite possible that they will also show good results for working with anxiety. However, if we are to go by current research findings based on randomised controlled trials, then practitioners need to consider whether there are at least some aspects of cognitive therapy that they could incorporate into their current practice when working with clients with anxiety.

There have been some interesting recent trials where counselling appeared to perform as well as cognitive behavioural therapy in the treatment of anxiety and depression in primary care in the UK (Bedi et al., 2000; Bower et al., 2000; Mellor-Clark, 2000). While this is very encouraging for counselling, the studies give little evidence of the methods used by the counsellors and by the cognitive behavioural therapists, or about the type and intensity of specific problems on which they were working. Further information will, we hope, show whether counsellors or therapists were using similar or radically different methods.

Disadvantages of the Cognitive Approach

Certain features of the cognitive approach have already been posited as advantages – its record of effectiveness, its focus, its short-term nature, its reliance on collaboration, and its detailed description in protocols which guide therapists to using the most effective approaches. Yet not all counsellors would see these factors as advantages. Like all therapies, cognitive therapy has its characteristic downsides, which have been pointed out by various critics. We like to say that cognitive therapy has its characteristic sins of both omission – things that should not have been left out – and commission – things that should not have been done (Wills and Sanders, 1997). Omissions usually cited are less care about the therapeutic relationship, lack of a spiritual dimension, lack of a developmental dimension, and lack of a 'liberating' framework (Rowan, 2000). While responses have been made to many of these failings, they perhaps remain as rather weak areas in cognitive approaches. Commissions may include an approach to goal-seeking which can be made to feel like *indecent haste*. While many clients undoubtedly like the business-like approach of the therapy, some clients may feel rushed. Cognitive theory itself tells us that people evaluate events according to their beliefs and cognition. Some clients have had miserable childhoods in which people around them were not prepared to give them 'quality time', and they may consequently carry the schema 'I'm not worth spending time on.' It would not therefore be surprising if such clients found themselves discomfited and their schema confirmed by too much emphasis on the short-term model. Cognitive therapy has sometimes been described as a therapy of the techno-logical age, an age which is perhaps stuffed full of information and commitments and yet gives less and less time to fulfilling them. In this way, it perhaps crystallises some of the key dilem-mas of our present form of society. Readers are likely to have a variety of responses to the fact that there may well be many more clients seeking help than they have the time for, particularly for counsellors working in time-limited settings. The cognitive approach at least offers evidence on effectiveness that supports its tendency to err on the shorter-term commitment rather than on the longer-term.

Cognitive approaches have much to offer in therapy for clients with anxiety problems. The central conditions of conceptual-isation, structure, collaboration and education give the meta-message that anxiety is containable and that clients can become empowered to help themselves in the long term. Cognitive therapy seeks to integrate an individual conceptualisation with more standard protocols applicable across many clients with similar problems. Counsellors need to be aware of the pros and cons of juggling the demands of the individual and the general – where being too individualistic short-changes the client of the active ingredients of therapy, and where protocol-based therapy may not hit the spot for the individual. Juggling these and other principles is the art of good counselling for anxiety. The container in which such work occurs, the therapeutic relationship, is discussed in the next chapter.

4

The Therapeutic Relationship in Counselling for Anxiety

Many of the texts we have read on counselling and cognitive approaches for anxiety pay only lip service to the importance of the therapeutic relationship. This is not because the relationship is not important, but rather that it is assumed that a good relationship is in place in order to do the therapeutic work, or that the relationship does not need to be the primary focus for counsellor and client.

As practitioners and teachers of cognitive therapy, we advocate that more explicit attention be paid to the relationship in cognitive therapy (Wills and Sanders, 1997; Sanders and Wills, 1999). Beck et al. (1979) by no means disregarded the importance of a good therapeutic relationship, and saw it as a necessary condition for therapeutic change. However, unlike person-centred approaches developing in parallel with cognitive therapies, Beck regarded the relationship alone as not sufficient for change. Cognitive theory proposes that the core conditions of a good therapeutic relationship create the context within which the therapeutic work takes place but the work requires both conceptual and technical expertise to be effective. The 'necessary and sufficient' statement, we feel, has meant that the relationship has often been taken as read, without explicit focus on the type or importance of counsellor–client relationship (e.g. Corrie, 2002). Cognitive approaches advocate a particular form of collaborative relationship and while it is true that very often, particularly in short-term work, we do not need to make the therapeutic relationship explicit in our work, it none the less needs attention during sessions and in supervision. Like any relationship, there can be strains and ruptures in the client–counsellor relationship and these may require attention for the therapy to proceed. The so-called 'non-specific' factors, that is, those connected with the therapeutic alliance, are often those factors that make most difference to clients over and above learning to understand and manage their anxiety: feeling understood, not being judged, and being given a listening space in which to explore problems by a congruent human being.

In this chapter we look at particular issues in working with the therapeutic relationship with clients experiencing anxiety problems. We begin by describing the central themes of collaborative working and of sharing a joint formulation, which provide the bedrock of the relationship. We then go on to look at how particular ways of working with anxious clients can impact on the relationship, identifying common challenges to the therapeutic relationship. These ways include the need to empower clients to face up to fears, at the same time creating a safe therapeutic space, dealing with avoidance and the clients' need for reassurance, and taking a systemic view of the clients' difficulties.

Therapeutic Collaboration in Counselling for Anxiety

Beck defines the collaborative relationship as one where 'there is a team approach to the solution of the patient's problem: that is, a therapeutic alliance where the patient provides raw data . . . while the therapist provides structure and expertise on how to solve problems . . . the therapist fosters the attitude that "two heads are better than one" in approaching personal difficulties' (Beck et al., 1985: 221). Wills and Sanders add a further note on 'expertise' in this regard; 'The counsellor can regard his expertise as expertise in people in general but this expertise will prove of little avail unless it can ally itself with the client's expertise about her own life' (Wills and Sanders, 1997: 71).

Throughout developing a collaborative relationship, we work reciprocally, keeping an awareness of the interpersonal exchange at all times (Safran and Segal, 1990). Both client and counsellor are working together to observe what is going on, to observe and comment on the client's way of being and on the interaction between that and the counsellor's way of being – all in the service of finding solutions to the difficulties facing the client. When the client is unable to see the way forward, or is unable to see alternatives to thoughts and beliefs, the therapist may be able to look from a different angle and to offer this to the client. Similarly, the client can see and offer a different perspective to the therapist. There can be a feeling in cognitive therapy at its best of both client and therapist rolling up their sleeves and getting on with the work.

Collaboration means being very explicit in what we are doing and why, and avoiding hidden agendas. The therapist does not form hypotheses or interpretations about the client and keep them to herself. Instead, everything is out on the table. If client and counsellor are working to different agendas, then the therapy is not likely to proceed smoothly. If the counsellor is trying to manoeuvre the client into seeing things from the counsellor's point of view, or is trying to get the client to be more 'logical', while the client simply wants to feel understood, therapy will be a rough ride. Instead the therapist is clear and explicit about what is in her or his mind, so that agendas for therapy as a whole, as well as for individual sessions and moment-to-moment interactions in the session, are known to both client and counsellor. This means that the therapist admits mistakes, is open to suggestions, and is willing to go where the client wants to go, without colluding with the client's difficulties.

A spirit of collaboration gives a 'ping-pong' quality to sessions: the time that therapist and client are speaking may be about equal; the therapist shares her thoughts about the client's thoughts, and asks for feedback. While questions may be asked by both therapist and client, both work together, collaboratively and empirically, to find answers. The client's thoughts, feelings and behaviours are reflected on, not interpreted. The spirit of collaboration may be clearer when it is absent: when, for example, the therapist tells the client what to do or to think; or when the therapist comes up with a brilliant suggestion about alternative views that the client may take of a situation, which then leaves the client cold. This kind of therapist behaviour is very easy to get drawn into. It is not always authoritarian in intent, and may be motivated by a genuine desire to get the client to a better place. Collaboration may also be absent when there are long silences in the session, when, rather than representing a meaning-laden pause, it leaves the client high and dry, struggling with where to go next. In true collaboration, the therapist is willing to help the client out without patronising, condescending or disempowering the client. In developing a good therapeutic collaboration, counsellors should be warm, open, empathic, concerned, respectful and non-judgemental. The process of developing such a collaborative relationship involves working with the client to set goals for counselling, determine priorities, maintain a therapeutic focus and structure both within sessions and across counselling as a whole.

Collaboration is built into the structure of sessions. Each session starts with working out an agenda for the work. There should be no sense of the agenda being 'set' by the therapist, but it should be collaboratively agreed. In practice, towards the beginning of counselling, it is not unusual for the counsellor to be more active in making suggestions as to what might be helpful, particularly when we are introducing the model and facilitating understanding of the client's difficulties. As therapy proceeds, the agenda should become more of the prerogative of the client.

We also suggest making frequent summaries throughout counselling, and for feedback on the session at the end: What went well? What are you taking away with you? Is there anything that you did not like or that was not helpful? We ask for feedback on the last session at the beginning of the next, to check that any problems that might have been brewing over the week can be looked at together. This constant process of feedback and adaptation to the client's views in cognitive therapy means that there is an ongoing 'rolling contract' (Wills, 1997) that keeps the therapy on track.

The importance of a shared formulation

Throughout our collaborative work in counselling for anxiety, we develop and work with a shared conceptualisation or formulation of the client's difficulties, based on a careful balance between what we know about the client as an individual and our knowledge of the client's difficulties as a general problem, with a specific model and mode for therapy. Working with a shared formulation is central to maintaining a collaborative relationship. It is also important to remember to build client strengths into the formulation. We have found the concept developed by Persons' (1989) 'old plan/new plan' a helpful way of doing this. It is possible to draw new patterns building strengths and new experiences into the formulation (Wills, 2002).

One problem that we have noticed when working with protocols for anxiety is that counsellors are tempted to rush to start 'treatment' before client and counsellor have worked out a shared formulation of the client's difficulties. For example, the counsellor may feel that he or she has a good understanding of the panic model and how this applies to the individual client, but has not spent sufficient time working through individual examples so both client and counsellor are clear about how the panic model fits their particular case. Where a client brings complex difficulties, it is vital to spend as long as is needed on the stages of assessment and formulation, before any therapeutic interventions are started. The therapist may well be tempted to do something, no matter what, when faced with clients' complex and painful difficulties and distress, or where formulation is difficult (Salkovskis et al., 1998). We stress the importance of delaying interventions until both client and counsellor are clear about what they are doing and why. The assessment phase is a time to develop a good working relationship, to ask relevant questions and help the client understand why such questions are being asked, and to use reflection and summaries to check that the issues are fully understood. With the information collected, client and counsellor literally draw up, on paper, a whiteboard or computer, a working model of the problems and a plan for therapy. We need to go back to revisit our formulation several times during therapy, a process that is aided when both client and counsellor have a copy, preferably well thumbed and scribbled on as therapy progresses.

Empathy and counselling for anxiety

Anxiety is a more or less familiar set of feelings for all of us. Using the conceptualisation models described throughout this text can often be a useful way of being aware of our sensitivities. In these conceptualisations applied to ourselves, we all find plenty of the avoidance and safety behaviours relevant to these problems. We will be able to find our own characteristic ways of dealing with anxiety. It is helpful for us to be aware of these patterns as we may find that they echo clients' coping styles. If, for example, we tend to make lists when we feel overwhelmed by life demands, we may find ourselves reacting against clients with OCD who do this. While the initial reaction to a client trait that echoes one of our own can be reaction formation, such an experience also offers the opportunity to develop our sense of empathy.

As one of the active ingredients in cognitive therapy (Burns and Auerbach, 1996), it is vital for empathy to be maintained throughout counselling. If the therapist has difficulty empathising with the client, this should be addressed both by the 'internal supervisor' (Casement, 1985) during sessions and by external supervision with a supervisor. Why am I having difficulty in empathising? What in the client or in me is getting in the way? If I or a close friend had the experiences of this client, how would I or they react? Are the problems totally understandable given the client's background and beliefs? Client reactions, especially anger and hostility, can get in the way of empathy, although these may have arisen because the client is feeling misunderstood.

Taking the client's problems seriously while exploring alternatives

One of the central aspects of working with anxiety problems is to help the client come up with alternative explanations for their difficulties. In essence we are saying: 'Yes, I know you think A, but have you thought that there may be other ways (B, C, D, etc.) of seeing things?' In line with cognitive theory, such an intervention may be viewed in different ways by clients: as welcome relief, an exciting challenge, or merely that the counsellor has missed the point entirely. We need to execute care, tact and high sensitivity in both how and when we begin the process of offering and exploring alternatives. When clients make apparently blatant or bizarre misinterpretations of their symptoms, it is particularly tempting to rush in with premature challenges. We should, however, rather be giving the message, 'Yes, I really understand why you think that this is the only way of seeing things. How can we find out if that is right? What do you think?' This way we are both reflecting our understanding of clients' experiences and maintaining collaboration, without belittling them.

Maintaining respect for the client

Maintaining respect for clients has always been a key value in all counselling approaches, and is highlighted by the work of Rogers and Egan (Egan, 2002). At first blush, some activities described in *The Skilled Helper*, for example deliberately increasing anxiety as part of a behavioural experiment, may seem at odds with a strong emphasis on genuineness and respect for the client. Recent research shows that counselling maintains great popularity with the public as a preferred treatment (Bedi et al., 2000), very possibly because of these values. Some of the interventions we describe in the book may seem game-like and even disrespectful. If interventions come to be seen in this way, then this is a very real concern from our perspective. There are, however, two key principles of cognitive therapy – collaboration and rationale giving – that should prevent cognitively orientated counsellors going down the disrespectful path. Collaboration stresses that the therapist takes the client with him every inch of the way. This usually involves giving clear rationales for adopting certain courses of action but leaving the final choice with the client. This, in our view, is a client-centred approach, especially in that it offers clients the chance to gain access to proven interventions, even though they might sound a bit risky.

The Impact of Avoidance of Anxiety on the Counselling Relationship

Avoidance is one of the central ways that clients deal with anxiety and one of the most important of the safety behaviours. Much of our work in anxiety involves confronting and overcoming avoidance in many varied ways, such as getting into a car when driving has been avoided or deliberately touching an area that feels 'unclean'. The confrontation activity can impact on the counselling relationship in two main ways.

Firstly, there is a need to encourage clients to do things that they may not want to do. This may feel highly uncomfortable for counsellors who fear damaging the relationship by being too pushy. We agree that pushing our clients to do things that they do not want to do is not our aim and not good therapy. We are aiming to work out collaboratively why the client avoids, and develop a shared understanding of how avoidance can be reduced by taking an experimental approach to exposure. All this requires a sensitive mix of collaboration and empathy, while at the same time we do not collude with avoidance.

Secondly, clients' avoidance can impact on the therapeutic relationship. People may avoid telling us particular aspects of their problems, because of acute embarrassment about their problems or their coping strategies. Some clients with anxiety problems, particularly those with obsessive compulsive problems or generalised anxiety and worry, are highly avoidant of emotions, wanting to avoid feeling anxious for fear of being overwhelmed or over-emotional (Salkovskis et al., 1998). They fear that the emotional floodgates will open if they start to get in touch with their anxiety feelings. We aim in therapy to find out the 'hot' areas for the client, the thoughts and fears associated with them. If a client is avoiding hot cognitions, it becomes difficult to access the most vital areas for therapy. Therapists should be wary of colluding with client avoidance for fear of upsetting the client. Our avoidance confirms the belief that emotions or anxiety cannot be coped with or tolerated, which is unhelpful in the long run. One way of identifying when there is avoidance in action is if the sessions start feeling dry, dull and intellectual, when the client is describing upsetting or difficult material in an emotionless or flat way. It is important to try to raise the emotional temperature, by reflecting back the unspoken feelings behind the words: 'When you thought you were going to die, that sounds terrifying'; 'Having to check so many times is so upsetting.' Reflecting back the actual words the client is using, along with appropriate affect, or saying how such events would make you feel: 'I don't know how you coped, I would have wanted to cry, I'd feel so upset' can also be useful. It might be necessary to precede such emotion-raising with a discussion of the pros and cons of expressing emotion, or with consideration of ways of coping should the emotions become overwhelming.

Many clients have very realistic worries that talking about their fears can make them worse, particularly where they have tried to cope by avoiding looking at their anxieties, or by keeping on in the same direction for fear that everything will collapse if unpicked. There is some truth in this, and it is helpful to acknowledge and discuss this at the start of therapy. Many of the ways of working described in this book have the flavour of paradoxical interventions, such as making the clients do or feel the things they most fear in order to find out that their fears are out of proportion. We know, for example, that confronting a phobic client with even the smallest first step of facing the feared object or situation will make them feel terrible, anxious, tearful, angry and upset.

These fears need to be elicited and explored at an early stage. Therapy, like much of life, is an experiment, and although we have evidence to make us feel confident that we can generally help anxious clients, we can offer no firm predictions about this particular client. Therapy can indeed sometimes make things worse, at least in the short term, and we are inviting clients to take a big risk by opening things out to change. However, many of the core fears of anxiety lie in this area and these need to be explored.

Zoe had been suffering from attacks of debilitating anxiety for years, following a series of stressful life events. She coped by 'keeping going', gritting her teeth and muddling through life, hoping the anxiety would not be too bad that day. The anxiety was so exhausting at times that she gave up and went to bed, finding that that somehow helped. She was in many ways very motivated to try to change, realising that her life had shrunk, but also was terrified of 'opening the floodgates' and ending up not being able to cope at all. We identified her specific fears and predictions as follows:

- If I begin to talk about it, I'll get so upset that I'll have to go to bed for ever.
- Talking about it will make me so anxious that I'll explode.
- Being anxious means that I cannot cope with anything.
- It is easier to bottle up the past than let it go, since the anxiety will kill me.

As with many clients with anxiety, Zoe had specific predictions about anxiety itself, which we then could explore before beginning work on her anxiety attacks. We looked at the pros and cons of staying the same versus trying to sort out her difficulties. We looked at 'what if . . .': what she could do to help if indeed things did get worse, and how therapy might introduce her to new ways of coping that she had not tried before. We acknowledged that therapy was a huge risk, but to stay the same seemed even more risky. She knew that she could stay in control of therapy and that she could stop it at any time. During therapy, we were able overtly to test out some of her predictions. In reality, Zoe found therapy very difficult at first, and did become more anxious. We used this to access her fears and central issues which she had avoided for several years, and Zoe's problems began to recede as she learned to look at things actively.

Avoidance can lead clients to want to stop counselling as soon as they feel somewhat better, rather than going on to look at what is underlying their fears. For example, a client with general anxiety and worry might find the initial stages of counselling helpful and reassuring, enabling her to talk through her worries and begin to put them into perspective. The client can feel better at first but may not have got to the bottom of her worries or have addressed the processes of worrying. This is what Dryden (1987) calls an 'inelegant' solution to the problems and may leave the client highly vulnerable to further episodes of anxiety and worry. The client may well wish to leave counselling at the stage of feeling somewhat better, rather than stay on and address the underlying concerns.

Confronting fears can be very painful. It may release strong emotions, directed at the counsellor. Some clients may experience a strong grief reaction, others may become very angry and blame the counsellor for making them confront what has been long avoided.

Anna had been confronting some of her fears that she would 'go mad' if she did not carry out her various safety behaviours – for example 'going blank,' silently praying etc. She was becoming markedly distressed and the therapist asked her if she would just stay with it a few moments longer. Anna blurted out, 'It's all right for you!!' The therapist acknowledged that it was indeed easy for him compared to her. She followed this up with, 'Well, can you guarantee that I won't go mad?' The therapist acknowledged that he couldn't. They sat in silence for some time until the therapist observed that the few minutes had now passed. For some reason it struck them as funny and they laughed and experienced a coming together again after the moment of disruption.

Sometimes there may be extreme emotions directed at the counsellor, with anger or abusive swearing at the counsellor, particularly when the client feels 'forced' to confront fears. We need to take a step back at these times. It is vital to acknowledge the client's feelings without reacting to them or getting caught up in the anger. We should acknowledge it when we are indeed pushing too hard, and then take a step back, or whether the feelings need to be stayed with in order to make the most of a potential breakthrough. The dilemma can be shared with the client, so they become an active participant in deciding the pace of therapy.

Working with the Client's Need for Reassurance

Clients with anxiety problems often have a huge need for reassurance from other people that their worries are not going to come true. The client with health anxiety, for example, needs to know that there is nothing wrong, and spends much time consulting doctors or textbooks to allay this anxiety. The client who worries about everything frequently needs to be reassured that their worries *will not at all costs* come true, for the client believes that he will not be able to cope in the circumstances. He therefore frequently asks friends and family for reassurance that bad things will not happen and, if they do happen, that help and support will be at hand. Clients with OCD frequently need reassurance that they have washed enough times; that they have definitely locked the doors or that their thoughts do not mean that they are going to do harm. Gaining reassurance means that the responsibility for making decisions is passed on to someone else. Such a need for reassurance can become active in the therapeutic relationship where, consciously or unconsciously, the client attempts to gain reassurance from the therapist that bad things will not happen.

On some levels all this seems fine: we all want and need to know that things are okay, that we are not alone and that things can be coped with. Reassurance can be a legitimate therapeutic goal – we have stressed how helpful 'normalisation' can be for many anxiety problems. However, the degree of need for reassurance can also cause significant problems, especially when it influences the therapist to pull back from facilitating the client to take necessary risks in confronting fears. This can result in clients not gaining in confidence and independence and getting stuck in cycles of worsening anxiety.

One of the main issues is that none of us can live our lives entirely without risk. If we go about our daily business, we may come across terrible accidents, violence, disease or sudden illness. Bad things may happen to other people, and we may inadvertently cause accidents. If we lock ourselves away, we may reduce the likelihood of such events but we can never completely eliminate the possibility that they may happen. We do, however, make it virtually certain that we will become socially isolated, bored, unfulfilled and terrified. People with anxiety problems are often looking for an infallible insurance policy that is prohibitively expensive (Salkovskis et al., 1998). We simply cannot protect ourselves fully and we cannot offer total reassurance to our clients. The only guarantee that we can offer is that if the client with anxiety problems continues to avoid taking any risks, such as going out of the house, for fear of having a panic attack, they will definitely continue to experience anxiety and agoraphobia. We cannot reassure that a panic attack will not occur, nor that anything else bad will not happen.

In a sense, at these points, therapy takes on a philosophical focus. Cognitive therapy texts (e.g. Beck et al., 1985) have sometimes suggested that such issues should not be pursued. We would agree that such issues are rarely pursued to a sense of full resolution but consider that some discussion of them can sometimes be part of a useful consideration of background factors that influence beliefs.

> Ben suffered from anxiety attacks at night just before going to sleep. A background discussion of this situation revealed a core belief 'You're on your own in this world.' Reflection of this belief identified that it represented a viable philosophical position. At a later time, however, it informed another series of exchanges that led Ben to reflect that he needed to 'become his own father', as well as to continue to seek succour from his inconsistent actual father.

Dealing with the client's reliance on reassurance as a way of coping means, firstly, being able to spot it in action, and, secondly, working with the client to look at its pros and cons and alternatives. In Chapter 11, we discuss the various ways clients with health anxiety seek reassurance from us in sessions. Sometimes reassurance is highly obvious, such as the client constantly asking questions; sometimes it is covert, such as the client slipping in innocuous questions at odd moments, where both client and counsellor may be unaware that reassurance is being sought. We then need to work collaboratively with the client to identify the need for reassurance and look for alternatives. At first it is likely that anxiety will spiral when reassurance is not gained; then over time it will decrease, leading to learning and a gain in confidence.

Alistair suffered from numerous obsessive intrusive thoughts and images. One such intrusion was a fixation on his very attractive girlfriend's waist. Her waist looked slightly fatter than he thought it should be. He attributed the thought, 'The fact that I keep noticing this means that I do not really love her', to the fact that he noticed her waist in this way. He kept asking me to reassure him that this meaning could not possibly be correct. After the therapist had noticed this pattern and fed it back to Alistair, they experimented with sometimes offering the reassurance and sometimes not offering it. Alistair eventually reached the conclusion that he generally felt more doubt after the reassurance had been offered than after it was not offered. After this he was more able to explore ways of dealing with this need himself – the main one being adopting the maxim: 'Tell myself once that it is only emotional reasoning making me think like this. Any further inner discussion will not help.' Although reassurance-seeking continued to be part of the picture of therapy with Alistair, it was increasingly dealt with more quickly, more satisfyingly and, sometimes, even with humour.

On occasions the need for reassurance may be expressed as total fixation on detail: the person with general anxiety and worry needing to tell us every detail of every worry at the beginning of every session; the client with OCD needing to go into great detail about their obsessions. This may arise from the belief 'If I don't tell my counsellor everything, they will never understand and I will never get better.' This needs to be directly addressed, if necessary interrupting the flow of detail in order to look at the process of what is going on. It is important to find out what the client believes will happen if they leave out details: how do they know what is significant and what is not? Are there other chances if one detail is forgotten? Preoccupation with telling every detail can be conceptualised as arising from the client's central lack of trust in other people's capacity to help, or their mistrust of their own ability to communicate with others. Salkovskis et al. (1998) suggest asking the client if it is better to itemize all the details of a picture or to stand back and gain an overall impression. It can be helpful to have a rule: 'If you forget something, if it is really important it will come back again.'

Working on Facing up to Fears: the Boundaries of the Relationship

Therapy for anxiety problems often involves exposure to feared situations or objects. This can have considerable impact on both the practical and psychological dimensions of running the sessions. The physical boundaries of sessions may be extended to other environments, such as supermarkets, shopping centres, trains, etc. We need to ensure that therapeutic boundaries are maintained while working in these situations. For example, once out of the counselling room, client and counsellor may relax into more general conversation, or may meet up with other people who want to talk or be introduced. How do we negotiate these boundaries without becoming a silent automaton? It can be awkward for both client and counsellor. While there are no absolute answers to these types of questions, some discussion of them before going out will mean that they should be less disruptive.

> Rebecca and her counsellor undertook a number of sessions that involved facing up to fearful situations both inside and outside the counselling room. She was concerned about dirt and contamination. Some sessions were to be conducted at home. On one occasion when the therapist called, Rebecca was in tears on her front path. An animal had knocked over and rummaged in her rubbish bin, creating a great mess in front of her flat. Additionally some people from the other flats had trodden some of this mess into the hallway. It seemed impossible to conduct the session as if this mess were not sitting out there, and they decided to go out to clear it up, tracking her emotional and cognitive reactions as they did so. This turned out to be a very 'can do' and 'helpful' way to work on the therapeutic targets. On another occasion, however, a pre-arranged joint trip to a council rubbish tip did not work out well. One aspect of the way that the tip was organised was unexpected and upsetting to Rebecca and she became very distressed. Client and therapist had to beat a quick retreat. Fortunately, they had worked out some ground rules for how she would deal with her feelings when such upset was still active at the end of a session. Knowing that she had coped well in a similar situation at the end of a previous session helped Rebecca and her counsellor deal effectively with the situation.

Besides the practical aspects of such situations, it is also helpful to track the interpersonal aspects of them. Because going out together carries a strong social symbolism and meaning, such activities can trigger interpersonal feelings in both client and counsellor. The counsellor had the distinct impression that Rebecca enjoyed 'outings'. Later on, she seemed to change her mind and was unable to say why. It was only towards the end of counselling that she was able to describe how she had enjoyed going out together, partly because she got the feeling of having an ally in the fight against her anxieties. On the occasion that they went to the tip, however, a friend had seen them and later teased her about her 'romantic' outing with an 'older man'. This teasing and the negative outcome of that outing changed the meaning of those situations for her and effectively put her off them for some time.

The Impact of the Client's Social Network on Counselling

For clients with long-standing anxiety problems such as agoraphobia, their family and social systems may sometimes get organised around the individual's problem. There may be overt or hidden benefits for either the client or the family. For example, some agoraphobic clients can run quite successful businesses by getting other people to become their 'messengers'. Sometimes being the person who operates outside the home for the client can be satisfying, even resulting in status or power from taking on this role. It is therefore important for the therapist to take a systemic view of the problem. Ignoring the system could mean that a therapist might not realise that another family member could feel threatened by the potential of the client's improvement. Family members may have evolved specific helping roles and may feel lost if the client gets better. Therapy may well need to have a systemic flavour, looking at the role of the individual within the wider system and at how he or she can make changes despite others being more set in the system. It can be helpful to make interested parties more involved in the therapy.

The Impact of Other Problems on the Therapeutic Relationship

Many of the clients we see have fairly straightforward problems amenable to the short-term and focused work described in this book, but many too will have more complex or long-standing difficulties, which impact on the therapeutic relationship (Beck et al., 1990; Layden et al., 1993; Wills and Sanders, 1997). Low self-esteem can have a big impact on the progress of therapy and can influence the therapeutic relationship (Fennell, 1998, 1999). We do not cover these issues in detail here, but realise the importance of recognising and working with therapeutic alliance difficulties arising from long-term and personality issues (Safran and Segal, 1990; Wills and Sanders, 1997; Sanders and Wills, 1999). Problems co-existing with anxiety, including depression, alcohol or drug abuse or general anxiety, can impact on the relationship. It is important to work out carefully with the client where the therapy should start and focus, given that these problems can get in the way of specific work on the anxiety itself. Many relate to common themes, such as depression arising from the inability to go out because of panic, or low self-esteem causing both depression and agoraphobia. In this case we need to balance attention to central themes with focused work on particular problems.

Counsellor Beliefs and Counselling for Anxiety

We all have our own beliefs and assumptions arising from our backgrounds and experiences, and these at times may impact on the relationship and progress of therapy. The kinds of assumptions and beliefs in counselling for anxiety include:

- If there is no progress, then I am a terrible therapist/the client is resistant/ the client cannot change.
- Anxious clients are difficult to work with.
- OCD clients are difficult so I must expect failure.
- Counselling for anxiety is a matter of technique.
- Anxious people are right to avoid things that worry them.
- The client 'should get a life'.
- No progress means that I must try harder.
- I have to reassure the client that things will come out right in the end.
- I cannot really understand why the client is so afraid.
- The client needs to meditate more/take homeopathic remedies/have acupuncture/learn to relax. (Magical cure beliefs.)
- It is better to avoid talking about this than to upset the client.
- If I challenge this client, he will think that I lack empathy.
- Clients should just be allowed to talk and talk.
- I must never interrupt the client.
- OCD clients are crazy: who really needs to vacuum every hour?

However good the therapist, however compassionate, it is likely that at times these kinds of thoughts and assumptions will be activated. We are after all humans interacting in a human situation, so our own views and experiences are bound to impinge on the relationship.

Cognitive therapy itself offers many tools for counsellors and therapists to identify and work with thoughts, assumptions and beliefs that may be getting in the way of therapy. At stuck points, think what is going through your mind about the client: Are there 'oughts', 'shoulds' or 'musts'? What is making it difficult to really understand and empathise with this client? Am I making assumptions? What does the client need right now? What do I need? Sometimes finding an image of the client can be helpful in pointing towards impasses in the relationship: seeing the client as an ever-hungry baby and seeing yourself as a wise owl or a helpful teacher may indicate that the pull for reassurance is active; feeling dragged down into the mud at the thought of seeing the client means that we may be feeling stuck because of chronic avoidance, by ourselves or the client.

We cannot stress too much the importance of taking supervision in these situations. The key is to tackle problems at an early stage and to be prepared to look at the process of the relationship when necessary. This does not mean that the relationship itself needs to be the focus of the therapy, but realising that – even in short-term, focused work – relationship issues can become a problem needing attention.

Diving in at the Deep End

Within cognitive therapy, and counselling as a whole, there are two approaches to working with clients: to start at the symptomatic level and work with current problems, and to work with background and longer-term issues. Within cognitive approaches for anxiety, the former has become predominant. Many of the models for particular anxiety disorders concentrate on the maintenance cycle. However, the role of past issues and long-term personality issues is beginning to take on more importance as models of working with more complex problems such as long-standing agoraphobia or obsessive compulsive disorder have developed (Young and Behary, 1998; Davidson, 2000). Such clients are typically very avoidant and have deep and long-held beliefs that underlie the disorders. Cognitive conceptualisation helps us to weave both past and present into our understanding of our clients, looking both at what is keeping the problems going in the here and now, and at what past factors have contributed to making this particular client vulnerable to his or her individual difficulties (Persons, 1989; Layden et al., 1993; Wills and Sanders, 1997).

When we are working with clients with long-term problems or personality issues, it is tempting to dive in at the deep end and aim to work with childhood and personality issues at the beginning: 'What is the point of helping clients to try things out differently if they have all these problems from the past to contend with?' Of course, the whole picture needs to be taken into account, and schema-focused models of cognitive therapy aim to help clients work with long-standing beliefs as well as current problems. There is a very real pull towards working where the action seems to be: counsellors coming from psychodynamic backgrounds may feel that they have not done a proper job without exploring the past and origins of the difficulties. We may spot huge schema issues early on in therapy and feel that that is where the action is, rather than concentrating on the seemingly more mundane intricacies of the maintenance cycle.

However, the evidence is that short-term work focusing on current difficulties, learning skills to cope with anxiety, and encouragement to try things out differently, can be extremely helpful for clients with complex problems, without necessarily looking at past issues. Clients with the range and complexity of difficulties characteristic of borderline personality disorder, often have never learnt ways of managing bad feelings, including anxiety, and feel swamped and dominated by extreme emotions. Helping these clients to manage bad feelings, and to learn basic skills such as staying with bad feelings and using anxiety reduction strategies, can be very beneficial (Linehan, 1993a, b). In addition, we have a huge amount of evidence that working at the day-to-day end of anxiety is effective, whereas developments in schema work are in their infancy and as yet we do not have much hard evidence to suggest effectiveness. Indeed, it may even be actively harmful and counterproductive to look at schema issues if maintenance cycles are not tackled. Clients may be short-changed if they are not offered the understanding, tools and methods for dealing with current problems. Delving too deep can at best be off-putting, and at worst actively harmful, if the client becomes overwhelmed by material that they cannot deal with (James, 2001).

Counsellors should not therefore be dismissive of working with the client to help the management of symptoms. We would encourage counsellors who are tempted to bypass this work in favour of targeting long-term difficulties, to pause before diving in. With our more complex clients, there is a danger that they are not being offered tools that can help them feel better in the here and now and this may be a necessary stage in tackling longer-term issues. At the early stages of counselling, while building up a good therapeutic alliance with the client, we can focus on achieving a balance between past and present. The past cannot be ignored, and needs to be woven into a conceptualisation of the individual client at an early stage. However, working at the symptomatic level is generally a useful first step, and helps both counsellor and client not to feel sucked into a morass of complexity.

5

Assessment of Anxiety Problems

Assessment is an integral part of all forms of psychotherapy and counselling. It means many things, from both counsellor and client 'assessing' each other to see if they can work together, to a detailed assessment for both client and counsellor to clarify what the problems are and to agree on a plan for counselling. Approaches from cognitive therapy advocate a structured approach to assessment, in order to elicit key information to begin to conceptualise the problems. During the assessment phase, the counsellor takes an active role in directing the assessment, asking particular questions at each stage in order to formulate the anxiety problem and develop a plan. We are aware that the concept of structured and explicit assessment of clients carries negative connotations for some counsellors (Dryden and Feltham, 1994), with concerns about assessment turning into a judgemental process involving labelling or diagnosis. However, our aims are to reach some early and therefore provisional agreements about what are the problems and the issues to be worked on (Wills and Sanders, 1997), and to work in a collaborative way throughout. We would argue that a structured and focused assessment phase provides a helpful container in which the work of counselling can begin, and is a reassuring and helpful process for both client and counsellor.

In this chapter we detail the stages of assessment, saying what we are looking for at each stage. We describe how to use specific problem examples to build up a detailed conceptual model of the anxiety problem, as well as taking a long-term and historical perspective. We outline how measures can be used to facilitate assessment, detail some of the pitfalls of using measures, and end with negotiating goals for counselling.

The Aims of Assessment

The structured assessment phase of therapy may take one, two or more sessions to build up a comprehensive picture of the client and his or her difficulties, leading to a collaboratively and mutually agreed plan for therapy. Assessment is a necessary part of the therapy process, and therapeutic in itself. Our clients should come out of an assessment feeling that their problems are more understandable both to themselves and to their counsellor, and that they have a clear idea of what will happen next. The assessment phase may last one or more sessions: for more complex anxiety problems such as health anxiety or obsessive compulsive disorder, it can take a few sessions to establish a working model of what is going on.

As counsellors, we aim to collect sufficient information to begin to build up the conceptualisation for the individual client, looking at how thoughts, feelings, behaviour and biology interact, so that we can formulate what kind of anxiety problem the client may be suffering from, and understand vulnerability factors and triggers. From this, we begin to devise a picture and plan for the counselling. Assessment enables the client to have answers to, and more understanding of, the following:

- What are my problems? Is there a name or way of understanding that is helpful? What exactly is going on?
- What is keeping my problems going? Why do I not just get better of my own accord? Are there feelings, thoughts, behaviours, physical symptoms or environmental issues that keep the anxiety going?
- How did the difficulties develop? Why at this particular time? What is going on in my life that triggered it all off?
- Why me? What makes me vulnerable?
- What can I do to help? What needs to change?
- What can I expect from therapy? What goals do I have? How might things be different when I am 'better'?
- What do I need to do to help myself?
- Can I work with this particular counsellor? Is now the right time for counselling?

Beginning Assessment

Assessment often starts before we see the client. For counselling in NHS settings, a referring general practitioner may give us an idea about the client in a written referral before we arrange to see the client, or we may have discussed the situation with doctor or client over the telephone as we arranged to meet. Other sources of initial information may be from employee or workplace counselling referrals. These initial assessment phases can colour our expectations of what the client may bring to the first session: we may be on the lookout for panic disorder, as diagnosed by the GP, or general anxiety as picked up in the difficulty in arranging the 'right' appointment with the client. We urge wariness in building up early preconceptions, since both client and counsellor need time to work out what the problems are: for example, a referral for a 'driving phobia' may mask problems of post traumatic stress disorder; 'classic' cases of panic disorder may mask social phobias or general anxiety and worry.

At the assessment meeting, we start with the flavour and philosophy of focus and structure, introduce the client to the agenda for the assessment, explaining that we will be asking about both past and present issues. Clients often come with preconceived ideas about meeting the counsellor for the first time, and it is helpful to find out at the beginning of the first meeting what their expectations are: we have heard clients with expectations of an in-depth analysis of their childhoods, an instant cure, advice on medication, being hypnotised, being admitted under section, and being laughed at. Many clients have fears of not being taken seriously, being told it is 'only stress', or that they are losing their minds. The early minutes of assessment aim to ensure clarity about what to expect during the first meeting. For counselling in medical settings the assessment can be introduced as follows:

> I have had a letter from your doctor, which has given me some information about the difficulties you've been having. She has told me [brief summary of the letter or referral details]. Today, we have about an hour, and I'd like to hear in your own words how you are, and about the problems. I'll ask you some quite detailed questions about what's been going on and how you are, and also some general questions about you and your background. How does that sound? Do you have any questions or concerns at this point?

Assessing the Maintenance Cycle and Building a Conceptualisation

Use of detailed examples

Part of the counsellor's role when assessing the maintenance cycle of anxiety is to help the client distinguish between different components of anxiety, thoughts, feelings, biology and behaviour. By understanding the different roles each of these have in keeping anxiety going, the client can become clearer about their difficulties and what to do. Each 'actor' in the play of anxiety has a different voice, and each needs a different solution. For example, a client with panic problems may be overwhelmed with somatic symptoms of anxiety, their 'spotlight' being on feeling churned up, hot and bothered, shaky, and experiencing headaches and stomach cramps, and may see the solution as getting rid of the physical symptoms. We, as cognitive therapists, would aim to widen the lighting on the stage, to look at how other components feed into and keep the symptoms going: how the individual interprets the symptoms (I'm dying, I'll lose it), what she does to cope with the fear and helplessness invoked by the voice of the symptoms.

The most valuable way of assessing anxiety problems is to ask the client for a recent, detailed example of the problem, where we aim to understand the links between thoughts, feelings, behaviour and biology. Although asking how the client generally feels is a useful place to begin the assessment, to really understand the problems we need to go into the detail of a specific example. Ask the client to think of a recent time when he or she felt anxious – an instance that is typical of the client's problems rather than an idiosyncratic episode. Then guide the client through a detailed description. When clients are avoiding any situations which trigger anxiety, they may have nothing specific to report when asked for a recent example, in which case they can be invited to imagine what they might feel, think or do if they had to, for example, go down to the shops alone.

Assessing physical symptoms, thoughts and feelings

Since, in anxiety, we are looking for vicious cycles, in some ways it does not matter where we start in terms of the interaction of thoughts, feelings, behaviour or physical symptoms. We start where the client starts in response to the question 'What did you notice first?' For many of the anxiety problems, clients initially describe their difficulties in terms of a range of physical symptoms. The list can seem endless, and incorporate all the bodily structures and functions altered by the 'fight or flight' adrenaline response. From here, clients can be asked what went through their minds when they felt the symptoms, how they felt in themselves, and what they did, as the following example illustrates:

Mavis, who had been referred by her general practitioner for help with anxiety and panic attacks, had not initially thought about the possibility that she was anxious, and did not know what a panic attack was. She had been feeling awful, with 'out of the blue' episodes of shaking, difficulty in breathing, tight-chestedness and tingling in her arms. She was extremely concerned that this was the beginning of heart disease, and had been checked by the cardiologist, who had diagnosed anxiety and sent Mavis off to 'sort herself out'.

The therapist asked Mavis to describe a recent example of feeling awful, in this case in the supermarket.

Counsellor: What was the first thing you noticed?

Mavis: I started to feel awful: really odd, completely out of the blue. I couldn't breathe, I started to get these pains in my chest and the tingling . . . I felt quite shaky.

Counsellor: So, you were feeling really awful . . . when you felt like this, what was going through your mind?

Mavis: Well, I know it's stupid since I know there's nothing wrong with me: the cardiologist said so . . . but I really thought I was having a heart attack and this was it!

Counsellor: It sounds like you were feeling pretty bad, but you sound a bit embarrassed about what you made of it. I guess it makes sense if you were feeling that bad.

Mavis: um . . .

Counsellor: So, you felt awful, chest pains, couldn't breathe, and you said to yourself, 'I'm having a heart attack . . . this is it.' When you said that to yourself, how did that make you feel?

Mavis: Terrified.

Counsellor: And when you felt terrified, what was going on in your body?

Mavis: I guess it didn't help: I felt much worse.

When clients like Mavis experience panic attacks, they initially say that the physical sensations occur first, 'out of the blue'. However, it is often the case that something else may trigger the sensations, for example the thought 'what if I feel anxious?' leads the client to feel anxious, and then notice their feelings, and then begins the interpretation cycle. However, when assessing panic problems, the order of asking the questions can enable client and counsellor to see how one thing triggers the next (Clark, 1986). The sequence is as follows:

1. 'What did you notice first?' Identify physical symptoms.
2. 'And when you felt that, what went through your mind?' Identify thoughts.
3. 'And when you said that to yourself, how did that make you feel?' Identify feelings.
4. 'And when you felt that, what happened in your body?' Identify physical symptoms.
5. 'And when you felt like that physically, what went through your mind?'

Then we begin to repeat the questions to ascertain the panic cycle. The sequence enables the client to look, perhaps for the first time, at how the way they interpret their symptoms leads on to increased anxiety and more physical symptoms, and thus more distress.

During therapy, we aim to discover those thoughts with the most explanatory value for understanding the client's emotions and difficulties – what have been called 'hot thoughts' (Greenberger and Padesky, 1995). For example, the thought 'I'm feeling anxious' may not be a negative thought but a statement of fact. Underneath this thought may be the hotter issue, 'I'm feeling anxious and in a minute something terrible will happen. How do I know this isn't a heart attack? Or I'll pass out.' The counsellor should be looking for appraising cognitions: those that give meaning to the events and feelings described. Self-appraising thoughts are often particularly salient. Appraisals may be hidden by a question: 'Why is this happening to me?' It is then useful to ask, 'Why do you think it is happening to you? What does it say about you?', leading to the hot appraisal, 'It just keeps on happening, I'll never get it right, bad things are always happening to me and there's no escape.'

In order for clients to clarify their anxious thoughts and feelings, diaries can be very valuable. A simple three-column diary of situation, feelings and thoughts is a useful starting place for the client to begin to clarify the difference between thoughts and feelings, and identify what triggers anxiety for them (Figure 5.1). The issue of which thoughts and appraisals to work with in therapy are discussed further in Chapter 6, on identifying and working with anxious thinking. At the assessment phase, it is important to be aware of the temperature of the cognitive material we are working with, and realise that it is not always helpful or appropriate to unearth the most salient issues right at the beginning.

Assessing behaviours

In assessing how the client behaves when anxious, we are aiming to distinguish between behaviours that might be useful to the client in tackling anxiety, and 'safety behaviours' that keep the anxiety going by not enabling the client to disconfirm their worst fears. The following example of Mike, a 24-year-old student with social phobia, mainly fears of speaking in public, illustrates how to distinguish these two types of behaviour. Mike is describing a recent incident in which he was required to make a presentation to the rest of his university course classmates. He had been

Date and time	Situation	How did you feel? Rate 0–10	What went through your mind? Rate belief in thought 0–10

Figure 5.1 *Diary of thoughts and feelings*

anxious and preoccupied about this for several weeks beforehand, but had worked out strategies to get him through. Notice that the counsellor asks Mike to describe what is going on in the incident as though it is happening now.

Counsellor: You're describing being asked to begin your presentation. How are you feeling?

Mike: Actually, I'm feeling as if I'm not really there, like my mind has gone off somewhere else, and that scares me. So, I try and really concentrate on what I've got to say, and keep an eye on how I'm feeling.

Counsellor: How are you doing that, keeping an eye on how you're feeling?

Mike: I'm scanning what's going on. I'm beginning to notice a sort of churned up feeling inside, like my guts are just getting busy, and I'm feeling quite shaky. I realise I've got to get a grip . . . otherwise . . .

Counsellor: Otherwise . . .?

Mike: Otherwise I'd lose it completely. Just spurt the words out all over the place and not make any sense at all. Like we've been talking about – like a complete prat.

Counsellor: Yes, a very awful image for you. How do you prevent this happening? What do you mean by 'getting a grip'?

Mike: I do everything in my power to relax – I bust a gut to relax. I say to myself over and over, 'Get a grip, Mike, get a grip', and try

and let my muscles go. I start taking deep breaths and concentrate on watching the air go in and out.
Counsellor: Does that help? How are you feeling now you're trying so hard to relax?
Mike: I know it is the only way I'll get through. I must relax, otherwise . . .
Counsellor: Otherwise . . .?
Mike: Well, it's back to the same old thing, the same old Mike being a complete prat.

From this example, Mike is trying to relax and breathe deeply in order to get through his presentation, and has very strong beliefs that if he did not do this, catastrophe would happen – in his case he gets a strong image of himself shaking, stuttering, saying words in random order, and being 'a complete prat'. The behaviours of trying to keep himself safe are not helpful for several reasons: they keep Mike focused on himself and how he is feeling, which means he takes many physical signs as evidence of losing control, and averts his attention from his audience; attempting to relax and breathe deeply may itself increase symptoms of anxiety (trying to bust a gut to relax makes most people feel highly stressed); and continually trying to control his anxiety means that Mike is unable to disconfirm his worst fears, that people will notice he is nervous, that the anxiety means he will spurt out nonsense, and so on.

When is a safety behaviour not a safety behaviour?

The range of what people do when anxious leads to an important question: when is a behaviour a safety behaviour and when is it a useful way of getting through life? Many of us might feel nervous before, say, an interview, giving a workshop or lecture, meeting our partner's parents for the first time, giving evidence in court. It is quite reasonable and helpful for us to calm ourselves down by some deep breathing, relaxing, or making sure we take time not to be stressed before the event by getting a good night's sleep. These can all be both helpful coping methods or safety behaviours, depending on the individual's beliefs. The key question is what the person believes would happen if they did not do these things, and whether they are the only ways of coping. If we know that, whatever happens, we will get through, that once we start talking we'll get interested and no longer be so self-focused, that the anxiety will recede and we will get on with the task in hand, then the coping behaviours are ways of helping ourselves feel better rather than a matter of averting catastrophe. So, as the example with Mike illustrates, it is important to check not only what someone does when anxious, but what they believe would happen if they did not do this.

Assessing the History of Problems

Taking a developmental perspective on the problems can be very helpful, in order to understand why the problems started in the first place, and to discover some of the key vulnerability issues for the client. Ask the client to describe when the problems first started, what was going on in their lives, what the client believes may have been triggers. The onset of a problem can be very clear: for example, the first time a client experienced a panic attack can be an unforgettable experience. The start of problems such as social anxiety and general anxiety, however, can be less clear: 'I've always been nervous around people'; 'I've always been a worrier.' We are looking for the time when such problems became so problematic that the individual sought help, and we are aiming to understand what triggered things then. Often there are external circumstances which conspire to lead to problems: for example, multiple external stresses may lead to overload of worry and flagrant and distressing anxiety symptoms; clients who are worried about social situations may have been able quietly to cope, but then go to University where giving presentations is an integral part of the work. We all have our 'last straws' and we are aiming to understand what these are for the client and why. From the trigger we can begin to build up ideas about the client's individual vulnerabilities to particular problems:

Frieda had always been a perfectionist, liking to do jobs competently and achieve good outcomes. She had done well at school, and was proud of her track record. At university, she worked successfully, coping with the pressure, making friends and generally being a star student. Two years after leaving university, Frieda started a job in market research. Because of her glowing references, she was fast tracked into a post with more responsibility and consequent longer hours. Initially she coped beautifully, enjoying the extra work and the praise that went with it. However, a number of difficult life events occurred at the same time and, shortly afterwards, Frieda began to experience painful bowel symptoms which woke her at night. She woke in the morning with a churning stomach, feeling tense and headachy. Her performance at work began to suffer, for the first time in her life. Frieda was eventually referred by her GP who was unable to help her with the bowel problems and had told her that they were stress-related. Frieda was at a loss to explain how she could be suffering from stress: she always coped with whatever life threw at her, she was one of life's copers and could take everything in her stride. We looked at all the events and life changes that Frieda had faced in the previous years. Seeing herself as a coper, Frieda had been reluctant to admit to herself that she could not cope with everything presented to her by life: however, by the end of the assessment, and by drawing a vivid map of her recent life events, Frieda felt somewhat relieved that there were explanations for how bad she was feeling. The assessment also brought up many feelings of shame at being 'unable to cope' to which we returned during the counselling.

Developmental History, Assumptions and Beliefs

During the assessment, we ask for a picture of the client's background, such as family details, and any difficulties or issues while growing up. Anxiety or depression, whether genetic or learned, may run through families. Interestingly, many clients describe their mothers as worriers. It may well be a universal trend for children to interpret a mother's care and responsibility as 'worrying' or 'fussing'. This fastidious care may, however, represent the high survival value attached to parents being over-protective as opposed to under-protective of their children, rather than a good indication of psychopathology in the family. We are aiming to begin to pick up on client rules and assumptions which may predispose the individual to anxiety. It can also be helpful to ask for themes and issues running through the family, or how the client was similar to or different from the rest of the family.

Henry's family moved several times during his childhood and travelled extensively. At a young age, the children were encouraged to test out everything, test their limits, and not be afraid, and would often go on camping expeditions miles away from anywhere where Henry felt at all safe. Henry was encouraged to take everything in his stride, but spent his childhood in terror. He never felt safe, found the unpredictability of it awful, and believed that he was the only one in the family with the responsibility for watching out for danger. He was always on the lookout, but any fears were dismissed by the family. Henry looked back on his childhood with feelings of insecurity mixed with regret, since his haphazard, rough-and-tumble upbringing 'should' have been idyllic for little boys. Later on in life Henry developed general anxiety problems and became apprehensive and worried about many aspects of his life. In counselling he could link this with his pervading sense of uncertainty and feelings of lack of safety in his early years.

There is much evidence in cognitive therapy to show that working with maintenance cycles alone can be highly effective; such work may produce changes in the client's assumptions and beliefs without these being addressed directly. From the assessment it may be clear to us that the client holds beliefs about themselves, others and the world which are likely to predispose her to anxiety; to begin to identify and address such beliefs too early on in the therapy can be counterproductive, and may not be necessary to produce change. To have our rules spelt out and challenged can be a difficult and threatening business. Frieda, in the previous example, felt she had done well with her beliefs about doing everything to perfection, and to begin to look at how such beliefs could be counterproductive would have been too difficult at an early stage. In Henry's case, the themes of vulnerability became central from the beginning of counselling: firstly we looked at his feelings of vulnerability about his health, and then at more general feelings of lack of safety in the world. During the assessment phase, we may begin to pick up on a client's core issues; the assessment phase is a time to make a mental or other note of these and return to them later on in the counselling, as and when the client is ready.

Assessing Health Issues

As well as assessing somatic symptoms, it is important to find out about medication and general health issues that might be involved (Hammersley, 1995). Clients referred by GPs or from other medical settings may come with written information about medication and pertinent medical problems. It is also important to check with clients who self-refer. We are now aware of the dangers of inappropriate or long-term prescribing of benzodiazepines for anxiety, and governmental guidelines from the Committee for the Safety of Medicines stress that tranquillisers should be used only as a short-term measure. However, it is not unusual to meet clients who are prescribed these medications to treat anxiety, and which may be causing further problems. While prescribing is not counsellors' responsibility, we can be helpful to clients who take medication, particularly benzodiazepines, by being knowledgeable about their effects and side-effects. There are a number of helpful publications on medication which give accessible information based on good practice guidelines (Hailstorm and McClure, 1998; Burns, 1999).

Anxiety symptoms may arise from a variety of medical conditions or medications, which are summarised in Table 5.1. Within

Table 5.1   *Medical and pharmacological causes of anxiety symptoms*

Medical causes	Medication substances
Cardiac conditions	Alcohol
Endocrine conditions	Caffeine
Hyper and hypothyroidism	Drug abuse
Hypoglycaemia	Prescription medicines
Neurological problems	Benzodiazepines
Asthma or respiratory problems	Withdrawal of substances
Hyperventilation	Withdrawal of benzodiazepines

counselling and therapy we are not required to be medical experts to test for all problems, and hope that these have been looked at for our clients referred through medical routes. We have only come across one client where blatant symptoms of panic were caused directly by a thyroid difficulty and which disappeared on treatment of the underlying problem.

Long periods of anxiety and stress may lead to problems such as headaches, aches and pains, stomach disorders and other stress responses (Palmer and Dryden, 1995). There may be co-existing medical conditions or illness which exacerbate the symptoms of anxiety. Physical symptoms may also be increased by some ways of coping with anxiety, or by general lifestyle issues, such as the consumption of alcohol, caffeine, tranquillisers or anti-depressants; constant physical tension in order to keep control; diet and nutrition; smoking; lack of or too much exercise; or over-the-counter medication. Christine Padesky gives an example of a client with panic attacks who turned out to be sitting right next to the coffee machine at work. This led to her imbibing up to 20 cups of coffee during her working day. As soon as she cut down on coffee, the panic attacks subsided.

We do not aim to provide an exhaustive list, more to show that the counsellor needs to be aware of other factors that may cause or mimic anxiety symptoms. Counsellors, doctors or clients do not always get the diagnosis right and we may all miss things on rare occasions, but it is important to be open-minded and cover various possibilities. If in doubt about what is going on, ask and find out more information. We urge caution, however, in over-medicalising symptoms where the client is looking only for medical causes, such as in health anxiety, as discussed in Chapter 11.

One of the main treatments for worry and anxiety used to be benzodiazepines, and these are still used more than is ideal. Valium and other tranquillisers can in fact cause many anxiety problems, particularly if the client attempts to cut down the dose and come off them. Benzodiazepines can be very effective in reducing anxiety in the short term, but unfortunately are so potentially dangerous in the long term, resulting in addiction, that they can cause more problems than they resolve. We need to be very aware in counselling about any medications the client is taking, and the potential impact on client's symptoms and the process of counselling (Hammersley, 1995). A number of clients have coped with anxiety by using drugs, prescription or otherwise, and alcohol, which can cause many other problems. These need to be carefully assessed and worked with.

Assessing Other Problems

Anxiety often goes hand in hand with other problems, particularly depression. Clients with anxiety problems frequently report feeling low at times, or claim that the anxiety has impacted on other areas of life. It is therefore important for the counsellor to assess how the client is feeling in him or herself, particularly looking for depression and its possible impact on the client's difficulties, and assessing any other problems. Tools such as the Beck Depression Inventory can be a very helpful aid to assessing depression.

When a client presents with both anxiety and depression, where should counselling start? It is helpful to work out which came first, since depression can lead to anxiety, or anxiety to depression. The timing may determine which the counsellor and the client decide to work on first. For example, if a client has anxiety problems, but is also feeling very low, unable to do much because of low energy, unable to enjoy much, feels hopeless and has poor sleep, these are indicators that depression may be a significant problem for the client. A client may need to decide which to concentrate on first: for example, low mood may result from not being able to go out and take part in activities because of anxiety, in which case the client may want to tackle the fears of going out as primary. Depression, however, can make it difficult for a client to work on other issues: depression produces a global negative view of the self, others and the world, which can make it difficult for clients to identify or believe in any alternative ways of thinking. In this case, counsellors would generally tackle the client's depression before working on anxiety, particularly when the client is moderately or severely depressed. Where to start in therapy depends, therefore, on balancing where the client wants to start, which problem has the most impact on the client's life, and where one problem is going to get in the way of effective resolution of another.

Anxiety may be a realistic response to threatening or difficult life circumstances. A client may, for example, be fearful of going out in case she meets a threatening ex-partner. Her concerns and worries about her children, health, or job security may well be realistic. We need to make a careful assessment of whether the level of anxiety the client feels is in fact a realistic adaptation to difficult circumstances, or an over-reaction, which is not helpful. The client has to be the best judge of this. It may be that the client needs to use other resources in order to deal more effectively with the threats, such as having more contact with the police if there are real threats from another person, or gaining more information and advice about problems such as work or debts. We need to be able to recognise when counselling alone is or is not appropriate for this client's needs.

Many of our clients have long-standing problems. Life issues will affect our approach within counselling, particularly in deciding whether long-term or short-term work is needed, whether a multidisciplinary approach may be helpful, and which problems we can tackle in counselling and which have to be worked with elsewhere. The evidence is that even clients with long-term problems can find focused work on tackling their anxiety problems helpful. However, it can raise the question of when to tackle the anxiety problem, and when other problems predominate.

Tracy came for an assessment with a long history of problems with social phobia and depression, which had led to difficulties in keeping jobs, to financial concerns and homelessness. During the assessment she described herself as a 'no hoper', far too damaged by her critical and abusive upbringing to be able to change. She had tried various forms of help, including counselling, medication and an anxiety management group, all of which she had dropped out of. Clearly, Tracy had a number of problems which we needed to prioritise. She was clinically depressed and becoming agoraphobic by avoiding going out, she was experiencing financial difficulties and debt because of neglecting to sort out benefits, and she suffered from long-standing social phobia. She had recently started drinking as a means of coping. Tracy felt that the overriding problem was her terror of other people, and her belief that everyone had a negative judgement of her: this was her priority for therapy. Over two assessment sessions, we both agreed that Tracy's other problems might well impact on being able to sort out the social phobia and we needed to tackle these first. We worked out a detailed plan and decided to 'call in the troops' to help. She had a more thorough review of medication with a psychiatrist, and, after the right dose was found, Tracy's mood and sleep began to improve. She was introduced to a community support worker who helped her to sort out her housing and benefits, and who went with her to the Citizens Advice Bureau to work out a plan for dealing with her debts. We met weekly to review how everything was going in tackling these problems, and to monitor her drinking. After a few weeks of hard work on everyone's part, Tracy was beginning to feel more in control. She had found accommodation and had sorted out her benefits so that she could make this a more stable home. She had a plan for dealing with her debts, by tackling the problems head on rather than avoiding them. She felt more in control of her drinking; and her mood was helped by the medication. We then targeted her depression and social phobia, conceptualising how these affected each other and how we needed to work on both at the same time. The work on social phobia started after four months of counselling.

Assessment Measures

Using measures is very valuable in clarifying the client's problems, in helping to be more specific and parsimonious with therapy, and in evaluating the effectiveness of our work. Using standard measures can help people to say things that would be difficult to say on first meeting, such as having very frightening thoughts, thoughts of suicide or experiencing physical symptoms which they find unacceptable. Measures, such as the Beck inventories, provide counsellor and client with more objective yardsticks for measuring change. Are we going in the right direction? Is one problem resolving only for another to increase? For example we may see a significant decrease in anxiety levels, but higher scores on the Beck Depression Inventory.

Some counselling traditions are against the use of measures, finding them contrary to the spirit and ethos of their particular model, invasive and over-medicalising of the problems. Using written measures can have their disadvantages – they can be off-putting if questions are seen as irrelevant or too challenging or detailed; they can cause significant problems for clients with difficulties reading or writing, and therefore have to be used sensitively and without assumptions being made. Our own views and experience is that questionnaires, used with clients' full understanding and consent, can have a real place in counselling for anxiety problems, so long as their use and limitations are accepted and the tools are used properly. They help to keep us on track, to see where we are going and to assess whether our counselling work is helpful or not.

Measures can take many forms, from standard measures such as the Beck Depression Inventory and Beck Anxiety Inventory, to measures designed specifically for individual clients, targeting particular issues and problems. Adrian Wells (1997) provides a comprehensive section on assessment measures, including copies of some of the measures, and we draw the following information from his source.

Standard measures

There is a variety of standard measures which might apply to all clients, such as the Beck Depression and Anxiety Inventories, which have a lot of data to support ranges of depression and anxiety in 'clinical' and 'normal' populations. Thus we can say that a client with a score of 10–19 on the BDI may be suffering from mild to moderate depression, whereas scores of 20–29 represent moderate to severe depression, and 30–63 severe depression. Similarly, scores on the Beck Anxiety Inventory can give a 'shorthand' as to how severe a client's anxiety symptoms may be. The following are useful measures:

- *The Beck Anxiety Inventory* (Beck et al., 1988) is a 21-item self-report scale, measuring severity of physical and cognitive aspects of anxiety.
- *The Beck Depression Inventory* (Beck and Steer, 1987), is a self-report scale with 21 items measuring severity of depressive symptoms. It includes a range of questions measuring different aspects of functioning, and questions about suicidal thoughts and hopelessness, which are very important to assessing the client's risk. We find these particular questions can be a way in to ask clients about suicidal thoughts and hopeless feelings, which may be difficult for clients to describe at the beginning of counselling, but are so important in terms of us being aware of risk and safety issues.
- *State Trait Anxiety Scale* (Spielberger et al., 1983) measures two related aspects of anxiety: 'state anxiety', the level of anxiety at a particular moment, and 'trait anxiety', the relatively stable individual level of proneness to anxiety.
- *Hopelessness Scale* (Beck et al., 1974) measures clients' level of hopelessness about the future, and predicts suicide intent, as well as suicidal behaviour. We tend to use this scale only where hopelessness and suicide risk are important issues, as identified during the assessment and from scores on the BDI.
- *Robson Self-Esteem Measure* (Robson, 1989) measures various dimensions of self-esteem. It is a valuable measure for many

clients, looking at how self-esteem may influence counselling. Interestingly, scores on the Robson have been shown to improve, indicating higher self-esteem, after cognitive therapy for anxiety and depression, possibly independently of whether a client's self-esteem was directly focused on during therapy (David Westbrook, personal communication, Oxford).

Specific measures for specific problems

Various particular measures have been developed to assess and measure specific problems such as general anxiety problems, worry, agoraphobia and social phobia (summarised in Wells, 1997). Specific measures are useful in determining what exactly are the clients' problems, in 'screening' for different anxiety problems, and in looking at outcome. The Fear Questionnaire (Marks and Mathews, 1979) gives an idea of the range of clients' anxieties in terms of social fears, agoraphobia and blood injury. Some questionnaires ask about very specific thoughts in specific difficulties, and as such help both client and counsellor to identify what kinds of issues and meanings are most pertinent. The Agoraphobic Cognitions Questionnaire (Chambless et al., 1984) measures specific thoughts about anxiety, such as 'I am going to throw up', 'I am going to pass out' or 'I am going to act foolish/go crazy/scream/babble and talk funny.' From this we can see whether the danger area for the client is in terms of physical danger or of how others perceive them.

Specific questionnaires can be helpful in a number of ways. A client with panic problems may be concerned about the physical or the social consequences of panic attacks, or both, and can see what is most pertinent through questionnaires which help to distinguish different issues. Questionnaires can help specify what kind of problem the client is experiencing: for example, a client with anxiety may be most affected by worrying thoughts, and it is the fact of experiencing such thoughts rather than their content which is most distressing. Using questionnaires such as those described below can provide useful short-cuts to assessment. Similarly, such questionnaires help us to assess change in the areas which are most important to the client.

Tailor-made measures

Rather than, or as well as, using off-the-peg questionnaires, specific measures can be designed with the individual client to measure change in whatever is of concern. For example, Tracy found it very difficult to say just how she was feeling and, for her, filling in questionnaires was difficult. She devised a 'global yeuch' measure, a 0–10 measure, which she called her 'yeuchometer', which gave us both useful feedback as to how she was. Other measures can be number of panic attacks, number of times going out was avoided, the amount of time able to stay in a room without checking for the presence of spiders, number of obsessional thoughts, happiness ratings, and so on. The list is as long as the number of clients we see, and clients can be very creative in coming up with their own measures.

Negotiating Goals for Counselling

The assessment phase ends when counsellor and client have some clarity about their goals for counselling. Most of our clients are clear about why they have come to see us: to feel better, to stop getting panic attacks, to be able to drive, to be able to go out alone, or to stop worrying about everything. Both client and counsellor need to be realistic about the goals that are possible, partly when constrained by a short number of sessions and partly when the client's goals may be unrealistic. Whether a client needs short-term or longer-term therapy can to some extent be assessed during the very early stages of counselling, but the ability to meet needs for longer-term work may be constrained by practical and resource limitations. Research evidence summarised in Chapter 7 shows that many clients' goals can be achieved in short-term work: for example, clients can stop having panic attacks, maintained at long-term follow up, after brief therapy of six sessions, which compares well with longer work. Even clients with long-term and enduring difficulties, perhaps characteristic of personality issues or 'disorders', can benefit from short-term and focused work, although longer-term work, focusing on underlying schema, may be necessary to look at underlying issues (Beck et al., 1990; Layden et al., 1993).

Clients may be unrealistic about their goals. To eliminate anxiety totally is not a realistic goal for most of us, given that anxiety is such a normal part of our human experience, and in order to define and meet our goals in life some anxiety-provoking extension into the unknown is usually necessary. We aim, therefore, to have realistic goals. Having said this, our journey in counselling may well end up in a place different from our original destination: for example, short-term work focused only on eliminating one specific phobia can dramatically improve self-esteem and quality of life, as well as eliminating other phobias. Counselling involves intrepid exploration as well as navigation.

6

Methods and Techniques

Anxiety and stress management is a therapeutic arena where techniques and methods abound. Many stress- and anxiety-management programmes focus on teaching clients a range of techniques, including relaxation and breathing methods, positive thinking or thought-stopping, goal-setting and problem-solving, meditation or massage. Many of these are highly effective and a good first port of call for most of us when stress or anxiety begins to take over.

While advocating a series of techniques can be very useful, it is likely that many of the clients who come for individual counselling or therapy for anxiety problems will have already tried various techniques and found them of only moderate value, or effective for a short time only. They may be wanting to understand more about their own anxiety problems as well as learning general methods to help. The key finding across many studies is that long-term changes arises from not just doing things differently but from feeling and thinking differently and holding different beliefs. Cognitive therapy has a well deserved reputation for being technique-based (Wills and Sanders, 1997). Some techniques have developed within the framework of the cognitively based therapies, and some are borrowed from other disciplines, including behaviour therapy, problem-solving or Gestalt. Techniques and methods are based on the client's individual conceptualisation described in Chapter 2. Using techniques aims to help change clients' beliefs about anxiety itself, leading to decatastrophising the symptoms, changing behaviour, and not allowing anxiety to govern life. In order to produce such cognitive changes, we use, strategically and expediently, a range of techniques, guided by the individual client's conceptualisation and our understanding of what is effective for different problems (Beck et al., 1985; Wells, 1997; Wills and Sanders, 1997).

We stress throughout the book the central philosophy behind working with anxiety problems: to help the client identify anxious predictions, and test these out, in order to come up with more helpful, non-anxious appraisals. So, we ask the reader to bear these principles in mind when thinking about techniques and working with individual clients. We also need to balance using techniques that have general value versus carefully matching methods to the individual client. Much of the development of cognitive therapy techniques has evolved in response to particular clinical *problems*: for example, the hyperventilation provocation test, described below, has evolved to help disconfirm clients' fears in the treatment of panic disorder, and specific behavioural experiments are used for different anxiety disorders. However effective the techniques may be in the treatment of particular problems *in general*, the approaches always need to be allied with the client's experience *in particular*, a point we return to through-out the book.

In this chapter, we offer a broad introduction to a range of methods used in helping clients with anxiety problems. In the chapters on individual problems, we give more guidance on how to match techniques to different forms of anxiety. Many anxiety-management methods, such as relaxation, are already well docu-mented, and rather than repeating them here we offer guidance on other reading. We aim not to just look at the techniques but to offer ideas as to when to use different methods, and give words of caution on inappropriate use. Other useful resources for methods include Butler and Hope (1995); Greenberger and Padesky (1995); Padesky and Greenberger (1995); Kennerley (1997) and Wells (1997).

Identifying and Working with Thoughts

Anxious thinking and anxious predictions underlie all the anxiety problems, and therapy very often starts with client and therapist working together to understand thoughts, images and beliefs which are driving the anxiety, and come up with more helpful reappraisals. There are a number of ways of identifying anxious thoughts (Padesky and Greenberger, 1995; Wells, 1997) sum-marised in Table 6.1.

Anxiety is such an overwhelming feeling that clients can find it difficult to identify what was going through their minds. Some clients cannot easily distinguish between thoughts and feelings, and find it very difficult to put their thoughts into words. A good question to ask is, 'When you felt so bad, what went through your mind?' or 'Did you get an image or picture in your mind?' It is important to elicit specific thoughts, in statements rather than

Table 6.1   *Identifying anxious thoughts*

Key steps in identifying anxious thoughts:

- Pick a concrete example.
- Ask about feelings.
- 'And when you felt that, what went through your mind?'
- Aim to identify specific thoughts.
- Turn questions into statements, e.g., 'What do other people think?' becomes 'They think I'm really stupid'. 'What if X should happen?' becomes 'If X happens, it would be a complete disaster.'

Sources of anxious thoughts:

- Shifts of mood in sessions or in real life: client suddenly looks or feels anxious.
- Predictions: what if you were to . . .?
- Role play anxiety-provoking situations.
- Asking the client to imagine themselves in anxiety-provoking situations.
- Self-observation and self-monitoring: thought diaries.

questions. For example, when the client reports the thought 'What if I couldn't cope?', he can be helped to rephrase it as 'If I didn't cope, it would be a complete disaster and I'd make a real fool of myself', thereby eliciting more emotion. The second statement gets to the heart of the matter.

A key point in identifying anxious thoughts is to separate out which thoughts are most salient from the numerous thoughts buzzing around. The most useful thoughts to identify are so-called hot cognitions (Greenberger and Padesky, 1995). Hot thoughts are those that are connected to emotions, as distinct from the numerous other anxious thoughts going through the mind. If the client's mood suddenly shifts, or the description of an event or problem is accompanied by emotion, then it can be useful to catch the immediate hot thought by asking 'What went through your mind just then?' These hot cognitions are likely to carry far more meaning for the individual than those which are not connected to emotion, and may in some cases be extreme or unhelpful to the client. For example, a client may report lots of worries about their health: 'There's something wrong'; 'I may be ill and it's not yet diagnosed'; 'What if they've missed something?' Although these are understandably anxiety-provoking, the thoughts connected with strong anxiety, fear or grief may relate more to the hot thought, 'I'll die young and leave my children.'

We think in both words and images: there is a great deal of mileage in identifying clients' images as well as words (Hackmann, 1997, 1998). We may ask, 'What went through your mind?' and the client will say, 'Nothing, I just felt awful.' The question 'Did you get an image or picture in your mind of something happening then?' may lead to identifying meaning: 'I saw myself in the restaurant, beginning to feel awful. My heart is pounding and I feel sick. I can just see myself suddenly throwing up over the table . . . such a mess, people's faces . . . or else I see myself getting up and rushing out, everyone staring at me . . . my face is bright red . . .'

Brewin (1996) suggests that it is helpful to distinguish between problems which have a very specific cognitive theme, such as misinterpretation of bodily symptoms in panic disorder, and more general themes such as in general anxiety and worry. Specific themes are likely to be easier to access in words and often respond well to cognitive interventions such as thought challenging, described below. More general themes are harder to target and less responsive to purely cognitive interventions. A range of more emotionally and behaviourally based interventions may be more appropriate.

Keeping records is vitally important, helping the client to pinpoint specific thoughts more accurately, and enabling distance to be created between the affect and cognitions. It is also valuable in recording specific predictions the client may be making, such as 'They'll think I'm stupid', or 'It'll be a disaster', in order to test out the predictions more accurately. A diary of thoughts is shown in Figure 6.1.

We have found in practice that some clients may be reluctant to write down their thoughts, believing that the act of recording what is going on will make the feelings worse, or preferring to avoid rather than focus on the thoughts. In this case, the client can be encouraged to try an experiment to test out whether keeping records does in fact make her feel worse, or whether, as is more common, writing down her thoughts enables her to begin to get them into perspective.

In practice, identifying thoughts can be very difficult for some clients: they may be able to describe their feelings, or what is happening physically, but find it hard to access exact thoughts. In this case, a period of learning how to access thoughts can be helpful, the counsellor asking the client to catch immediate thoughts and images when they notice a change in mood or physical state, and to write these down. Some clients may find it difficult to describe their thoughts in words, or be unable to keep written records. Here, we need therapeutic creativity: some clients may find it helpful to record their thoughts on a tape recorder, some may mark thoughts in a pre-prepared anxious thoughts diary, or some may find drawing their thoughts or images helpful.

Date	Situation	Anxiety: How did you feel? How bad was it (0–100)?	Automatic thoughts: What went through your mind? How much did you believe each thought (0–100)?	Alternatives to automatic thoughts: How much do you believe each alternative thought?	Results: How do you feel? What can you do?
Monday	Standing outside the supermarket	Panicky (100) Breathless (80) Heart racing (70) Sweating (80) Trembling (80)	I'm feeling terrible, I'm going to pass out. (100) What if I pass out in the supermarket? I'll look a complete fool. (80)	This is just the same old anxiety again. Nothing bad is going to happen. I'll just feel a bit bad for a while, then forget about it. The symptoms are not dangerous, do not mean I'll pass out. (80)	Feeling better, still a bit anxious but I know nothing bad will happen so can just ignore how I feel and get on with the shopping. Thought about planning dinner.

Figure 6.1   Diary of anxious thoughts and alternatives

There are situations where recording and working with anxious thoughts can be counterproductive. For example, when people have difficulties with obsessional thoughts and ruminations (Chapter 12), the process of identifying and challenging individual thoughts feeds into the rumination, and becomes a source of further worry and rumination. Similarly, asking clients whose problem is primarily worry to record all their worries can increase the thoughts, and set the client off on an endless search for the answers (Chapter 8). For these problems, taking a meta-perspective, considering and working with overall thinking processes rather than individual thoughts, is far more helpful.

We need to watch out for thought-recording becoming a safety behaviour in itself. The client may believe they have to catch and challenge all their anxious thoughts, otherwise they will be overwhelmed and lose control. Carrying a thought record and writing things down can be used as a safety behaviour: one client was diligently completing reams of records for each session, and reported that he felt vastly reassured that his thoughts could be kept under control. He dared not go out without the diary in case he became overwhelmed with anxious thoughts and went mad. So, as for all techniques, we need to be sure that they fit well with the aims of our work with individual clients.

Modifying Anxious Thoughts

Once specific anxious thoughts are identified, client and counsellor can work together to test out the validity of their way of thinking, treating anxious thoughts and predictions as hypotheses to be tested rather than facts. Such an approach is named 'collaborative empiricism', using guided discovery and experiments to test out thoughts and beliefs and explore alternatives. Exploring the link between events and our interpretation must be done in a friendly and understanding way, and not give the message that there is a 'right' or 'wrong' way of seeing things, just that there are many alternatives influencing our reactions. It is vital to be empathic and non-judgemental; putting the thoughts into context is particularly important: 'Given your experience, it makes sense that you keep saying x to yourself.' Regular summaries can help to check that the client and counsellor are on the same wavelength.

There are two main approaches to challenging thoughts: the process of guided discovery using Socratic questioning, and behavioural experiments.

Socratic questioning and guided discovery

The ideas of guided discovery arise from the work of Socrates. It may help to understand what has been written about him:

> Socrates (469–399 BC) was famously ugly, seeming to recall facially the half-human, half-animal satyrs who in Greek myth were the lewd attendants and drunken companions of the wine god Dionysus. But in a dialogue written by his less famous pupil Xenophon, Socrates is said to have joked that his bug eyes, although aesthetically unpleasing, were functionally superior to normal eyes, since they enabled him to see side-ways as well as straight in front. (Cartledge, 2001: 126)

> When told that the Delphic oracle had replied to a questioner that Socrates was the wisest man on earth, he reportedly said, 'Ah yes, but that is only because I know that I know nothing for certain'. . . . Such a stance may plausibly be interpreted as marking the beginning of wisdom. (ibid.: 137)

Socratic questioning does not mean we all need to be famously ugly. It defines a way of working with the client primarily using a question-and-answer format, to look at things not only from the side of the head, but from different angles, understanding that the way we think about things is but one way in a sea of uncertainty. Anxiety makes our minds work towards exaggerating the seriousness and likelihood of feared consequences, and undermining our abilities to cope. By using guided discovery and Socratic questioning, we aim to guide client discovery (Padesky, 1993), to explore alternatives and come up with more measured ways of thinking. It is not about positive thinking: many human fears are real and need to be taken seriously. Working with anxious thoughts aims only to find a more helpful and realistic balance which does not feed into the vicious cycle of anxiety (Wells, 1997; Wills and Sanders, 1997).

Useful questions are as follows:

- What is the evidence that x is true? What is the evidence against x being true?
- What might be the worst that could happen?
- And if that happened, what then?
- What leads you to think that might happen?
- How does thinking that make you feel?
- How would that work in your body?
- Is there any other way of seeing the situation?
- What might you tell a friend to do in this situation?
- Is there something else you could say to yourself that might be more helpful?

- What do you think you could change to make things better for you?

The guiding principles in asking Socratic questions is never to ask questions for which the client has no answer (Padesky and Greenberger, 1995). 'Why do you think that way?' is likely to elicit 'I don't know, I just do.' 'What kind of effect is it having on your life?' is more likely to elicit a useful answer, such as 'It makes me feel so anxious, I can't even get out of the house.' Socratic questioning draws the client's attention to relevant information which may be outside the client's focus. For example, the therapist might ask a client who fears collapsing during a panic attack, 'When you say you're terrified that you might faint when you feel so panicky, have you ever felt really faint but not actually fainted?' The question can help the client think about the realities of fainting, moving from a vague fear to remembering information which may be useful. He may answer, 'I've felt really awful lots of times, but I've never actually collapsed.' The questions can then move to discovering why this might be so: 'How might you have stopped yourself fainting?'; 'If you feel faint, but don't actually collapse, what does this tell you?'

Padesky and Greenberger (1995) suggest that there are four stages to Socratic technique:

1. Asking informational questions, to uncover information outside the client's current awareness.
2. Accurate listening and empathic reflection.
3. A summary of information discovered.
4. Asking synthesising questions which help apply the new information discussed to the client's original thought or belief.

The aim of guided discovery is for the client to learn how to question their thoughts and beliefs themselves. Rather than just asking questions in sessions, the therapist teaches the client the kinds of questions to ask in order to look for alternatives. When thinking 'I'm losing control', the client learns to ask himself: 'What does this mean?' 'What is the evidence I'm losing control?' 'Is there anything to indicate that I'm not losing control, but just feeling that way?' 'Why am I ignoring this at the moment?' – and other questions to reduce the potency of the anxious thoughts.

Behavioural experiments
Despite its close association with behaviourism, Beck's cognitive therapy developed quite separately, and became a magpie,

thieving from the nests of other therapeutic models, including behaviour therapy. Changing behaviour was not seen as the primary aim of cognitive ways of working, but could be used in the service of finding different ways of thinking. Thus, the idea of behavioural experiments was born, where a range of tasks are used to test out beliefs. Behavioural experiments aim to allow the client to make belief changes within the experiential mind as well as the rational (Epstein, 1998; Padesky and Mooney, 2000). No amount of logic and rationality can replace a very real human experience of doing things differently and learning at a gut level. Asking clients to test their beliefs and predictions is like asking them to find out the depth of an area of water in front of them. The anxiety and fear makes the water seem a bottomless, cavernous pool. Jumping in, the client learns that it is a splashy, shallow puddle.

A behavioural experiment aims to help the client test out thoughts and beliefs in order to discover their relative validity or truth (Beck et al., 1979, 1985). In sessions, the client may come to see that the likelihood of some terrible catastrophe occurring should he become anxious is in fact exaggerated; but he will not totally believe this until it is put to the test.

Matthew had many problems with social anxiety and panic attacks, but one of his problems was a terror of wasps. He felt this fed into his other problems, making it more difficult for him to get out and about and act normally in company with other people: when invited to the pub in the summer by work colleagues he wanted to go but always declined, which he felt made him seem more unfriendly. We tackled the wasp phobia as part of an overall plan for help with anxiety. Matthew believed that when he encountered a wasp, it would immediately make a 'bee line' for him, and take out its total aggression on him. He stopped this happening by running away, flapping his arms, screaming and totally avoiding, as far as possible, going outdoors during the wasp season. We spent some time exploring his beliefs that wasps single him out, and that they were hostile and aggressive without reason. We discussed how useful it was to a wasp, from an evolutionary perspective, to try and avoid creatures that are obviously bigger and more dangerous than they, rather than deliberately attacking them, and how most angry behaviour from wasps was in self defence. While Matthew agreed, in principle, with this argument, he still did not believe that wasps were at all benign. The experiment for Matthew, after some weeks of preparation, was to meet up with a wasp, but stop himself from flapping and running, and observe the wasp's behaviour. He noticed that the wasp did mind its own business, was more interested in looking for sugar than in unleashing its fury on Matthew, and was more likely to pay attention to him when he was afraid than when he was relaxed. From this experiment he concluded that his beliefs about wasps were exaggerated, and partly caused by his reactions to them rather than anything inherent in the wasp's make up.

Other forms of disconfirmation are used in panic disorder and social phobias. Clients with panic problems often believe that if they did not sit down, relax, breathe deeply and otherwise try to control the panic, they would faint, pass out or make a fool of themselves (Salkovskis, 1991, 1996b). Therapy involves working with the client to disconfirm what they most fear. By going into a public place and deliberately hyperventilating in order to induce panic, and then stopping themselves from sitting down, the client can see whether it is possible to pass out. Disconfirming the fear has a powerful effect on the individual's beliefs.

Collaboratively working out suitable experiments involves the following steps:

- Find out the exact prediction, in so many words: 'If I panic, I'll make a complete fool of myself'; 'I need to worry in order to do anything'; 'If people see I'm anxious they will think I'm an idiot.'
- Find out the worst possible prediction, the one holding the most anxiety and emotional reaction, and aim where possible to disconfirm the client's worst fears, or come up with feasible alternatives.
- Use guided discovery to find out possible alternatives: 'Panic is pretty harmless and nobody notices'; 'Worrying paralyses me rather than being helpful'; 'Lots of people are anxious and not everyone judges everyone else.'
- Review evidence for and against each belief.
- Ask the client: 'How can we test this out?' Work together to find some feasible experiments, in session or for homework. Make experiments manageable and 'no-lose', so the client can find it helpful whatever happens.
- Do the experiment and review in the light of the predictions.
- Keep practising.

It can be helpful for the client to keep a diary such as shown in Figure 6.2 to record specific predictions and the outcome of experiments.

Behavioural experiments can be as simple or as complicated as the situation requires. The same task may be used in different

Date	Situation	Prediction: How will I know if my prediction comes true?	Experiment to test prediction	Outcome?	What I learned
Monday	Standing outside the supermarket.	I'm feeling so bad I am going to pass out. Unless I get out of here fast then I may be very ill.	Stay in the supermarket. Stop trying to do anything to control the anxiety and see what happens.	I felt quite uncomfortable but I did not pass out, or even need to sit down. I stayed there and was pleased with myself. The bad feelings went away after a few minutes. Found some nice new ice cream!	Stay with it, things are not as bad as they feel. Anxiety won't make me pass out. I enjoy things and feel good if I don't avoid and run away. Buy this ice cream again!

Figure 6.2   Behavioural experiment diary

ways depending on the beliefs that are being tested. For example, the task of using relaxation techniques can be used as an experiment to test out a client's belief that they need to do everything at maximum pitch all the time, a teeth-on-edge rush through life. Using relaxation methods throughout the day, the client may find out that they get more, not less, done as a result of a calmer approach. Another client who practises her relaxation techniques several times a day as a way of warding off panic may practise not trying to relax and learning that panic goes away of its own accord, and that 'trying to relax' actually keeps her on edge.

Another experiment is to design the circumstances in which the feared catastrophe could happen.

Jean feared fainting at work. Her predictions were that she could faint very easily, at any time when she was feeling anxious or light-headed. The evidence was that she had never fainted, but in order to understand her beliefs more, we explored what she would have to do in order to faint at work, given that she had never fainted so far.

Jean: Well, I could not eat breakfast for a start.
Counsellor: And how many times have you done that and fainted?
Jean: Well, none – I often miss breakfast, but it doesn't seem to make much difference.
Counsellor: You'll need to try harder! What else?
Jean: I could feel really anxious
Counsellor: Have you ever felt really anxious at work?
Jean: I've been anxious at work loads of times, but that hasn't worked, has it – even when I've not tried to stop fainting? So, I could have the most terrible flu, and a heavy period, and not have slept for weeks, and not have eaten, and walked a long way into work. . . and then I'd faint!
Counsellor: So if you did faint, what would that tell you about the conditions in which you might faint?
Jean: Well, they're quite extreme really – if I felt like that I probably wouldn't go into work at all. Or if I did, everyone would be very sympathetic and send me home.

Further experiments for Jean were to test her fears about fainting itself. The counsellor conducted an anonymous survey of 30 people to ask what they would think if they saw someone faint at work. This showed that people were unanimous in being concerned and non-judgemental, and most would offer to help. The next experiment might be for Joan to feign a faint at work to test out whether it is as catastrophic as she fears.

Behavioural experiments involve creativity on the part of both therapist and client. From our own clinical experience, we have accompanied clients into shops where they have tried to have a panic attack and faint; we have asked our clients who worry about their thoughts being true, to worry for a week that their therapist has won the lottery in order to test out whether their thoughts do indeed have magical powers; and asked clients to conduct a survey of their friends to find out if the client is the only person who ever gets anxious in social situations. Behavioural experiments have one important precondition: they must be no-lose experiments, aimed at both gathering information and testing out alternatives. Whatever the outcome, something has been learned. It is preferable that the outcome will not be as the client fears, although if it is, this can also be used as an opportunity to assess whether the client's fears were exaggerated, or how the client can learn to deal with difficult situations. We as therapists may be nervous about experiments going wrong or backfiring, and we need always to build in no lose strategies whatever the actual outcome. The following illustrates a situation where an experiment provokes the worst scenario to happen to the client, but she found that she had underestimated her coping resources and overestimated the catastrophe.

Sue often felt so anxious she felt very sick, and at times would be sick at the thought of going into public places. She mainly avoided going out without her husband or daughter for support, and carried mints and antacids to avert being sick. She had a distressing image of suddenly throwing up all over the place, and people looking at her with disgust and labelling her an alcoholic. We used an experiment to test out whether being sick in public was an option, and Sue hyperventilated in the session to induce feelings of anxiety. She did start to feel very sick and unwell, and after a couple of minutes was sick in the basin in the counselling room. She felt initially very upset by this, and at the end of the session I was worried I had caused irreparable harm and she would never come back. In fact, she returned the following week saying that it had been very useful. She knew that if she got very anxious she could be sick, but it was not nearly as bad as she thought. She actually felt in control enough to reach a basin, and her images were not borne out in reality. She felt more confident about going out, and realised 'If the worst happened, it is not the end of the world and I can cope.' Further experiments involved Sue going out alone, without her mints and antacids, and allowing the feelings of being sick to come and go. Sue learned that 'Whatever happens, it is never as bad as being stuck at home all the time: and I can cope!'

Using Imagery to Identify and Modify Fears

Verbal discussion cannot always reach beliefs and meanings, particularly when they are charged with emotion, or if the individual has an intellectualising style, perhaps avoiding emotion by excessive talking. Working with the client's images can be a powerful way of identifying anxiety-provoking meanings to the individual (Edwards, 1990; Hackmann, 1997, 1998; Hackmann et al., 1998, 2000). Images are often far more charged with meaning than are words, and hold much power for the client in terms of identifying more about their underlying fears. Images can be useful where the client has difficulty putting fears into words, or where she may want to avoid talking through the fears. Imagery can be useful when working with a client's 'felt sense' of fear or other emotions, where the feeling element predominates without necessarily being accessible in words (Gendlin, 1981). Memories and meaning may not be encoded in language but in images or bodily sensations, depending partly on the age at which meanings develop, and how feelings and emotions are expressed or accepted early on (Layden et al., 1993).

Ways of getting in touch with images include asking: 'Did you have a picture in your mind just then?' Once the individual has come up with an image, the client can be asked to describe it in greater detail. Questions such as 'What is happening? Who else is in the image? What are they doing or saying?' can help the client to be more specific about the image. Once the image is identified, the types of questions shown in Figure 6.3 can be used to help the client unpack the image and explore its personal meaning, implications and origins.

Although anxious thinking is very much focused on the future, people's thoughts, fears and images get 'stuck' at a certain point, often at the most frightening or awful stage, where there seems no hope of rescue.

Felicity was terrified of driving, particularly fearful of being in an accident and being trapped in the car. She had avoided driving for some time, but now needed to drive to meet changes in her job requirements. She was coping with driving by being very alert and on the lookout for danger, trying to relax when driving, and avoiding driving in any situations where she might get trapped in her car for a long time. Although she had a vague image in her mind of being trapped in the car, she was initially unable to elaborate on it: 'I don't even want to think about it.' However, she was encouraged to elaborate on the frightening image going through her mind. She saw herself stuck in the car, with the roof caved in above her, and being unable to move. Although this image was upsetting, the worst of it was her crying out for help and nobody hearing her. She saw herself screaming and screaming for ages, getting colder and more uncomfortable, and feeling totally forgotten. The image brought back memories for Felicity of being accidentally locked in the garden shed by her younger sister, and it being what seemed like a very long time before she was discovered. Using imagery, Felicity was encouraged to complete the image of being trapped in the car. She imagined herself crashing and her worst fears coming true, but then she was able to imagine how quickly the rescue services came for her, and how she was rapidly surrounded by police and firemen who were able to help her. She wound the film forward to being taken out into an ambulance, and taken to hospital, then walking out of hospital in order to rebuild her life. Felicity also built other rescue factors into her image – that if she was trapped, she would be able to fall back on her own coping resources, keeping herself calm, talking to herself. She was helped by a television rescue programme that showed how a woman was rescued from being trapped in her car.

Obviously, Felicity's fears are realistic in many ways – many of us would avoid driving if we really thought about the risks involved. However, she was constantly dwelling on the worst aspect of what might happen, increasing the probability and cost sides of

- What is so bad about the events in the image?

- What does that mean to you?

- What is the worst that can happen?

- How do you feel right now, emotionally and in terms of body sensations in the image?

- How did you get into this situation?

- What is going through your mind in the image right now?

- Does the image remind you of anything?

- What are your earliest memories of the feelings/thoughts/sensations/experiences in the image? Where were you? How old were you?

- What was happening in your life at the time? How did you feel about yourself at that time? What does that mean?

Figure 6.3   *Questions to explore imagery*

Source: Wells and Hackmann (1993)

the equation while not thinking at all about rescue factors. Completing the image, and also making connections to a frightening episode in her life, enabled Felicity not to need to dwell so much on possibilities, and focus on the benefits of driving and on being a good driver.

Relaxation Techniques and Counselling for Anxiety

Relaxation techniques in many forms have long been used in the treatment of anxiety problems and have a very important place. However, in the last few years, with the introduction of concepts of safety behaviours, relaxation techniques are being used with more caution. Rather than being widely advocated, relaxation is applied strategically depending on the individual client's conceptualisation. One major disadvantage of relaxation techniques is when they are used as safety behaviours and avoidance, preventing disconfirmation of anxious predictions. For example, a client might use relaxation methods to cope with a situation that has previously triggered panic. Where this is successful, it could lead the client to conclude he has now developed a skill that can help him with a truly dangerous situation. Counselling for anxiety aims to help the client discover that these situations are very frequently much less dangerous than the client imagines. Following cognitive restructuring of the danger of situations, the client can drop their safety behaviours, including using relaxation. This may be particularly true in the treatment of panic. Some studies (Clark et al., 1994) have shown that CBT is superior to relaxation; others (Padesky, 1995) have claimed that the inclusion of relaxation in therapy for panic slows or even reverses the effectiveness of therapy. Some, for example Wells (1997), have argued that a purely 'cognitive' approach should not include relaxation at all with any of the anxiety disorders.

In general, there is strong evidence that relaxation methods can be unhelpful and contraindicated when working with clients with panic attacks. Some clients who experience panic attacks find that relaxation actually triggers their attacks (Leahy and Holland, 2000). This may be because actively trying to relax involves becoming more aware of bodily reactions such as breathing or muscle tension, and such awareness sets off catastrophic interpretations characteristic of a panic attack. Relaxation for these clients can be actively counterproductive: a client may find that if an advocated technique makes things worse, then there is no point in continuing with counselling. Paradoxically, much of the early work with clients with panic problems involves trying to induce anxiety in sessions (Chapter 7). For these clients, it is important to start with their fears and work on decatastrophising their fears of anxiety itself, rather than trying to reduce anxious symptoms.

Advantages of relaxation techniques

While relaxation is currently less in vogue in cognitive therapy, it is important to distinguish between when it is actively unhelpful and when relaxation can be positively beneficial. Relaxation can be used as a behavioural experiment, for example to test out beliefs about having to keep going at all costs: 'If I relaxed then I'd never get anything done.' The client can try their normal strategy, then learn relaxation methods and see whether being more relaxed during the day and having time off means that they actually work more efficiently and productively. Slow controlled breathing can be a useful first aid, and used as a behavioural experiment for clients to learn that something as simple as changing breathing can make them feel better, then that their original fears were out of proportion. For example, clients with benign chest pains can be very anxious about the possibility of heart disease. The pain can be increased or reduced by changing their pattern of breathing, enabling the client to discover that symptoms were not of heart disease but more of benign physiological changes arising from something as simple as breathing (Sanders, 1996). Some cognitive-behavioural approaches (Bourne, 1990) take an integrative approach and advocate wide usage of relaxation and visualisation techniques, more usually associated with other therapeutic models. In our clinical experience, many clients find relaxation methods highly useful in increasing comfort and is a means of getting rid of unpleasant anxious and stressful feelings following the core cognitive work to decatastrophise the symptoms. Relaxation may be a positive element of therapy if it is seen as a way of helping the client to cope with his own reactions to a situation which may not be as dangerous as he has imagined in the past.

Relaxation strategies

There is a wide range of relaxation strategies allowing for idiosyncratic choice for a particular client with a particular disorder. Padesky (1995) describes seven main approaches to relaxation:

- distraction
- controlled breathing
- muscle relaxation

- active relaxation
- biofeedback
- hypnosis
- meditation

These have been well documented in sources such as Palmer and Dryden (1995), Bourne (1990) and Kennerley (1995, 1997). Padesky (1995) advises that clients may well report that they have 'tried relaxation before and it didn't work'. In this situation, it is always worth getting the client to show what they have learnt or tried. In Padesky's experience, they are frequently following wrong procedures or are only trying the method for very brief time periods, insufficient to allow for relaxation to begin.

People for whom relaxation does not work

There are certain people who do not seem to respond well to relaxation. Padesky (1995) cites three types of clients with whom she has experienced this difficulty:

- clients who fear the sound of their breath, such as clients with panic disorder;
- clients who have strongly held core beliefs and assumptions on the necessity of control, and experience relaxation as a feeling of losing control;
- clients who have been sexually abused and who have learnt the need for vigilance.

In the latter case and other related cases, it can be very hard for clients to 'put themselves in the therapist's hands' while learning the procedure. This does not necessarily mean that they cannot learn to use it by themselves but it should lead to a discussion of the likely outcome of such efforts.

The importance of 'down time'

Despite, or even because of, technological advances, we seem to be living in an increasingly busy and stressful society. It is important therefore to talk to the client about the wider aspects of their anxiety. Not only can people find it very hard to relax in this kind of life but they may also find it difficult to 'do nothing' and 'hang out'. We have noticed that some clients react to this kind of stress build-up by a response of 'drop everything'. This response can be equally dysfunctional and have serious implications in terms of their future lives.

Fay was a teacher who did a lot of part-time sessional work. She took her work very seriously and put a lot into it. As a part-time sessional worker, however, she did not enjoy good working rights and was also frequently overloaded with work by her boss. Despite all this, she loved her work and found ways of muddling through. At the start of one academic year, however, she had a severe relationship crisis. She dropped all her teaching just as the term began. Although her employers were quite sympathetic to her situation, they had a lot of trouble replacing her and were reluctant to give her further work later. In retrospect, Fay came to the conclusion that it would probably have been better to cut down on, rather than drop her work at that point.

A review of current tasks and some time-management analysis can therefore be a useful additional dimension to working on anxiety. While it is obviously sometimes necessary to drop everything, it can also be helpful to try to find more down time. Sudden life shifts are hard to make good and may contain risks. Sometimes it is necessary to work patiently towards gradual improvement by beginning to factor in self-care rather than going for the total solution of dropping everything.

Mindfulness

We hesitate to include mindfulness on a chapter which looks at tools and techniques, since it is more a philosophy of being than something that is applied as and when necessary. Mindfulness is both age-old, part of the philosophies and spirituality of Zen and Buddhism, and more recently borrowed and adapted to the service of cognitive therapy. Mindfulness is a way of being in the present moment, of being mindful of now, regardless of how acceptable, unacceptable, painful or difficult this might be. The practice of mindfulness meditation is a means to stay focused on the here and now, learning to be aware and observe what is going on rather than getting involved in automatic patterns of reaction. Kabat-Zinn (1990) describes the methods of mindfulness meditation, and how these are successfully used to help people with the various stresses of life, arising from the 'full catastrophe of living' (a term borrowed from Zorba the Greek) – pain, physical illness and psychological difficulties. The daily practice of mindfulness meditation has been shown to reduce anxiety for people with a range of anxiety problems (Kabat-Zinn et al., 1992; Astin, 1997), and forms the backbone of 'dialectical behaviour therapy', helping people with long-term personality issues and self-harm (Linehan,

1993a, 1993b). It is also being developed for depression (Segal et al., 2001).

Teasdale (1999) has incorporated mindfulness into cognitive models of emotional disorder. He describes different modes of being:

- mindless emoting, where the individual is immersed in their emotional reactions and unable to evaluate them in any way;
- focusing on the self or emotions in a detached way;
- mindful experiencing, or 'being there', where one is aware of thoughts, feelings and felt senses in a non-evaluative manner, enabling us to use these as a guide to self-understanding and problem-solving.

Being aware of thoughts and feelings is very central to cognitive therapy, and a level of non-judgemental awareness is integral to being able to label and identify thinking, and evaluate it in a helpful manner. Being mindful, not judgemental, can help people to stay with their bad or anxious feelings, being aware of them rather than having to leap automatically to control or try and get rid of emotional pain.

The applications of mindfulness within counselling and cognitive therapy are in the developmental stage, but may well prove helpful to clients where feelings are difficult to tolerate, and where learning to stay with and observe can begin the process of change. It may be that some anxiety problems are characterised by people being too aware of themselves, and using their 'felt sense' too much, for example socially phobic individuals using their feelings as a basis for reality. For these individuals, mindfulness may be less helpful (Wells, 2000). This remains open to speculation and debate, but for those readers wishing to pursue it further, we recommend Kabat-Zinn (1990, 1995), Teasdale (1999) and Segal et al. (2001). Another useful source is Gendlin (1981) writing on focusing.

Problem-Solving

Problem-solving encourages the client to work out practical and psychological ways of dealing with problems, using their own skills and resources as well as help from others. It can be particularly helpful for individuals where life stresses are contributing to their problems, and where the individual is finding difficulty in addressing or solving these problems or is avoiding tackling the problems. The stages of problem-solving are shown in Figure 6.4. Problem-solving can be particularly helpful for people with

1. **Identifying and clarifying the problem**: Client and counsellor work together to identify exactly what the problem is, and other questions such as: Who is affected? What are the components of a problem? When do I need to do something about it?

2. **Setting clear goals**: The client identifies what exactly she or he wants to achieve, and by when.

3. **Generating a range of solutions**: Client and counsellor brainstorm what solutions might be possible. The client can also ask others for possible ideas about solutions to the problem.

4. **Evaluating the solutions**: The client looks at the list of possible solutions and identifies which ones might be helpful and which can be rejected.

5. **Selecting the preferred solutions**: The client ranks the solutions in order of feasibility and selects one or two to try.

6. **Trying it out and evaluating progress**: The client tries out the selected solution and then thinks about how successful it was. If the solution was not helpful, the client picks another solution and puts this into practice.

Figure 6.4   *Problem-solving exercise*

chronic worry (Chapter 8), enabling them to take charge of their problems and resolve those that can be changed, rather than being paralysed by worry. For more details, see Butler and Hope (1995) and Palmer and Dryden (1995).

Identifying and Working with Assumptions and Rules

There is substantial evidence that working at the level of thoughts and assumptions is sufficient and effective for many clients with anxiety, and is the place to start counselling. For clients with straightforward anxiety problems, perhaps triggered by life stresses, and without huge underlying issues, it is unnecessary to begin to tackle core beliefs in order to produce substantial improvement. Even for clients with long-term issues, going into core beliefs can be counterproductive or dangerous without initial groundwork to enable clients to cope with strong emotions or difficulties that emerge from working on past, core issues (James, 2001). Even for clients with long-term issues, tackling levels of thought and assumptions is often sufficient to enable the client to make lasting improvements in current symptoms. Unhelpful assumptions leave the client vulnerable to the risk of relapse: although therapy may help the client deal with and work through the present episode of the problem, unless the rules underlying the problem are also worked through, the client may experience similar problems in future. Working with assumptions helps the client to develop skills to deal with future problems.

Identifying assumptions

The information for identifying a client's rules and assumptions comes from many sources (Fennell, 1989):

- themes which emerge during counselling
- patterns in the client's way of thinking
- labelling the self or others
- highs or lows of mood
- the client's response to therapy

Despite all the drawbacks and difficulties our set of rules may pose, our assumptions and beliefs are very central to our frame of reference, fitting like a comfortable old pair of slippers. They feel right, and to act or think against them may seem dangerous and anxiety-provoking. It can, therefore, be very threatening to have these beliefs exposed or challenged, and can imply to the client that they have 'got it wrong', sometimes for many years. Therefore the counsellor needs to proceed with empathy and sensitivity and work with, not against, the client. There should be no sense that some beliefs are 'right' and others are 'wrong', or a sense of the client and counsellor getting into an argument: the counsellor's task is to understand the client's viewpoint however much the counsellor may disagree with it or see it as irrational. Should there be a sense of counsellor and client arguing against each other, the focus should become the counselling process, not the relative merits of each view. The counsellor must work at the client's own pace and be sensitive to cues, spoken or unspoken, that the client is uncomfortable with the process of counselling.

The process of guided discovery is a key way by which a client's assumptions are clarified. Asking questions, being curious, finding out how the client thinks and what makes them think that way enables rules to be made explicit. Rather than accepting the client's rules at face value, guided discovery enables probing to understand the underlying mechanisms. Rather than saying, with empathy, 'Yes, that would be terrible', or 'It sounds like you're very scared of that happening', when a client is talking about the fear of fainting when feeling anxious, the therapist's mode of inquiry is along the lines of 'What if that did happen . . . what would that mean?' The therapist pursues this form of questioning until a clear rule emerges, a process called the downward arrow technique (Burns, 1999). The downward arrow approach involves peeling away the layers of meaning to identify what is beneath the client's specific fears, the questions being repeated several times until a 'bottom line' is reached. The aim is to arrive at a statement which makes sense of the client's fears: 'If I believed x, then I would feel the same way.' The process is illustrated with Claudia, an adult education tutor, describing her terror of having a panic attack in front of her class.

> *Claudia*: [describing a recent attack] I felt really faint: I just knew I was going to pass out.
> *Therapist*: Suppose that really happened, that you did faint – what would be bad about that for you?
> *Claudia*: Well, I'd fall over in front of all these people.
> *Therapist*: And suppose you did fall over: what next? what is the worst that could happen?
> *Claudia*: Well, I'd just be lying there like a complete fool.
> *Therapist*: Suppose what you say did happen: what would that mean to you?
> *Claudia*: It would mean I'm really out of control: just not as good as others: can't even stand up and do my job without making a complete mess-up.
> *Therapist*: And if that were true, what would that mean?
> *Claudia*: It would just show what a fake I am.
> *Therapist*: Is this something that keeps coming back to you: some form of rule?
> *Claudia*: I guess I have to be in control: If I'm not in control, people will see me for what I am: a fake.

Modifying and revising assumptions

For some clients, simply identifying the rules enables the client to begin to change. Once articulated, the client may well be able to see that it is not realistic or helpful to hold such extreme black and white views. The counsellor can encourage the client to look at the grey area between the black and white extremes posed by the assumption. The assumption may be seen to be an ideal, or a preference, rather than an absolute necessity.

The process of working with assumptions is, in many ways, similar to the approaches described above to challenge anxious thoughts: the overall aim is for the client to test the assumptions

- What is the assumption? What are my exact words to describe the rule?

- In what way has this rule affected me? What areas of life has it affected – school, work, relationships, leisure, domestic life?

- Where did the rule come from? What experiences contributed to its development? Rules make a lot of sense when first developed, but may need revision in the light of subsequent, or adult, experience.

- What are its pros and cons? What would I risk if I gave it up?

- In what ways is the rule unreasonable? In what ways is it a distortion of reality? What are the ways it is helping or hindering me?

- What would be a more helpful and realistic alternative, that would give me the pay-off and avoid the disadvantages? Is there another way of seeing things, which is more flexible, more realistic and more helpful, giving me the advantages of the assumption without the costs?

- What do I need to do to change the rule?

Figure 6.5   *Questions to help the client discover alternative assumptions*

Sources: Beck et al. (1979, 1985); Burns (1999)

empirically, to find out the relative 'truth', helpfulness or unhelpfulness of the rules, and, if found not to measure up, to come up with alternatives. Guided discovery, Socratic questions and behavioural experiments all enable more information to be gathered about the client's assumptions in order to test out their validity. Some key questions that can help to guide the client towards alternatives are shown in Figure 6.5.

Challenging assumptions: taking risks

One powerful way of testing out rules is to devise experiments in which the individual does not act in accordance with the rule, but behaves as though a different rule is in operation, and tests out the consequences. For example, Claudia believed 'I must be in control all the time: if I'm not it'll prove I'm a fake'. An experiment might be for her to practise being slightly less 'in control' at work, occasionally preparing her lessons slightly less thoroughly than usual, leaving something in the staff room and having to go and get it during a class, or feeling ill in class and having to sit down, to test out whether this proved that she was 'a fake'.

It is extremely important for any experiments that the client and therapist negotiate to be no-lose situations. Whatever the outcome of the experiment, the client must be able to learn something useful. Taking risks is, by definition, threatening to the client; therefore the client needs to be supported in the decision to try something new, with a good outcome, whatever happens.

Homework

Despite having such loaded connotations for most of us, the term 'homework' has stuck within cognitive therapy to describe the plethora of tasks and activities clients engage in between sessions to tackle their difficulties. Homework, home tasks, practice-time or problem-busting activities, or whatever name the client chooses, has been found to be a predictor of successful therapy (Burns and Spangler, 2000). Homework is popular and encourages an ethos of self-help and learning things that are useful to life in general. It helps build bridges between sessions, and acknowledges that the therapy hour is but a tiny drop in the ocean of a client's busy life. It is also in the spirit of working on the experiential mind as well as the rational, trying things out to see how they work, and learning by practice, not just talking. Homework can take many forms, including reading, listening to the tape of therapy sessions, filling in diaries, recording thoughts and feelings, and a range of behavioural experiments described throughout the book.

The key in working with homework is to move away from the flavour of setting tasks, with the connotations of them being marked and judged, towards collaborative agreement in the session. Working with protocols, it is tempting to be protocol-driven with homework: 'If it is session three, then the client ought to be challenging their thoughts, and challenge their thoughts they will!' Being prescriptive may or may not be helpful, but goes against the spirit of collaboration. We need to balance being aware of things that we know can be helpful, with being led by the client as to what might be appropriate for now. Asking the client what they think might be useful to work on in the week is a good place to start, and we are often surprised by the answers. However, if the client says they need to 'go away and think about it', this might be too vague for useful activity to arise. Alternatives are for the client to write down more specific tasks, or set aside half an hour in the week to write down the results of the thinking. We also need to do our homework. Remembering to ask about the client's homework is a good first step and more likely to motivate all concerned.

Anxiety Groups

For many people with anxiety problems, group work can be as effective as individual therapy (White et al., 1992; White, 2000; Morrison, 2001). Jim White's work involves setting up large 'stress-control' groups – structured, didactic groups of up to 50 people – with very much an educational flavour. Participants are encouraged to 'become their own therapists'. In the six, weekly groups, clients are given information and taught techniques to manage anxiety, in categories such as 'controlling your body' (using relaxation methods), 'controlling your thoughts' (using cognitive therapy methods), 'controlling your actions' (including exposure and behavioural advice), and 'controlling your future' (relapse prevention). Interestingly, clients are actively discouraged from talking about their own problems, which may be necessary to work in large groups, and also helps focus on anxiety reduction methods rather than symptoms and difficulties. The two-year follow-up studies on these groups are extremely encouraging (White, 1998a), with up to three-quarters of participants maintaining improvements at two years. Large day-long workshops on anxiety management have shown very good results (Brown et al., 2000), and are as effective as small-group format. There is good evidence to show that self-help methods can be very beneficial (e.g. Gould and Clum, 1993; White, 2000). Clients using the self-help package 'Stresspac' (White, 1998b, 2000), which follows the format for stress-control groups, showed significant improvements maintained at three-year follow-up. Clients who had received the pack showed reductions in GP consultations for anxiety, use of medication and referrals to secondary care. Self-help materials can be very useful to clients on long waiting lists, instilling hope and beginning clients on the process of helping themselves, and may cut down the number of sessions. The effectiveness of different forms of anxiety management groups may relate to specific techniques that are introduced but may also relate to general factors across group work (Yalom, 1995; Dryden, 1998): instillation of hope, meeting people with similar problems and finding that one is not alone with difficulties, sharing others' experiences, and translating an individual painful problem into a common, shared understanding.

Results from group therapy and self-help are very encouraging. But, can they replace individual work? The evidence to date is that while many clients can find groups helpful, they may not be appropriate for others. Individual work is more helpful for clients who are depressed, those with complex difficulties and those with obsessive compulsive disorders (Morrison, 2001), although it may be that group work has a place while these people wait for individual therapy. Groups probably have higher drop-out rates than individual work, and face the challenge of being relevant to mixed groups with a variety of individual problems. Depending on the setting, it can be difficult to recruit sufficient numbers to groups without some clients having to wait a long time until groups are ready to start. A detailed discussion of group work is beyond the scope of this book, but useful sources include Dryden (1998), Scott and Stradling (1998) and White (2000).

Overall, groups and self-help methods enable large numbers of people, who would otherwise remain anxious or have to wait a long time for individual work, to receive effective help. Groups are cost-effective and an efficient use of scarce therapy time, particularly in the NHS. Technological advances in the use of computer programmes and the Internet mean we have a growing rate of creative methodology for self-help. Ideally, a combination of individual, group and self-help work should form part of the range of services for the many anxious people in the community.

This chapter has shown the wide variety of techniques and methods that may be used collaboratively with clients. Techniques are only as good as the use to which they are put, and need at all times to fit well with the individual client and his or her conceptualisation. The next section of the book considers the different variants of anxiety, and looks at how general methods and techniques can be used within the particular approach to each anxiety problem.

PART II

COUNSELLING FOR SPECIFIC ANXIETY PROBLEMS

--------------------- 7 ---------------------

Panic Attacks, Panic Disorder and Agoraphobia

> The Uncertainty of what they fear'd made their Fear get greater . . . And this was what in aftertimes men called a Pannick. (Earl of Shaftesbury, seventeenth-century historian, quoted in the *Oxford Shorter Dictionary*)

The Greek God, Pan, was said to have helped the Greeks at the Battle of Marathon by coming on the Persian enemies with great suddenness and infecting them, by means of a shout, with overwhelming and unreasoning terror or 'panic'. The onset of panic is so swift that the victim experiences it as coming out of the blue, and so unbalancing that victims are unable to mobilise their usual coping responses. A vicious cycle arises, where fear builds on fear until the panic attack builds on itself to a crescendo, at which point the victim assumes that some impending catastrophe must occur.

Panic attacks and panic disorder are a frequent reason for clients to seek help and counselling. The experience is often of extreme physical symptoms, leading many to seek initial help from medical services. Some people have such severe panic attacks that they are mistaken for heart attacks or other serious illness, and panic may be diagnosed only after extensive medical testing, adding to the anxiety experienced. Other clients will have had one or two panic attacks, realise that their anxiety has become a problem and seek help at an early stage. Panic attacks are highly physical experiences, and many earlier models of therapy focused on helping clients to overcome these symptoms, using anxiety-reduction techniques. The very specific nature of panic attacks, and the finding that physical therapy could only go a certain way towards helping clients, led to more sophisticated cognitive understandings of the problem, looking more at the role of cognitions and meaning. Therapy for panic attacks has been largely revolutionised by the work of David Clark and colleagues in Oxford in the 1980s. We now have very effective forms of therapy which can be easily learned and used to focus on panic attacks and panic as part of other anxiety problems. The central role of panic attacks in agoraphobia has also meant that we can now offer more effective forms of help for agoraphobic clients who were traditionally regarded as difficult to help.

In this chapter, we describe panic attacks and panic disorder, and look at how they relate to agoraphobia. We describe how to build up a step-by-step conceptualisation of panic, and the stages of identifying and working to disconfirm the client's specific anxious interpretations of panic symptoms. We look at how panic and agoraphobia are very closely associated, and how to adapt counselling for panic attacks to clients with agoraphobia.

Defining Panic Attacks and Panic Disorder

Josie is a 23-year-old trainee manager who is preparing for important exams. She has had problems with her eyes, made worse by the extra reading for her revision. She is also contemplating going to live with her boyfriend. She has come for counselling after experiencing a frightening panic attack during a revision course. She describes this attack as follows:

> I feel like I am going mad. I don't trust my brain any more. I was doing a revision course and it was one of those all-day Saturday things. I had no food all day but I drank lots of coffee. Afterwards I felt very dehydrated so I went off to the pub with the others. I felt okay when I was in there but when I came out . . . my eyes started to ache so I took my glasses off. Then things started to go trippy. I was feeling terrible and had a sense of real dread. I went into Boots because I knew that they had air-conditioning there. I found a chair to sit on. A lady asked if I was okay and brought me water. After a while I began to feel a bit more normal. I sat until I felt calm enough to go round to Ray's to tell him that I'd had a funny turn.

The central features of a panic attack relate to the interpretation of benign physical symptoms, often of anxiety, as evidence for impending catastrophe causing further anxiety. This interpretation triggers a vicious cycle, where the anxiety causes further symptoms, further catastrophic interpretations and further anxiety. The *Diagnostic and Statistical Manual* (*DSM*) criteria are shown in Table 7.1.

Table 7.1   *Definition of a panic attack*

A discrete period of intense fear or discomfort in which four or more of the following symptoms develop abruptly and reach a peak within 10 minutes:

Palpitations, pounding heart
Shortness of breath
Chest pain or discomfort
Sweating
Trembling or shaking
Choking sensations
Nausea or stomach distress
Numbness, tingling
Chills or hot flushes
Dizzy, unsteady, light-headed or faint
Derealisation or depersonalisation: feeling detached from oneself
Fear of losing control or going crazy
Fear of dying

Source: APA (2000)

The *DSM* definition of a panic attack stresses its abrupt nature and specifies that it reaches a peak within 10 minutes. Intense fear is described in terms of highly physiological reactions including heart palpitations, shortness of breath, or feelings of choking. More cognitive symptoms include a sense of unreality and fears of losing control or dying. Panic attacks appear out of the blue, without immediately obvious triggers, increasing the individual's sense of unpredictability and anxiety.

Diagnostic criteria make distinctions between panic attacks and panic disorder. A panic attack is not in itself a disorder in the terms of the *DSM–IV*. However, panic attacks are frequently cited as criteria for other anxiety disorders (APA, 2000). When panic attacks become recurrent and persistent, defined as one attack followed by at least one month of worrying about attacks, then the client is likely to meet *DSM* criteria for panic disorder.

Panic attacks are extremely common, with some studies citing as many as 40 per cent of the population experiencing one or more attacks in their lives. Community surveys in the UK indicate that between 7 and 28 per cent have had a panic attack at some time in their lives but only a small percentage of those go on to develop panic disorder. Occasional panic attacks are very common, particularly in response to stress. Such attacks are usually infrequent, provoked by known stressors, and do not have any long-lasting effect on the individual. Even when such problems fall short of the panic disorder criteria, they can still have great effects on the person's life. Living with the constant fear of an attack is liable to reduce the person's ability to work, sustain relationships and even enjoy leisure time. Not surprisingly, people want to avoid the fear and discomfort of attacks and start to avoid situations and places in which attacks may be or actually are triggered. This can have a significant impact on the individual's social and work life and means that important tasks may be indefinitely postponed. As a result of avoidance, the client's fears are not confronted and overcome, increasing anxiety and the likelihood of panic in the long term. Panic may be linked with specific phobias, such as of crowded shopping areas or certain animals. When feelings of panic have no obvious triggers they can be more frightening and difficult to deal with than those with known causes: it is harder to tackle or avoid the unknown than the known.

The definitions of panic and panic disorder help to focus on two fundamental aspects of what has become a highly successful psychological approach to treating panic disorder. Firstly, panic attacks arise from the way the individual interprets physiological symptoms, often of anxiety itself; and, secondly, worrying about attacks over time becomes part of the problem.

Conceptualising Panic: David Clark's Cognitive Model of Panic Disorder

The frightening nature of panic attacks means that they are very likely to prove to be events to which strong meaning will be given. The fact that people are so physiologically aroused during a panic attack interferes with the slower logical functions of the processing system, perhaps enhancing the power of emotional reasoning (Wills and Sanders, 1997). This explains why people having panic attacks frequently feel like they will die, even though they may have survived many such attacks previously, and know logically that they are unlikely to die right then. Clark and his colleagues in Oxford began the search for specific meanings associated with panic disorder, building up the model over a number of years and basing the therapy methods on solid research findings (Clark and Fairburn, 1997). Clark found that people with panic disorders did indeed have a highly specific way of reacting to attacks. This is well summed up in the statement:

> Individuals who experience recurrent panic attacks do so because they have a relatively enduring tendency to interpret certain bodily sensations in a catastrophic fashion. The sensations that are misinterpreted are mainly those involved in normal anxiety responses. . . . The catastrophic misinterpretation involves perceiving those sensations as

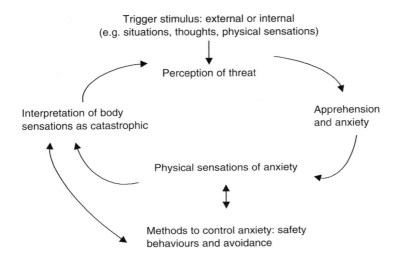

Figure 7.1   *The vicious cycle of panic*

Source: Reprinted from *Behaviour Research Therapy Journal*, 24, D.M. Clark, 'A cognitive approach to panic', 461–70, 1986, with permission from Elsevier Science.

much more dangerous than they really are, and, in particular, interpreting the sensations as indicative of an immediately impending physical or mental disaster – for example, perceiving palpitations as evidence of an impending heart attack. (Clark, 1988: 149)

The combination of physical symptoms, interpretation and fear led to the development of the vicious cycle of panic (Figure 7.1).

Physiological symptoms which trigger panic attacks can arise from a variety of causes, including anxiety, stress, hyperventilation, tiredness, caffeine, being hungover, dehydration or small dizzy attacks. Clark's model implies that although people who suffer from panic disorder experience strongly aversive physiological reactions, they probably do not have any more major physiological problems than other people, but react to the attacks in a significantly different way. This view does not rule out the possibility that panic disorder sufferers are somewhat physiologically different, perhaps having a more sensitive nervous system. People with a tendency to hyperventilate may experience more panic attacks. Panic sensations are sometimes associated with physical complaints such as mitral-valve prolapse or hyperthyroidism and it is therefore advisable for clients to have a thorough physical check as part of the preparation for therapy.

Whatever the causes of the physical symptoms, what leads to panic is the individual's *interpretation*. The interpretation of the symptoms involves true catastrophes and includes (Wells, 1997):

- I'll faint.
- I'm having a heart attack.
- I'm going to die.
- I'm going crazy.
- I'm having a stroke.
- I can't see – I'm going blind.
- I'm going to suffocate or run out of air.
- I'm going to be sick.
- I'm going to be paralysed.
- I'm choking.
- I'll panic for ever.
- I'm going to lose control.
- I'm going crazy, will start to babble or talk funny.

Clients can also have a number of catastrophic interpretations about the social consequences of panic attacks, such as fainting in public or making a fool of themselves, characteristic of social anxieties or agoraphobic fears.

Given these interpretations, it is hardly surprising that a panic attack provokes further anxiety and panic. The model of panic is not an attempt to define panic sufferers as irrational. The basis of their misinterpretation of what is, after all, ambiguous information is an understandable attempt to comprehend a frightening situation with limited information and while one is in a frightened state of mind. It also makes sense to err on the side of caution. Taking note of physiological symptoms is a normal part of human behaviour, and is adaptive, enabling us to pay attention to and respond to anything that might be amiss. However, while the client's interpretations may be useful, they can also be contradicted by other evidence and be counterproductive. Again, being self-conscious as social beings can be adaptive, but in anxiety and panic the role of attention and interpretation has gone well beyond what is helpful.

There is much research evidence substantiating the reciprocal relationship between physiological symptoms and their misinterpretation, posited by Clark. For example, it has been found that clients with panic disorder are more likely to make catastrophic interpretations of ambiguous physiological symptoms than are individuals who do not experience panic (McNally and Foa, 1987; Harvey et al., 1993; Clark, 1996). Clark et al. (1994) showed that clients with panic disorder who had shown significant reductions in symptoms also showed consistent cognitive change. Conversely, those who continued to be liable to misinterpretations were more likely to relapse.

Why do Panic Attacks Persist?

Why do people keep on interpreting physical symptoms as evidence of impending catastrophe, even when over and over again the catastrophes do not occur? The research on panic now suggests that the answer to this question is connected to three main factors.

1.   Selective attention (hypervigilance)

Panic sufferers become extra alert to any of the kind of symptoms associated with their attacks. For example, they may repeatedly check how they are breathing, being very aware of any changes in breathing sensations. This focus means that they notice any normal and benign changes, which are then open to misinterpretation. Such focus feeds into a vicious cycle of extra attention leading to extra worry and extra symptoms. Hypervigilance was demonstrated in a series of elegant studies by Anke Ehlers (Ehlers and Breuer, 1992; Ehlers, 1995). Normally we are not tuned into our heartbeats and cannot estimate our heart rate particularly accurately. Compared to non-panic controls, panic clients were more accurate in identifying their heart rates, indicating hypervigilance to normal changes in heart rate.

2.   Safety behaviours

Studies by Salkovskis (1991) and Salkovskis (1996a, b) have shown that panic sufferers have a number of distinctive behaviours which they use to deal with attacks. For example, people who think that they are having a heart attack will tend to sit or lie down. As panic attacks are self-limiting, they will eventually calm down. They may well then conclude 'I would have had a heart attack if I hadn't sat down.' Sitting down therefore becomes a safety behaviour because it prevents them from learning that they would not have had a heart attack, even if they had not sat down. Other safety behaviours in panic are shown in Table 7.2.

Safety behaviours to control panic can be strategies that clients have specifically learned to control anxiety. For example, slow controlled breathing or relaxation may prove to be unhelpful to

Table 7.2   *Safety behaviours in panic and agoraphobia*

Slow controlled breathing
Relaxation
Trying not to lose control of mind or behaviour
Trying not to think anxious thoughts
Sitting down
Keeping very still
Focusing attention on body
Asking for help
Distraction
Counting
Holding on to or leaning on someone or some thing
Carrying water
Carrying mints
Carrying medication
Checking out availability of exits, toilets, help, telephones
Using a shopping trolley and clutching on to it
Tensing up legs

clients where they believe that only by controlling their anxiety is catastrophe averted. Some safety behaviours are very subtle, such as tensing up the legs when feeling anxious to prevent fainting, or apparently commonsensical, such as always using a trolley in the supermarket, or making sure of always carrying a mobile phone. We need, therefore, to fully understand the significance of all the clients' safety strategies to decide whether they are part of the problem or part of the solution.

3.   Avoidance

Clients experiencing panic understandably learn to avoid the situations which trigger their attacks. As a result, it is more difficult for the individual to learn that situations are not as dangerous as they imagine them to be. A vicious cycle of avoidance is set up, which reduces confidence and leads to more anxiety and panic. Avoidance behaviours can be very subtle and we need to keep asking about them. Josie, for example, mentioned being driven to work by her mother. Further exploration established that, for her, getting a lift with her mother was motivated by the desire to avoid the possibility of having a 'mental breakdown' when driving herself. The therapeutic process itself can be diverted by client avoidance. Clients can steer the discussion away from vital areas, and sometimes a therapist's implicit empathy with their client's pain may collude in this, as discussed in Chapter 4 on the therapeutic relationship.

Agoraphobia

Agoraphobia is generally defined as a fear of being alone in crowds outside the home – hence the fear (from the Greek word *phobos*) of the public place (from the Greek work *agora*, the market-place). The more specific hallmark of agoraphobia is fear of being in places from which escape might be difficult or embarrassing. This fear, as with many of the anxiety disorders, leads to marked avoidance. Although the stereotype of people with agoraphobia is being unable to leave the safety of the home, agoraphobics may be able to get out and about but avoid more specific situations where the exits are not easy to get to. For example, some clients fear being in crowded cinemas or theatres where making an exit would be noticed by other people. Agoraphobic individuals may fear making fools of themselves in public places, fears similar to those of people who are socially anxious (Chapter 10). For example, fainting in public would be seen as terrible, because of being the centre of others' hostile or judgemental attention (Hackmann, 1998).

Table 7.3   *Definition of agoraphobia*

Anxiety about being in places or situations where it would be difficult or embarrassing for the individual to escape, or where help would not be available, if the person were to feel anxious or panicky.

Agoraphobia involves clusters of situations which the person dislikes, such as being outside alone, travelling in public transport.

The individual avoids these situations where possible, and is very distressed and anxious about getting panic attacks should they be unable to avoid.

The person may or may not meet criteria for panic attacks, but remains very fearful of the possibility of panic.

Source: APA (2000)

Links between panic and agoraphobia

It is increasingly recognised that agoraphobia is closely associated with panic, fear of having panic attacks in public being central to the agoraphobic's fears. The fear is not so much of the public place itself but of what may happen in it. Panic disorder is most usually accompanied by agoraphobic fears but these do not always reach the level that justifies the term 'agoraphobia'. The position is often unclear because fears may be under-reported due to cognitive avoidance: the client may not want to talk about or acknowledge some fears. Where panic occurs with agoraphobia, panic attacks are experienced and reported as being triggered by particular situations. In comparison, panic without agoraphobia is more likely to be experienced as coming out of the blue. In Josie's case, described at the beginning of the chapter, before the onset of panic she had had an active social life, but during the depth of her difficulties she became unable to go to many of her usual every-day places for fear of panic attacks.

As the relationship between these two problems becomes clearer, it is acknowledged that agoraphobic problems do compli-cate therapy for panic and, when severe, reduce the effectiveness of therapy (Hackmann, 1998). Clients with agoraphobia may have a long history of the problem, often with various attempts at treatment which have not worked. Years of staying in, or years of being dependent on others for much of life, mean that the individual's life and that of the family may be bound up with the client's difficulties. Agoraphobia is more likely to be a result of long-standing problems, rather than of specific stressors (Hack-mann, 1998). Agoraphobic individuals may have a long pattern of insecure attachments, dependence on others, low confidence in their abilities to cope with life on their own, or a mistrust of others helping (Liotti, 1991). An insecure base in childhood means the child avoids painful feelings, since problems seem insurmoun-table, leading to chronic anxiety and fears of feelings themselves. They may find it difficult to put meanings on to the emotions arising from threats of separation from others. When bonds with other people change, the individual finds it difficult to manage the emotional pain, perhaps not recognising it as grief, loss or anger, but will attribute their feelings to physical illness (Goldstein and Stainback, 1991). The individual may never feel able to cope on their own, due to lack of or too much protection when younger; the idiosyncratic meaning of being in public is that there may not be people around to help or that other people are not trustworthy.

Adapting Counselling for Panic and Agoraphobia

The major aim of counselling for panic is to enable the client to identify and test out alternative interpretations of their physical symptoms. The main tools of therapy are guided discovery and Socratic questioning to clarify specific meanings and fears, and behavioural experiments to test out the client's fears. Counselling involves building up and testing an alternative model, and decatastrophising clients' fears about anxiety itself.

The benefit of a strong model for panic with good research backing is that it enables the therapist to offer highly credible interventions that can proceed on a step-by-step basis. There are prescribed steps that therapists can follow in the particular order presented below, with well defined protocols available (Zuercher-White, 1999). We discuss more about the pros and cons of protocol-directed counselling in Chapter 3, and we are well aware that protocols can be reassuring for some but an obstruction for other counsellors and therapists. Since there is strong evidence that therapy proceeding along set paths is very useful for helping clients overcome panic attacks, we urge therapists always to consider following the protocol first unless there are good reasons for not doing so.

Protocols for panic do not emphasise the influence of unhelpful beliefs and assumptions integral to the cognitive model. This is not to say that these underlying issues are never relevant in working with an individual client with panic. However, there is such strong evidence for the effectiveness of changing the maintenance cycles in panic that it is now regarded as conventional wisdom to work on this area first. Only when the panic symptoms are well under control should one normally consider working on patterns of schemata and assumptions (Wells, 1997), and then perhaps only when there is a clear rationale for doing so.

The key stages in working with panic:

- Build up a shared model of panic during the assessment phase, using Socratic questioning and guided discovery.
- Induce feelings of panic in the session to identify and work with hot thoughts and appraisals.
- Identify specific hypotheses about the causes of symptoms, and use Socratic questioning and behavioural experiments to test different hypotheses.
- Use behavioural experiments involving dropping safety behaviours.

Build up a shared model with the client

The first stages of counselling for panic aim to introduce the client to the model of panic, and to work collaboratively with the client to individualise the model for his or her particular difficulties. In introducing the model, we work not to disprove their misinterpretations but rather to build another way of looking at their experiences. Throughout working with panic, we introduce the idea of testing out different hypotheses. Building up the model of panic is best achieved by asking the client to give a specific recent example of an attack, and by 'walking through' the attack step by step with them, using Socratic questioning throughout. We also physically draw out the model on paper with the client, as shown below.

Josie is describing a recent panic attack in a supermarket.

Josie: Well, you know, there is such a glare in those places. When you walk in, the light sort of hits you between the eyes. So I started to feel very trippy. It was horrible.

Counsellor: Sounds a bit like the revision thing. Did you have body feelings like that?

Josie: Yes. I was really dizzy. With a lumpy dry throat. I felt quite sick actually. And my heart was racing.

Counsellor: So what went through your mind at that moment?

Josie: Shit. Get the hell out of here!

Counsellor: And if you really had not been able to get the hell out, what is the worst that could have happened to you?

Josie: Just gone totally out of control . . . anything could happen, I could die, I could kill . . . anything.

Counsellor: And how much do you believe that now, you know, as a percentage, as we have done before?

Josie: Now, I guess 30 per cent, but then it was like 95 per cent.

Counsellor: That sounds terrifying – how did it make you feel?

Josie: Really frightened . . .

Counsellor: And when you felt so frightened, what was going on in your body?

Josie: I guess I felt much worse, more shaky, sick, my heart was racing . . . I guess it just set me off again?

Following this exchange, therapist and client work out an individual vicious cycle and draw it up as follows:

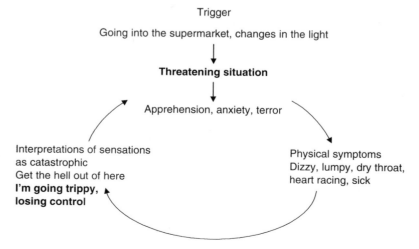

Figure 7.2   *Josie's vicious cycle of panic*

The discussion then goes on to look at Josie's safety behaviours:

Counsellor: So what did you do next?

Josie: Well, I noticed that I was quite near the loos . . . you know they are quite near where you go in. So I went in there and locked myself in a toilet until I calmed down.

Counsellor: Right so here's that old problem we have hit before. This model says that you actually were never going to go mad, out of control or die – even if you had stuck it out in the supermarket. Whereas you are now left wondering if going into the loo 'saved you'? So how are we going to find out which is right?

Josie: The problem is that even if it is only a small chance, it would be a huge price if the model is wrong.

Counsellor: And is there a price associated with continuing to have panic attacks?

Josie: There certainly is!

The information about behaviour is then added to the vicious cycle as follows:

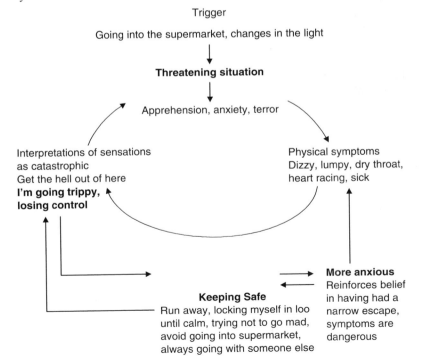

Figure 7.3   *Josie's vicious cycle*

Wells (1997) suggests that the best moment to start work on the vicious cycle is in the middle of the panic attack cycle when the sensations are at their peak. This allows therapist and client to uncover and realise the really hot thoughts, sensations and feelings. The therapist may have to push for the true hot appraisal in the thoughts. Notice that, in the Josie extract above, the first cognition given is 'Get the hell out of here.' This cognition, however, conceals the real fear of the consequences of not getting out of there, so the therapist asks 'And if you were not able to get out, what was the worst that could happen to you?' This then gets to the catastrophic misinterpretation quickly.

Induce feelings of panic in the session in order to identify hot thoughts and appraisals

In order to begin to explore the meanings the client gives to symptoms of panic, it can be helpful and necessary to activate panic symptoms in sessions. By activating emotion, we are activating the emotional mind, allowing emotional learning as well as intellectual learning.

Activating anxiety in a therapy session is unlikely to hit the temperature of a fear in outside life. The therapist should make the environment safe and comfortable for the client. This indeed is probably all to the good, as overwhelming anxiety would be likely to block the client and lead nowhere. Additionally, client and therapist can agree how excessive anxiety will be tackled should it arise, for example by having 'calming time' involving calm low-key talking, relaxation or distraction or by invoking safe images. It is often useful to develop an image such as that of a safe place early in the therapy. The therapist needs to be careful not to construct safety behaviours out of these interventions, by being clear that they are being used as a means of making ways of confronting fears work and are therefore very much a temporary means to an end.

A full list of induction techniques is given in Wells (1997) and includes:

- Asking the client to repeat aversive paired words such as Breathlessness – Suffocate . . . Chest pain – Heart attack . . . Light-headed – Collapse . . . over and over again until the feelings of panic begin to rise. This can be an excellent way of bringing home to the client the role that internal dialogue and thoughts play in panic disorder.
- Hyperventilation provocation test, asking the client to hyperventilate for five minutes and report the symptoms

they experience. This can be combined with the client trying to make their fears happen: for example, trying to faint, trying to fall over by standing on one leg, or trying to have a heart attack.

- Body-focus tasks: asking the client to concentrate on one part of their body and report the sensation they get. This invariably brings up symptoms such as a throbbing finger, or a sense of unreality from staring. This shows how selective attention can easily enhance a feeling that something is wrong.

Clients understandably do not like doing these tasks and some refuse outright. We need to proceed with sensitivity and caution, always being willing to demonstrate the tasks ourselves before asking the client to do it, or break down the induction techniques into smaller manageable tasks. However, within these tasks is powerful learning and re-attribution of meanings. Clients learn that if panic symptoms can be evoked by simply reading paired words or hyperventilating, then it is likely that the symptoms are benign and of anxiety rather than anything more sinister. Evoking panic symptoms and then encouraging clients to stay with the feelings helps clients to learn that the symptoms do not lead to catastrophe, but eventually go away of their own accord.

Identify alternative hypotheses

When clients are in the middle of a panic attack, logical thought and meaning goes out of the window, and interpretations become based on worst-case scenarios. Thus, the meaning of physical symptoms is always seen to be much more catastrophic than it actually is. We aim to take into account the client's anxious view, but also begin to build up alternatives, by identifying and testing out different hypotheses as to the meaning of symptoms.

One factor in Josie's history that turned out to be relevant to her situation was that she had taken quite a lot of drugs at university, including hallucinogenic drugs. This drug taking had finally come to an end when she had had a 'bad trip'. This explained her frequent use of the word 'trippy' to describe her feelings of dissociation during panic attacks. It also enabled her to talk about her deeply felt fears that she might have damaged her brain irreparably as a result of taking these drugs. This new information was built into her conceptualisation in the form of two rival hypotheses regarding the panic disorder that could then be tested out. In this case, the two hypotheses were written out as follows:

My panic attacks may result from either:

Hypothesis 1: Doing drugs at university has completely done my brain in. The damage to my brain is causing these attacks and will get worse and worse as time goes on. In the end, I will go mad or even die.

or

Hypothesis 2: My bad trip at university has understandably led me to be frightened that I have done permanent damage to my brain. I get very frightened when I feel out of control. My problem with my eyes means I can't see as well and that makes me feel lost and scared at times. When I get these sensations, I have frightening thoughts such as 'I am going mad' and that makes me even more hyper, building up into an attack.

Behavioural experiments – dropping safety behaviours
The most powerful way of changing catastrophic misinterpretations of symptoms is for clients to put themselves in situations where they experience symptoms of panic but do not do anything to control them. This gives the client experiences in which the catastrophic misinterpretations are found to be invalid, allowing for disconfirmation of misinterpretations and the beliefs underlying them. This is known as 'dropping safety behaviours'. The therapist can set up such tasks as homework assignments but it is more powerful initially to conduct experiments with the client in the session or out in the world. A real life exercise might involve leaving the therapy room and going to a situation that the client fears, for example going to the supermarket with Josie, and asking her to try not to control her symptoms. Sometimes a panic may arise in the session itself and may provide material to work on in the 'here and now'.

An experiment is described for Josie:

Counsellor: I wonder if we tried very hard, whether we could actually make you go mad?
Josie: I don't like the sound of this!
Counsellor: No, it's hard, isn't it. But let's give it a go? You reckon that if you lose control, you will go mad. So what are you doing now to maintain control?
Josie: Do I have to do this? Well, I'm paying attention to you and I am sitting tight sort of thing.
Counsellor: Okay, try a few minutes of not paying attention to me and sitting tight?

After a certain amount of giggling, they sit for a few minutes.

Josie: Can we stop now?
Counsellor: Of course, but did you go mad then?
Josie: Not this time!
Counsellor: How come? Were you doing anything to stop it?
Josie: No, I really tried to go mad but I couldn't – I guess going mad isn't so simple, is it? I can feel mad but not go mad.

The above examples can be regarded as in-session behavioural experiments. Experiments can also be devised to run outside the therapy room, either as homework assignments for between sessions or as assignments with the therapist available but not in the immediate presence of the client. For example, the client might do some physically stimulating exercises to increase heartbeats in order to tackle situations where strenuous activity is avoided because of false concerns about the heart or breathing. However, we need to be sure that this is safe for both client and counsellor, and is inadvisable with cases of known risk, such as heart disease, asthma, high blood pressure or pregnancy.

Two other classic behavioural experiments for panic and agoraphobia are as follows:

The Hyperventilation Provocation Test in Panic

Belief: My symptoms mean I am going to go mad, die, collapse or have a heart attack.
Alternative: My symptoms are a result of hyperventilation and nothing bad can happen.
Experiment: Hyperventilate for two minutes and try to go mad, die, collapse or have a heart attack.
Outcome: Client stays sane and alive. Learns that panic is not as dangerous as thought, but problem lies in the way symptoms are interpreted.

Agoraphobia

Belief: If I go out, I will have a panic attack, pass out and make a complete fool of myself. People would think I was completely mad.
Alternative: Panic does not lead to passing out. Even if I did, someone would help and be understanding.
Experiment: Client watches while counsellor 'passes out' in shopping centre and observes other people's reactions. Then, hyperventilates and tries to pass out herself in shopping centre.

Outcome: When counsellor mimes passing out, one person stopped to see if she was all right but everyone else just got on with their business. No great drama. When client tried to pass out, could not and no one paid any attention.

A fuller list of behavioural experiments is given in the table below.

Table 7.4   *Behavioural experiments for working with panic*

Experiment	Goal in changing misinterpretations
Over-breathing task Getting the client to hyperventilate will produce panic-like symptoms	The experiment shows that symptoms do not come out of the blue It can also show that they will subside without safety behaviours
Physical exercises such as jogging and going upstairs	Panic-like symptoms can be induced by exercise and therefore cannot be dangerous
Chest pain exercises: taking deep breaths and inserting a finger into the ribs	As above, especially where chest pains are a major symptom
Staring exercises: eye fixation or staring	As above, especially where visual disturbances are a major symptom
Daydreaming combined with over-breathing	Feelings of dissociation can be deliberately provoked
'Acting as if': faking a collapse in public	Can disconfirm catastrophic fears about how others will react if the worst happens

Source: Wells (1997)

Once the client has done the experiment, it is very important to spend time looking at what has been gained, in terms of a reappraisal of the original belief. In Josie's case, the experiment gave weight to Hypothesis 2, that feeling mad is not the same as going mad. A client who tries hard to faint in the session, without success, learns that faint feelings arising from panic do not lead to faints.

Words of caution in encouraging clients to drop safety behaviours

Knowing that a client's way of coping with anxiety is a safety behaviour does not automatically mean that it is right, or safe, to work to challenge such behaviours too early in counselling for all clients. We need to proceed with caution and sensitivity, remaining collaborative so that the client knows what we are asking, and why, at all stages. We hold on to safety, and being asked to change too much, too soon, may be counterproductive. Clients may feel overwhelmed, frightened and defensive about the idea of dropping safety behaviours, and it may not sit well with some counsellors' ethics. At all stages experiments are carefully negotiated with the client in a spirit of collaboration, and should be construed as 'no-lose' experiences.

Counselling for Agoraphobia

While much of counselling for panic can be done at the level of symptoms and re-evaluating interpretations, working with clients with agoraphobia may well need to be longer-term with more focus on past issues and core beliefs. Graduated exposure, working on a step-by-step hierarchy of feared situations, has been a well-used and effective therapy for agoraphobia (Rachman, 1997). Now it is realised that agoraphobic problems are often closely associated with panic, it is generally assumed that a treatment combining exposure and cognitive strategies will be an effective treatment for panic with agoraphobia (Eysenck, 1997), using exposure as a series of behavioural experiments to test the client's beliefs and predictions. Much work can be done with agoraphobic clients using methods of working with panic, particularly helping clients to drop their safety behaviours and test predictions about becoming anxious in public places (Salkovskis et al., 1997). But because these clients often have more complex difficulties, we often need to work in a different way. The active ingredients of therapy with agoraphobic clients are (Hackmann, 1998):

- Working on changing catastrophic interpretations by finding out true causes and consequences of symptoms, using guided discovery and behavioural experiments.
- Using imagery when verbal methods alone are not powerful enough.
- Overcoming avoidance.
- Working on underlying assumptions and beliefs, as and when necessary.

Given the problems underlying agoraphobia, much of therapy can focus on helping the client to disengage from dependence on others. It is important to ensure that the therapeutic relationship provides a secure base for the client to form attachments during the therapeutic process. One problem when working with agoraphobic clients is that they can find it difficult to get to sessions. Their fear and avoidance may mean they frequently do not turn up, or cancel sessions, and find it difficult to do home tasks. They may also avoid any painful feelings necessary for working with their fears. One option is to hold sessions in a safe place for the client, such as at their home, at least initially. In practice, home-based sessions are far from ideal: many issues about boundaries arise, the client may feel so safe that it is impossible to activate their fears, and we may be competing with the telephone, television, children, family and dog. If working at home, setting boundaries to the work is extremely important, in terms of not making the boundaries so safe that no therapeutic work can be done. It can help to negotiate that only the first few sessions will be held at the client's home, after which sessions will move to the clinic or other counselling setting. Often clients are able to get to their GP surgery if to nowhere else, and this can be a good place to start seeing clients. We need to be open about breaches of boundaries and keep re-negotiating with the client, particularly when we are working on more active challenging of fears and dropping safety behaviours in feared situations.

Using imagery with agoraphobic clients

Working with client's images can be a very helpful part of working with agoraphobia. For example, therapy involves planning experiments consisting of gradually more difficult tasks, while dropping safety behaviours. This means breaking down goals like going to visit a friend into separate achievable tasks, such as going on to the street, walking to the end of the street, going to the bus-stop, while doing nothing to control the panic. It can be very helpful to facilitate a mental rehearsal of these steps and tracking the process by getting the client to imagine doing each step and reporting their sensations as they imagine them. Clients may also have frightening images of previous traumas underlying specific fears, such as memories of being left alone as a child or being lost. Imagery work can help the client both to identify specific fears and to begin to find psychological completion by the working through of their images in order to re-evaluate the meaning of them (Hackmann, 1997, 1998). For example, one client got strong images of becoming hysterical as she stepped onto a boat. The 'working through' of the image saw her calming down. The meaning of the image was changed from 'I can't cope with sailing' to 'sailing might be difficult for a while but I'd calm down and cope'. Hackmann (1998) cites using imagery with a client who feared fainting in public. This fear related strongly to the memory and image of being taken against his will to hospital. The image was connected back to a childhood experience of becoming ill and being taken to hospital where he was separated from his parents. He interpreted this as due to his parents not loving him. Imagery was used to change the meaning of his childhood memories in order to 'repair' the memory and enable the client's beliefs as an adult to change, by using techniques described by Edwards (1990). The client re-imagined the situation, seeing himself as an adult warning his parents not to send him to hospital, or, if it was necessary, to reassure him that they did love him and would be there to collect him soon. In our experience, we see a number of clients whose fears about abandonment relate to experiences of being hospitalised as children in the 1950s, when it was thought bad for the child to have any contact with parents.

The Effectiveness of Cognitive-Based Interventions for Panic

There are a growing number of outcome studies demonstrating the efficacy of the therapeutic approaches described above. Beck et al. (1992) compared results of cognitive therapy versus 'supportive therapy'. Cognitive therapy results were significantly superior. Other studies have replicated the effectiveness of cognitive therapy (Clark et al., 1994; Arnz and van de Hout, 1996). A shorter version, involving around seven sessions plus self-help work, has also been found to be effective (Botella and García-Palacios, 1999; Clark et al., 1999).

Most of these studies have been in the form of clinical trials, with extensive exclusion criteria, for clients with a primary diagnosis of panic disorder without agoraphobia. There is some evidence that treating panic with agoraphobia is not as effective as treatment for panic without agoraphobia (Williams and Farbo, 1996).

Despite these reservations, the collective work on cognitive therapy for panic is a good example of how a researched and tested model of a disorder can provide an invaluable template for the practitioner (Rachman, 1997). Such a template gives information that the practitioner can use to assess and understand the client and to plan interventions in such a way that the chances of success are maximised. Most of the work described above focuses on disrupting the maintenance of the disorder rather than disentangling all the underlying vulnerabilities associated with it. Counsellors may often be more attracted to the exciting search for underlying causes than to paying attention to the detail of the maintenance cycle (James, 2001). In our view, the two factors need to be taken together. Therapy for panic is unlikely to be successful without paying strong attention to changing the maintenance cycle, but attention to underlying causes, even though they may be in some senses unknowable, is often essential for maintaining the bond within which the therapy is conducted. Our conceptualisation needs to include consideration of why the client is likely to have developed a tendency to misinterpret symptoms, without necessarily overly focusing on background or childhood issues, particularly when clients are benefiting a great deal from work only on the maintenance cycle. There is perhaps some irony in our experience that when therapy proceeds on the assumption that there *must* be an underlying cause, the client may seek more attention for his presenting problem, whereas if therapy proceeds on the assumption that an underlying cause should not be assumed, the client may ask for more consideration of his or her childhood. Like many things in life, we need to strike an effective balance.

8

General Anxiety and Worry

Last night, while I lay thinking here
Some WhatIfs crawled inside my ear
   Shel Silverstein. From: *The Kingfisher Book of Comic Verse*, 1991.
London: Kingfisher Books. (And thanks to my client who contributed it.)

Don't tell me that worry doesn't do any good. I know better. The things
I worry about don't happen.
Author unknown

Feeing generally anxious and worried is a common reason for
people to come to counselling. The problems include a combination of physical symptoms, feeling on edge and tense all the
time, and worry. Such a combination of symptoms is what most
of us would call 'anxiety'; if the anxiety reached levels which
began to be seriously disruptive of life, it might well begin to
meet diagnostic criteria for generalised anxiety disorder, a
central feature of which is worry. Many of us have experienced
episodes when thoughts and concerns go round and round in
our heads, without our being able to come to conclusions or take
action which might make us feel better. The more the worry
process goes on, the more our fears seem to be realistic and
highly probable. Looked at objectively or in the cool light of day,
we can see that the worries were out of proportion; but at the
time they seemed very real. For clients with high degrees of
worry, the worries never stop, and can never be got into proportion. Clients with general anxiety and worry often feel
misunderstood: people respond to their concerns with 'Don't
worry about it; it won't happen', an impossible task for someone
locked into worry. They may not be taken seriously, are dismissed as neurotic and not given a chance to feel that their
concerns are valid.

  Help for people with general anxiety and worry problems has
mainly targeted the physical symptoms, using methods such as
relaxation training and biofeedback. In our experience, clients
we have seen with general anxiety problems have tried various

forms of help, such as anxiety management groups or relaxation training and a variety of different medications. Some arrive for psychological help already dependent on benzodiazepines, perhaps used for some time with little success. Other counselling and psychological strategies have looked at the problems the client was facing and attempted to tackle these. While such approaches are effective in helping clients in the short term, many clients remained vulnerable to worry: while the content of the worries could be examined, the process would keep going.

In the last few years, established approaches to anxiety and worry have been supplemented by exciting new strategies. The main focus has been to bring to psychological therapy a greater understanding of worry, developing a metacognitive perspective to the process of worry and how this can be more effectively tackled in therapy. Many of the techniques of anxiety management, focusing on reducing physical tension, learning to relax, focusing on the content of worries and sorting out problems or cognitive restructuring may be far more effective once the individual can target the process of worry itself, and work out effective ways of reducing it. We introduce these newer approaches in this chapter and look at how to adapt counselling where worry is a central feature for our clients.

Defining General Anxiety and Worry

People with general anxiety are persistently anxious and worried, far out of proportion to 'real' circumstances. What they worry about may be serious and realistic: the possibility of bad things happening to themselves or family such as illness, debt, theft, loss and other catastrophes, or worries about work, money, relationships and whether they will be able to cope with the demands of life. While the specific content of worries is normal and common, for people with general anxiety and worry, the worries feel out of control: they do not respond to attempts to stop worrying, rationalise or get things into perspective. Worries have the quality of ruminations, being persistent and never ending. Alongside the worry, people also feel very uncomfortable and anxious, their fight or flight responses working overtime. This results in feeling tense, wound up, unable to relax, irritable, on edge, and in suffering physical problems such as pain due to muscle tension, insomnia, irritable bowel syndrome, or needing to urinate all the time. The worries and anxiety symptoms can cause difficulties sleeping, which in turn increase the person's feeling of being

Table 8.1   *Definition of generalised anxiety disorder*

Excessive anxiety and worry about a number of events or activities, which the person finds difficult to control

The worries are associated with:

Restlessness, feeling keyed up or on edge
Tiredness
Difficulty concentrating
Irritability
Disturbed sleep
Tension

The worries cause significant distress and impairment of normal functioning.

Source: APA (2000)

unable to cope (Table 8.1). People with anxiety problems such as panic or phobias may experience episodes of anxiety in relation to particular events or circumstances; in contrast, the problems of general anxiety and worry are very unpleasant and can seem never ending.

Various themes characterise general anxiety and worry. Beck's work (Beck et al., 1985) highlighted how anxiety arises when perception of threat exceeds the person's perception of their ability to cope. In general anxiety, the balance of this equation always seems shifted against the individual, who feels persistently overwhelmed and unable to cope. The actual threat is seen as constant, but often vague or unspecified, and mainly linked to uncertainty: not knowing what is around the corner and how to cope with the unknown gives rise to constant worry and anxiety (Wells and Butler, 1997).

General anxiety and worry go along with many other problems such as panic attacks, phobias and social phobia. However, a distinguishing feature can be the focus of the client's concerns and worry, which can be much wider-ranging than for clients with other anxiety problems: almost anything can be worried about, whereas, for clients with panic or health anxiety, their concerns are more specific. General anxiety can be chronic and very disabling and can result from, as well as cause, low mood and depression. People with disabling worries may well have low confidence and low self-esteem, both being a cause and effect of the anxiety, and may have a long-standing tendency to avoid difficulties and depend strongly on other people in order to manage their lives. Many of these individuals report a susceptibility to feeling anxious and worried since childhood, 'I've always been a worrier' is commonly reported.

Mary, a 45-year-old publishing assistant, was referred for help with her anxiety, which had gone on for at least 20 years. She had tried various forms of help, including anxiety management groups, counselling, medication and relaxation, all of which had helped for a while but her anxiety had always returned. She had recently learned that her company was to be making redundancies, and there was significant uncertainty about her job, which triggered off extreme anxiety and worry. When we met, Mary said that she had been feeling awful all the time for weeks: tense, on edge, shaky, experiencing difficulties sleeping, bowel problems and headaches. Thoughts were going round and round in her mind, not only about the situation at work but about 'everything'. Her whole life felt threatened and she worried about getting through each day, as well as about her family, the dog, housework, money and the problems of the country. Objectively she knew that her life was not under threat: even if she lost her job, her family were financially comfortable and she would find something else. The 'facts' were small consolation to her, and the worries seemed to grow each day. 'I can worry for England, if not the world.'

Raised anxiety and worry can be caused by a number of medical conditions, by caffeine, alcohol, or withdrawal from these or other drugs, and can be a side-effect of various medications, including benzodiazepines. General anxiety is, not surprisingly, linked with stressful life events: sometimes people go through a period of stress and difficulties where their worries are totally realistic, but cannot be switched off once the problems are resolved. Early childhood experiences of not feeling safe, adequately protected, or able to exert control over their lives may lead the individual to feel unsafe and worried throughout their lives (Butler, 1994). The child may have been the responsible eldest who looked after younger children or the parents. How the child's family copes with uncertainty and ambiguity can be important – whether uncertain events are seen as hovering in the background and therefore with the potential to strike at any time, or as so unlikely as to be not even worth thinking about.

Conceptualising General Anxiety and Worry

Understanding the cognitive mechanisms

A model is shown in Figure 8.1, showing the central role of different types of worry in the maintenance of general anxiety, and how worry keeps worry going.

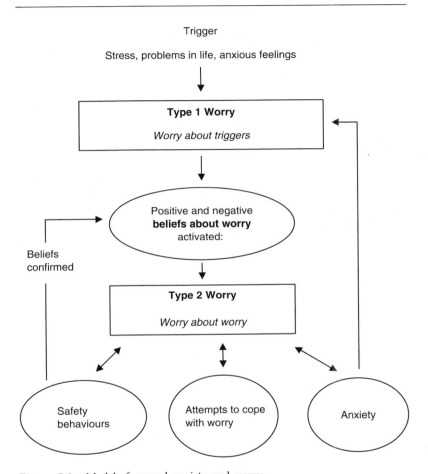

Figure 8.1   *Model of general anxiety and worry*

Source: Ricketts and Donohoe (2000), adapted from Wells (1997)

Worry is a cognitive activity: the person ruminates, coming up with all sorts of ideas, images and fears so that she experiences thoughts constantly 'going round and round my mind'. Many worries have the qualities of negative automatic thoughts, with marked catastrophising, black and white thinking or ignoring one's coping abilities. However, focus on the content of worrying thoughts is not where the action is: take away one negative thought and another stream will follow in its wake. Conceptualising worry needs to take into account the stream: the process of worry.

Why do people worry?

A lot of research has focused on *what* people worry about and how much they worry: that is, the content of worry. More recently there has been interest in *why* people worry. Wells (1995, 1997) divided people's worries into Type 1 and Type 2. Type 1 worries are about external or internal events, such as work, money, health, family, friends, coping with particular difficulties, the world situation, being socially acceptable. These worries can be worked with, using methods such as thought monitoring and looking for alternatives. In contrast, Type 2 worries are concerns about the fact that worrying thoughts occur and the content of the thoughts: that is, worry about worry or meta-worries. Where Type 2 thoughts are a major problem, it is unlikely that attempts to challenge worrying thoughts themselves will be successful (Wells and Butler, 1997; Wells, 2000). We need to understand people's beliefs about worry itself, both negative and positive.

WORRY ABOUT WORRY: NEGATIVE BELIEFS AND WORRY   Specific worrying beliefs about worry include:

- I'll go mad if I don't stop worrying.
- My brain will explode with all these worrying thoughts.
- I'll never be able to stop worrying if I start.
- I must stop worrying.
- One worrying thought and I'm off for ever.
- My worries will take over and control me.
- Worrying about bad things makes them happen.

As a result of worries about worry, the individual takes measures to try and stop worrying. Trying to stop worrying does, paradoxically, increase the worry. The 'white bear' test shows that trying to 'stop thinking' about something actually increases the likelihood that the thought will come to mind (Wegner et al., 1987; Wegner, 1989). Try for a moment not to think about a white bear . . . or a purple giraffe . . . or an orange hippopotamus. The process of trying not to think about something actually increases the focus, making it almost impossible to not think. Thought suppression increases the likelihood of thoughts coming to mind, and so increases the sense that worries are uncontrollable, in turn increasing attempts to control them, and so on in a vicious circle.

   The worries also mean that the individual is extremely vigilant about the possibility of danger, noticing any threats in the environment, overestimating dangers, making the individual feel more insecure and anxious. Worrying produces more worrisome possibilities, things that may never have occurred to them before, which then need to be worried about, causing more anxiety. The more anxious the person, the more the brain is in worry mode.

Worry may also be a means of avoiding looking at what the individual is really concerned about and may block out more distressing thoughts and images that may help the person avoid looking at worse fears or feelings in the short term. When the deeper worries are not looked at, however, they continue to be problems increasing the person's anxiety and worry (Borkovec and Inz, 1990). If worry helps the individual avoid more painful issues, then the worry is reinforced and likely to continue.

WORRYING ABOUT NOT WORRYING: POSITIVE BELIEFS ABOUT WORRY
Most of us would agree that too much worry is a bad thing – it makes us feel worried, harried and bad, and paralysed rather than being able to take action. However, people worry for good reasons. There are no doubt some advantages to a certain level of worry: it helps us work out possibilities, mull over solutions to problems, motivates us to take action and so on. A moderate degree of worry gives us the ability to see problems that may crop up, and may have evolutionary survival value. Research shows that people also have positive reasons for worrying (Freeston et al., 1994; Wells and Butler, 1997; Wells, 2000), although they may not be aware of these without discussion and analysis. Worrying is seen as a way of preventing bad things from occurring, or as minimising the effects of negative events by making the person feel less guilty, less disappointed should negative events occur, and providing distraction from thinking about even worse things. Worrying is also seen as a means of making positive things happen, such as finding a better way of doing things, finding solutions to problems and helping the individual feel more in control (Freeston et al., 1994).

This may be translated into certain positive beliefs about the effects of worry:

- If I don't worry, it might actually happen.
- I worried about it – so it's not my fault if it happened.
- If I worry about it, I'll be prepared when bad things happen, and not so disappointed or upset.
- I have to worry in order to do anything.
- If I didn't worry, I'd never get around to doing anything.
- I worry in order to feel in control.
- I have to worry more just in case I missed something.
- If I keep on worrying, I'll eventually sort it out in my mind.

Rina, a second-year sociology student, felt overwhelmed by the amount of work she had to do. She was working constantly, and was exhausted. Her mind simply could not switch off her work, and she spent hours worrying about working – 'I'm not doing enough', 'I have to do more', I mustn't stop thinking about it', and so on. To begin with, we looked at ways for her to challenge her thoughts – how much is enough? Is she doing enough work? She carried on worrying, although knowing it was not 'rational'. When we explored the process of worrying, Rina found that she had many positive beliefs about the benefits of worry: 'If I didn't worry about my work, I'd never do anything'; 'Worrying means I'm working'; 'Worrying about my work shows [my father] I do care about getting a good degree.'

Some beliefs about worry can be almost superstitious, like mascots that are given the power to prevent bad things happening. As a result, people do not dare risk trying out life without the mascot, but believe that the worries themselves have a protective function. Worrying can be confused with thinking things through helpfully, and occasionally the worrier will hit upon a useful solution or insight during worrying, which reinforces the message that worrying was helpful in arriving at something useful.

A university lecturer in quantum mechanics and theoretical physics who came for help with general anxiety said that he was reluctant to give up worrying, since all his life he had worried away at complex issues of physics, and come up with many ideas and solutions through this process. We discussed how there were two types of 'worrying'. His academic life was enhanced by his mind churning over complex problems, like a computer processing in the background and eventually hitting upon useful connections. While of great interest to him, these 'churnings' were not personally laden or threatening. When worried, he was consumed with fears and anxieties about himself, his health, the family, job certainties, coping with his mind slowing down as he got older, and about whether he would eventually lose his mind. He learned to distinguish these two types of thought processes, and how to reduce 'worry worry' without losing 'creative churning'.

RUMINATION AND WORRY   Rumination is an integral part of worrying: thoughts go round and round in one's head, being chewed over without any particular conclusions being drawn. Ruminating can increase anxiety levels, making the person feel anxious about the various possibilities that arise in the mind, while decreasing their confidence in being able to deal with problems. When in the process of ruminating, the individual is unable to examine their thoughts in the detached way necessary to gain some perspective, reduce anxiety levels, and increase problem solving. Ruminating drains the individual of resources necessary to evaluate and come to more useful conclusions (Wells, 2000).

Behaviour and worry

People who worry and experience general anxiety try many ways of coping, including asking for reassurance from other people and wanting certainty that their feared catastrophes are not going to happen. Mary, for example, had no confidence in her ability to make decisions, and needed to check out with her husband what she should wear, what to buy, whether she was well enough to go to work, whether to ask her daughter to help more with house-work and what to do over the weekends. Other people often try to reassure: 'Don't worry, it'll never happen, you'll be all right', which offers reassurance in the absence of certainty. Asking for reassurance can also lead to a range of responses from others, which can add to the individual's uncertainty and feeling out of control. Worries about worry itself also lead to 'safety behaviours' designed to keep the individual safe from the effects of worry, such as trying to control their thoughts or using distraction as a means of avoiding worrying itself, which may, as we have seen above, actually increase worrying thoughts.

Avoidance is another coping strategy: people may avoid doing things that make them anxious, which can lead to significant restrictions on the individual's life and also reduce confidence. Mary avoided making any plans for evenings and weekends, finding herself thrown into worry at having to make decisions on whether she would be able to cope. People also avoid worry itself, avoiding anything that might trigger the worries, rushing around and keeping busy to avoid having to think, which both confirms the dangers of worry itself and prevents the individual learning that worry itself is not dangerous. Worry itself may be a form of avoidance: people report worrying about something rather than doing it; as we have discussed above, worrying and ruminating can help avoid looking at and tackling the person's real, under-lying fears. People can attempt to avoid uncertainty in their lives by sticking to rigid routines, always doing everything the same way or trying to prepare for every eventuality, but be thrown into acute distress if their plans change or unexpected events happen.

Assumptions and beliefs

People with generalised anxiety and worry often have low self-esteem, see themselves to be poor copers, lack confidence in their own decisions, and find uncertainty very difficult or intolerable. Clients with long-term anxiety and worry may come from backgrounds where there is uncertainty, absence of good secure attachments to others, or where their abilities to make decisions and become self-reliant are not developed. Some always felt out of their depth, having to cope with things beyond their means as children. Mary, for example, came from a large family where she was asked to look after her baby brother from a very young age, a responsibility she found overwhelming at times. She constantly tried to cope but was always fearful that something awful would happen.

People with general anxiety may have global beliefs, such as 'you never know what is around the corner', or 'whenever things go right, they always go wrong'. Such beliefs are no doubt true for most people, since life tends to have its ups and downs, and both good and difficult things happen during our lifetimes. When clients are highly anxious, such shifts in life are connected as being cause and effect, the good times causing the bad. These beliefs also feed in to central lack of confidence in coping with change. These clients may believe that the world is always against them and nothing works out. This may be a combination of personalising and catastrophising common events. For example, a client was distraught at having difficulties in buying a new house, taking it as evidence that nothing ever worked out simply for her, rather than as evidence that house-buying is a stressful business. They may feel unsure of their ability to cope with difficulties, and use coping strategies that might increase the likelihood of things going wrong, such as avoiding tackling financial problems until they build up to crisis point.

Adapting Counselling for General Anxiety and Worry

General anxiety and worry are common to many anxiety problems, and it can at times be difficult to distinguish what is going on. We may start counselling with standard techniques such as thought monitoring and challenging, and one key that worry is a central problem is the experience of 'yes . . . but's': for every answer to every negative thought there is another stream of negative thoughts. We may as counsellors experience a level of frustration at this – the client holding on to their worries at all costs while we are attempting to reduce them and help the client gain perspective. One of the tasks for the counsellor, therefore, is to maintain a curious and questioning attitude, not only towards the content of the client's difficulties ('Why are they so worried about x?'), but also towards the process of worry itself ('Why is my client worrying?').

Counselling for worry requires keeping slightly detached from the content, and not getting sucked in, without losing therapeutic empathy. Many clients with worry problems have had bad experiences of not being listened to, of their worries not being taken seriously by others, or being dismissed. On the other hand, to spend a long time in counselling listening to the outpouring of worries can be counterproductive. While clients' worries are real and objectively worth being concerned about, and we can understand why the individual is concerned, counsellors need to keep in mind the 'umbrella' of processes above the concerns, and help form hypotheses about the process. One way is actively to interrupt the client's stream of worries, and empathically reflect on the client's emotions and worry processes. 'There are so many worries going round and round in your mind . . . you sound really desperate when you tell me all these concerns . . . it sounds like they are never ending: we talk about one and another hundred worries pop up.' A useful counselling skill is immediacy, being in the here and now and actively commenting on what is going on: 'Sometimes when I'm listening to you, I feel confused or lost . . . I wonder if it might help for me to interrupt and help you to refocus?'

Using the two-hypothesis model, described on pages 123–4, can be useful. Rather than focusing on answering worries, the counsellor can offer two alternatives:

1. That all these terrible things are the problem. Mary is going to lose her job and it will be completely catastrophic.
2. That *worrying* about these terrible things is the central problem. The problem is that Mary is worried about what might happen if she lost her job, and the worry is getting in the way of her thinking through alternatives to feel better.

People have usually spent much time trying to resolve the first alternative – worrying to prevent bad things happening, seeking reassurance, avoidance – but little time on effectively focusing on the second alternative, which involves tackling the worry. Our task is to maintain a collaborative stance throughout, enabling both client and counsellor to be clear about the rationale for interrupting worries in order to look at overall processes. Clients may well come to counselling to be reassured about their worries, and we need to negotiate the boundary between being empathic and understanding, without maintaining the client's difficulties.

The key adaptations to helping clients with general anxiety problems are:

- Working with the process of worry: identifying and testing out specific beliefs about worry.
- Helping the client build up a repertoire of skills to cope with worry and anxiety.
- Working with underlying assumptions and beliefs.
- Working with ways of dealing with uncertainty.
- Building up self-confidence.

Working with the process of worry

During counselling we need to identify the client's specific beliefs about the effects of worry, gain understanding where these beliefs may have come from, and help the client test them out and come up with alternative beliefs that are less likely to generate more worry. People have specific reasons for believing that worry itself is harmful, often that it will lead to serious mental illness. This particular worry is reinforced by images from the media or literature of the neurotic personality, mental illness and madness, such as provided by *Cold Comfort Farm* and *Jane Eyre*. Clients say that once they start worrying they cannot stop, which is often the case: we need therefore to look at the meaning of not being able to stop worrying. Socratic questioning helps us to identify worries about worry: 'What might happen if you were to worry and worry and never be able to stop?' 'What would that feel or look like?' 'Do images come to mind?' Similarly, we aim to find out the client's positive beliefs: 'What would happen if you were not to worry?' 'What would that feel like?' 'Would anything bad happen?'

Once client and counsellor are clear about the client's positive and negative beliefs, a combination of guided discovery and experiments helps test out the beliefs. For example, a client who believes that worrying will drive her mad or cause her to lose control increases her worries, tries to worry and worry, and test out what happens. While this may be very uncomfortable, the client may find they worry more, but do not go mad, or lose control.

Mary had a clear image of herself driven mad by worries, a mad woman with hair awry, face locked into a tortuous grimace, in the corner of a room, unable to cope. In the session, she spent 15 minutes really getting into her worries, worrying more and more and trying to go mad. She then looked in a mirror, and saw herself as poised and as well dressed as she usually was. She continued to practise this for homework, and was able to laugh at her images and the reality. We discussed the discrepancy about how often she had felt overcome by worries, and how often her scenario had happened. We also thought about what would need to happen for her scenario to come true – a combination of severe life events, losing everything, brain injury or poisoning, and failing to go to the hairdresser, an unthinkable event for Mary.

A client who believes 'I have to worry, otherwise catastrophe will be around the corner', can be encouraged to use distraction to take his/her mind off the worries, or switch to worrying about something else, and monitor whether the catastrophe actually happened. This way they have some exit point for the worries. The following example illustrates how Liam worked this out for himself, as he wryly describes:

I was worrying and worrying about the business – had I made the right decision in taking on more staff? What happens if we get behind financially? Will I get the accounts in on time? What if we don't break even this month – what is ahead for us? And so on and on. I then realised that I'd forgotten to worry about my health – so I switched to that, and had a good worry about getting older and the pains in my back and whether the doctors had missed something after all. This kept me going for the rest of the week. I then remembered that I'd forgotten to worry about the business, although it was rumbling on as usual, and it occurred to me that it doesn't really matter what I'm worrying about, worrying doesn't stop things happening or make them happen – so I can pick a topic at random to worry about each day – or maybe I don't need to worry at all?

Strategies to reduce worry and solve problems

There is a range of strategies and methods that help reduce or control worry (Butler, 1994; Butler and Hope, 1995). While these are very helpful, to increase their power in cognitive therapy, they can be used not only to get relief from the symptoms of worry but also to test out and undermine underlying specific beliefs about worry.

One very helpful technique is the 'worry decision tree' (Butler and Hope, 1995: 181) – a series of questions to help decide what the worry is, whether anything can be done, what to do and when to stop worrying. The sequence of questions is as follows:

1. What am I worried about?

    Be specific about the worry, spell it out in so many words.

2.   Is there anything I can do?

> If *yes*, work out what needs to be done and do it rather than worrying.
> If *no*, accept that it is out of our hands, or unsolvable, or unpredictable, and use distraction or other techniques to stop worrying.

3.   Is there anything I can do now?

> If *yes*, do it.
> If *no*, make plans to do it later, then stop worrying by distraction or other techniques.

Techniques to reduce worry include:

- Interrupting the process of worry: using distraction, physical activity, talking about something else, doing soothing activities, being kind to oneself.
- Writing down the worries.
- Counting the number of worrying thoughts rather than becoming involved in their content.
- Worry-busting images: mentally putting the worries in a computer file then in the wastebasket; e-mailing them to the dump; watching them float away in a bubble.
- Worry time: condensing worries into a planned slot each day, and interrupting them at other times.
- Mindful meditation: learning to observe the worries without judging them or taking action; realise they are just thoughts. (Kabat-Zinnn, 1990, 1995)

Clients who feel that worry is unpredictable, and just comes along without any prompting, can learn that periods of worry are often predictable, triggered, for example, by an uncertain event (in Mary's case, possibility of redundancy), when tired, premenstrual, hungry, unwell, in the middle of the night, or waiting for medical test results. Clients can then normalise their worries, and predict in advance when their worries will strike, 'I am worrying because it makes total sense that I will worry, given the circumstances', and so be more prepared and accepting.

People who are generally anxious may not have developed effective problem solving skills, or lack confidence in their ability to solve problems. Problem solving skills, such as described in Chapter 6, involve learning how to turn general worries into specific problems, work out specific solutions, take action and evaluate. Problem solving is very helpful in enabling clients to take action rather than worry, and to improve their confidence in being able to deal with problems. Clients may find it hard to see difficulties that arise in life as problems that can be tackled, rather than as overwhelming threats: so once a problem arises, worry is the first, incapacitating response, which inhibits the individual in even trying to problem-solve (Dugas et al., 1995). Worriers can have difficulties in discriminating between problems that they can do something about, and other problems that are insoluble, the latter often taking up a great deal of worry time. So, helping clients to redefine challenges as problems rather than threats helps mobilise problem solving skills.

> For Mary, it was a revelation that she was able to solve difficulties herself rather than worry or ask for help, and also ask herself whether there was anything that could be done at all. Once she learnt to stop and identify life difficulties as problems rather than overwhelming threats, she found she was better than she thought at working towards solutions: this in turn boosted her confidence. Her company made her redundant: she dealt with this by seeing it as a problem and opportunity, and looked for creative alternatives to a job which she realised she had not enjoyed much anyway.

One theory mentioned above is that worrying is a means for the individual to avoid looking at more difficult issues: although it feels painful to worry, the process of rumination and worry means that the 'top layer' of concerns may be chewed over while pushing down the underlying issues. Counselling offers an opportunity for clients to look at their underlying fears and images, and understand and work with these fears. The fears may be catastrophic, unpredictable, uncontrollable and terrible issues, yet with very low probability and unpredictability; once they can be identified, the client can be encouraged to look at the value of thinking about such possibilities, or problem solve how to manage should the worst happen. Discussing the client's fears enables them to be relegated to the 'I'll cross that bridge if I come to it' category; many of the difficult things that happen to people are in fact totally unpredictable and we cannot plan for their occurrence or our reactions.

> During counselling, Mary and I used downward arrows to look at what underlay some of her fears. One thought that kept her awake at night was the thought that something bad might happen to her

daughter. She would go over and over what might happen, coming up with some distressing images based on stories in the media, but then get upset and try and block out the images, often by worrying about something else. I encouraged her to look at some of her worst fears, rather than avoiding looking at them, and she came up with many powerful images accompanied by tears. She kept on saying 'I couldn't cope . . . that would be it', which again we looked at. During this work, Mary began to realise that she was spending a lot of emotional energy on events that had not happened, and might or might not happen, but no one could have any idea of the future. She realised that she wanted to channel some of her emotion into improving her relationship with her daughter now, into remembering to tell her how much she loved her, and spend good time with her during her life, as far as possible. We worked, too, on increasing her sense that whatever happened to her in her life, she would be able to find resources to cope – even if this meant going to pieces for a while – and others would always be there for her. She symbolically put her fears for her daughter into a mental drawer, and opened another one called 'today'.

Building confidence and ability to cope with uncertainty

Central issues for people with persistent worry problems and general anxiety include feelings of inability to cope in the world, difficulty in making or trusting decisions, fear of change and high intolerance of uncertainty. All these can be usefully looked at during counselling. Looking at the process of worry, and testing out some different ways of coping, such as problem-solving rather than worrying, can begin to improve clients' sense of being able to deal with their lives. General strategies to build up the individual's confidence and self-esteem can be integrated into the counselling (Fennell, 1998, 1999). Trying different things, and breaking fixed, 'safe' routines, helps one to learn that change is a manageable part of life.

Mary identified making decisions as a central problem: she had avoided doing so as much as possible or always checked with others and asked for reassurance. She planned a 'decision programme', listing things that she wanted to decide on herself, and asked her family not to get involved or try and reassure her even if she asked. She began to practise, and realised that her decisions were mostly fine, and that even if she made decisions which in retrospect were not the best, she could practise managing and living with the consequences. She decided she wanted to learn assertiveness skills, and take up swimming: she found out where classes were held and went along herself, without consulting friends or family first.

Fear and intolerance of uncertainty is a central theme i
anxiety. Counselling can focus on the meaning of uncerta
on finding other ways of managing in an uncertain world (Wells
and Butler, 1997). People often have areas of their life (such as
driving) in which they are prepared to take risks despite a fairly
high probability of bad things happening. They do not worry or
think about this, but spend much time on the uncertainty sur-
rounding remote, unlikely and uncertain events which none of us
can plan for. This work is philosophical in nature, all of us needing to work out how we manage the uncertainties of our lives, and
how much we live our lives with a degree of tolerance of
uncertainty. Clients can come up with a different 'tee-shirt slogan'
for life: 'If it could possibly happen to anyone, it will happen to
me', may change into less anxiety-inducing slogans such as 'So
what if it happens? I'll just have to deal with it at the time'; 'Bad
things are always unpredictable so there's no point even trying to
predict them'; 'What is now is now'; 'Live for today, not for what
might happen.' We then look at how life might change when
wearing the new tee-shirt.

Effectiveness of psychological therapies for general anxiety and worry

For many clients with low-level worries and anxiety who are
seeking help at a relatively early stage, general, non-directive
counselling is effective, enabling them to talk over their worries
and gain a different perspective (Boulenger et al., 1997). Other
helpful strategies include learning to relax and reduce the physical
aspects of anxiety and thereby avoid getting into a negative spiral.
For clients with persistent and disabling general anxiety and
worry, such counselling may be less effective, and even cause the
clients to dwell more on the content of their worries rather than
find ways of effectively tackling the process of worry. Research
reviewed by Wells and Butler (1997) shows that taking a cognitive
perspective is more effective than more standard anxiety-
management techniques such as applied relaxation. Many of the
newer cognitive behavioural approaches to general anxiety and
worry are very effective for this client group, when compared to
no help at all, other psychotherapeutic help, or medication (Barlow
et al., 1997). Clients whose general anxiety problems improve with
psychological help also experience improvements in accompanying anxiety problems such as social and simple phobias, and low
mood (Borkovec et al., 1995).

Overall, psychological therapies are, at present, only able to
help a proportion of those disabled by persistent anxiety and

worry: in a meta-review, Durham et al. (1999) found that only about half of clients with severe and disabling general anxiety, according to *DSM* criteria, made very good progress. Wells (2000) describes new developments in cognitive ways of understanding and working with the processes of worry and metacognition, which may well prove useful in providing more targeted and effective ways of reducing worry and general anxiety.

9

Specific Phobias

If your child shrieks and runs away at the sight of a frog, let him catch it and lay it down at a good distance from him; at first accustom him to look upon it; when he can do that, to come nearer to it and see it leap without emotion; then to touch it lightly, when it is held fast in another's hand; and so on until he can come to handle it as confidently as a butterfly or sparrow. (John Locke, *Essay Concerning Human Understanding*, 1690 (cited in Saul, 2001: 36)

The Greeks have a lot to answer for in our labelling of phobias. The word phobia derives from the Greek phobos ($\phi o \beta o \sigma$), meaning flight, panic and terror. The image of the god Phobos was used on shields and masks to strike terror into the heart of the enemy and paralyse him with fear. A phobia, in more modern times, is a persistent and excessive fear attached to an object or situation which is not in itself significantly dangerous. It can help to know some Greek to understand the origins of many of the names given to phobias: xenos ($\xi \epsilon \nu o \sigma$), the fear of strangers expressed as xenophobia; agora ($\alpha \gamma o \rho \alpha$), the market place; arachnophobia, from the Greek for spider ($\alpha \rho \alpha \chi \eta$); or claustrophobia, from the Greek $\kappa \lambda \epsilon \iota \sigma \tau o \sigma$, to shut, or close.

Phobias are extremely common, and most people either have or know someone with a specific phobia. Some objects of phobias carry a degree of inherent danger, or trigger fear or disgust, although other phobias are of apparently benign objects or situations. The difference between something people are able to live with or enjoy and a phobia, lies in the perception of cost, risk, coping resources, and the degree and uncontrollability of the anxiety experienced. While many would not deliberately confront certain objects or situations, yet are able to cope should the need arise, the phobic individual will sometimes take extreme steps to avoid their fears.

Our clients are very clear about what they are afraid of, and believe that their fears are out of proportion, yet are unable to confront the feared object or situation. They may feel other people do not take them seriously, and have had experiences of jokers deliberately setting them up for a head-on meeting with their fears. They describe their fears as 'stupid' or 'trivial', which undermines the fact that phobias can have a significant and painful impact, causing distress and chronic anxiety if the individual knows he has to face the fears on a regular basis. Many life difficulties can arise from the need to avoid situations. A lorry driver may be unable to work after developing a fear of motorways, or the spider phobic may be unable to go out of the house.

Despite their prevalence and impact, phobias can be easy to treat, and enabling clients to overcome phobias is enormously rewarding for all concerned. Treating just the phobia has side-effects of improved self-confidence, better relationships and increased ability to conquer other fears, without necessarily looking at these issues in counselling (Saul, 2001). Successful therapy for one phobia results in the reduction of other fears (Rachman and Lopatka, 1986). Many phobia treatments can be conducted in one long therapy session (Davey, 1997; Öst, 1997; Antony and Barlow, 1998), rather than prolonged counselling, which increases their availability to clients where resources are restricted, and its acceptability to clients. There are many resources for clients, such as those offered by airlines for flight phobia, and by zoos for a range of animal phobias (see Appendix for details). The effectiveness of brief therapy means that counsellors and therapists can, if necessary, resolve their own phobias if they need to see a client with similar problems.

Treatment for phobias has traditionally been behavioural, involving exposing clients to their fears until their anxiety reduces. Due to the emphasis on behavioural methods, and on very short-term work, and to lack of focus on background factors, many counsellors have not recognised their role in helping clients with phobias, the work mainly going to psychologists or community nurses. We hope that this chapter encourages counsellors to think again about directly working with clients' phobias. Newer cognitive behavioural approaches are described, which enable counsellors to combine the effective methods of exposure with working within a counselling and cognitive framework. Combining cognitive and behavioural methods, rather than undertaking a purely behavioural approach, fits better with a counselling ethos. Cognitive counselling focuses on collaboration and the search for meanings, and actively uses a good therapeutic relationship, while equipping clients with methods to help them literally face their fears.

> A marked and persistent fear that is excessive or unreasonable,
> triggered by the actual or potential presence of a specific object or situation.
>
> Exposure invariably provokes immediate anxiety.
>
> The individual recognises that the fear is excessive or unreasonable.
>
> The feared object or situation is avoided where possible, or tolerated only
> with intense distress and anxiety.
>
> The anxiety, distress or need to avoid significantly interferes with the
> individual's life.

Figure 9.1   *Description of specific phobias*

Source: APA (2000)

Defining Phobias

The *DSM* criteria for specific phobias are shown in Figure 9.1.

People can be phobic of many different objects or situations, as shown in Table 9.1. The characteristic of a phobia is that exposure to the feared object or situation leads to severe symptoms of anxiety and a profound need to escape. If the individual cannot escape, they experience significant anxiety, either short-term if the threat disappears, or chronic anxiety if the threat does not easily go away or cannot be avoided. The person will as far as possible try and avoid their fears, which can place great restrictions on their lives. Phobias can be highly circumscribed, so an individual with a specific phobia can be completely comfortable in situations which others would label as dangerous: the steeplejack terrified of water; the oil rig diver terrified of spiders; or the parachutist who had to stop her hobby because of an overwhelming terror of landing near a snake.

Away from the phobic situation or object, clients recognise that their fears are exaggerated, but are unable to control their reactions when exposed to their phobias. People's beliefs about the dangerousness of objects or situations increases the closer they are to them: for example, as a height phobic, I know that the Millennium Wheel is extremely safe and provides an amazing view, and that I would survive the experience. If I was inside a capsule, I would believe 100 per cent that, any moment, the capsule would fall off, the wheel would stop and we would be stuck there for days, the whole structure would disintegrate and fall into the Thames, and I would die of fright. Similarly a spider phobic realises that in this country spiders are harmless, peaceful

Table 9.1   *Common phobias*

Animals	Environment
Spiders (Arachnophobia)	Lightning (Astradophobia)
Wasps (Spheksophobia)	Thunder (Vrontophobia)
Snakes (Ophidiophobia)	Bridges (Gephyrophobia)
Birds (Ornithophobia)	Darkness (Nyctophobia)
Dogs (Cynophobia)	Sea (Thalassophobia)
Cats (Ailorophobia)	Water (Hydrophobia)
Mice (Musophobia)	Heights (Acrophobia)
Horses (Hippophobia)	
Feathers (Pteronophobia)	

Bodily functions and health	Situations
Blood (Haematophobia)	Driving
Injury involving bleeding	Flying
Needles, Injections (Trypanophobia)	Lifts
Vomit/vomiting (Emetophobia)	Moving staircases
Choking (Phagophobia)	Enclosed spaces (Claustrophobia)
Fear of contracting illness	Crowds (Ochlophobia)
Dentists	Being alone (e.g. in the house at night)

creatures, but when a spider is spied in the room, it becomes a huge, dangerous and aggressive threat.

60 per cent of the population will experience fear out of proportion to an object or situation at some point in their lives, and around 12 per cent meet diagnostic criteria for a specific phobia (Curtis et al., 1998). Most phobias are more common in women than in men, with the exception of height phobia (Curtis et al., 1998). There are at least 250 different phobias (Saul, 2001). Apart from social phobia, the most common are fears of insects and small animals, heights, water, public transport, storms, closed spaces, tunnels and crowds (Davey, 1997).

What Causes Phobias?

Early understandings of phobias gave prominence to behaviourist ideas of learning theories and classical conditioning, phobias being thought to arise as a result of objects or situations being paired with traumatic events. Fuel for such models arose from dubious experiments such as Watson and Rayner's deliberate attempts to induce a young boy, 'Little Albert', to become phobic of a white rat. Some, but not the majority, of people with phobias can pinpoint a specific traumatic event that triggered their phobias, which would be necessary for classical conditioning models. Choking phobia nearly always has a sudden onset following a traumatic choking episode; driving phobias can link closely with trauma following road traffic accidents. Many dental phobics have had unhappy dental encounters, particularly before the advent of effective pain control.

While some phobias can be traced back to obvious trauma, this is by no means the whole story, and simplistic models of classical conditioning are not borne out by the evidence (Davey, 1997). Not all people experiencing trauma develop phobias; and, conversely, it is difficult to produce fears and phobias with aversion therapy, pairing electric shocks or drugs inducing sickness with stimuli, such as so called 'treatments' for homosexuality too few decades ago. Learning theory would predict that anything can be the object of a phobia, and phobias ought to be equally distributed between many objects. Unfortunately for the behaviourists' argument, they are not. An interesting example is snake phobia, which is common even in countries such as Britain and Denmark where poisonous snakes are virtually non-existent in the wild, and the majority of snake phobics have never been bitten by a snake (Murray and Foote, 1979). This implies that fear of snakes is not learnt but is an acquired 'hard-wired' response, dating back through aeons of time to an age when poisonous snakes were a deadly threat to our ancestors (Rachman, 1997). Many phobias relate not to learning but to inherent fears that have not changed from childhood, such as fears of the dark, blood, animals or thunderstorms. People may be inherently predisposed to develop phobias, such as having a well-developed sensitivity to disgust, leading to increased likelihood of blood, spider or vomit phobia. Height phobia appears to be unrelated to specific trauma. Poulton et al. (1998) found that children who had had a serious fall between the ages of 5 and 9 were less likely to develop height phobias. We are writing following the traumatic events of 11 September 2001 in America, which have potentially increased the actual or perceived likelihood factor in the fear equation for flying. Whether this produces an increase in people who develop full-blown phobias of flying remains to be seen.

Phobias may only come to light when an individual's circumstances change. For example, a builder who has never particularly liked heights, whose working conditions change so that he or she needs to work above ground; a flight phobic whose job requires more travel; the individual with a vomit phobia who wants to get pregnant; or someone with a fear of needles requiring dental treatment, blood tests or surgery. Change in circumstances can lead to appraisal of risk changing. For example, a woman who had no problems with driving developed a driving phobia when she had her second child, becoming more aware of the potential costs of driving should she have an accident and consequently not be there for the children. Having children means a dog phobic has to face her fears when taking the children to the park.

Conceptualising Phobias: Looking for Meanings

Phobias can be conceptualised as a cycle of anxiety triggered by exposure to the phobic situation, maintained by specific interpretations the individual gives to the phobic stimulus and to their anxious response itself. As for many anxiety problems, the way the individuals try to cope with their fears, their safety seeking behaviours, helps them to feel better by avoiding further contact, but stops disconfirmation that their fears are unfounded (Figure 9.2). Our search when counselling for anxiety is to help the individual find out the specific meanings and appraisals, and use planned exposure to disconfirm these fears.

While many of the objects of phobias do possess inherent dangers, people with phobias have developed beliefs about the danger of phobic situations, to do with overestimating the degree of risk and harm, and underestimating their coping resources. Phobias have specific meaning for individuals, which they may not be explicitly aware of. For example, a driving phobic may see driving as a potentially risky activity, but their anxieties lie in the specific possibility of being trapped in the car for hours without anyone helping, should an accident occur. The spider phobic may be fearful of becoming so scared that they lose control of their bowels. These meanings given to phobic objects or situations can explain why people can be phobic of apparently unrelated things (Beck et al., 1985).

George came for help with a phobia of driving, but also experienced fears of flying in large aeroplanes (but not small four-seaters), of lifts, tunnels, or going down escalators. He was happy using the London Underground, but always walked up and down staircases. The meaning given to each of these situations was the possibility of being trapped and unable to escape. While lifts, tunnels and car crashes may be self-explanatory, George thought he could easily escape from a small plane if necessary, but not a large jumbo with all the doors sealed. Fear of escalators started when he saw one of the ever more popular television disaster programmes showing a man who slipped and became trapped when his tie caught between the moving stairs.

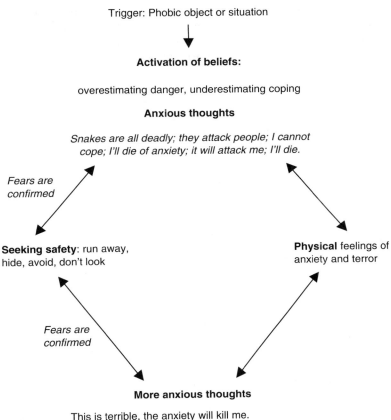

Figure 9.2   *Vicious cycle in phobias*

Clients may interpret their feelings during exposure to phobic situations as evidence of danger. For example, people with height phobias can experience feelings such as being sucked to the edge or feeling the floor tilting, which they then take as evidence of reality. Some clients experience highly visual and real flashbacks of an original trauma, such as being bitten by a dog as a child, which means they cannot distinguish the reality of the present situation (seeing a friendly dog in the distance), from the past trauma. Safety behaviours used by the client can increase their anxiety and discomfort and may in some cases increase the risk of danger (see below).

Phobias such as dental phobia can relate to specific meanings, connected to early experience not only of dental treatment but other experiences when the individual felt out of control or in pain. Clients' fears include (Chapman and Kirby-Turner, 1999):

- fear of loss of control
- fear of the unknown
- fear of betrayal and lack of trust
- fear of pain, or anticipation of pain
- fear of intrusion, belittlement and humiliation.

Counselling for Phobias

Historically there have been two approaches to dealing with phobias: the tip of the iceberg approach, and behavioural exposure treatment. According to the former, phobias represent the tip of the iceberg of much deeper entrenched fears, which need addressing in order for the phobia to resolve. Progress may be slow, in case discussing these fears unleashes unknown and uncontrollable terrors, ideas influenced by Freudian concepts of the seething unconscious. At the other extreme is the behavioural approach, concentrating only on the tip of the iceberg and ignoring what may lie beneath. In a cartoon advertising a phobia clinic, a client is seen looking out of a tiny box containing spiders, snakes, birds and other feared objects, and dangling from the thirtieth floor, presumably a one-session treatment aimed at covering all possibilities. Translated into real-life behaviour therapy, the behavioural approach involves exposing the terrified clients to increasing magnitudes of their fears in a graded hierarchy, allowing the client to relax until their anxiety reduces, before moving on to the next step. Behavioural treatment alone has produced very good results for many phobias, and the reader is referred to texts such as Davey (1997) for detailed descriptions of behavioural methods.

More recent approaches to therapy for phobias combines behavioural and cognitive methods, allowing for the highly active ingredient of exposure with cognitive formulation and understanding of what underlies and maintains the client's fears (Davey, 1997). The research to date indicates that there is not a great deal of difference between the two forms of therapy in terms of outcomes (Craske and Rowe, 1997).

In this chapter, we advocate an active combination of behavioural and cognitive approaches, each being necessary but not alone sufficient for helping our clients in counselling practice.

Some clients are unwilling to go through purely behavioural treatments, since it requires them to become very anxious and face their fears head on. There is a high drop-out rate in treatments involving pure exposure, limiting its value for all clients. Exposure may be effective because of complex cognitive changes. For example, the individual changes beliefs about threat, harm and coping factors through their experience of being able to stay in feared situations without significant ill effects. Cognitive approaches directly and overtly target changes in beliefs, which leads to more acceptable treatments for clients, particularly those who will not engage in a directly behavioural approach (Thorpe and Salkovskis, 1995). By exploring underlying beliefs, we are taking into account what is underneath the tip of the iceberg as well as concentrating on changing the tip, thus providing a link between the two: neither getting stuck on explaining phobias rather than changing them, nor ignoring their origins and links with our complex beliefs. For counsellors, working cognitively and collaboratively, gaining the whole picture and paying attention to therapeutic relationship issues is more consistent with their ethos and ways of working than applying a standard behavioural treatment.

However much cognitive approaches are being used to help clients with phobias, exposure is the most active ingredient. Without exposure, therapy is unlikely to be successful. Some clients are able to go on to make behavioural changes based on cognitive shifts, without going through a formal exposure programme in therapy. Counselling enables the client to understand the origins and distortions in their fears and the client is then able to experiment with reducing avoidance and conquering their fears. However, the research shows that without actual exposure, the phobia is likely to remain: when our clients walk out of the session saying that they will now go and try it all out, the ones who actually do are likely to be those we do not need to see again. In-session exposure work for spider phobia has been shown to be more effective than self-help programmes (Öst et al., 1991).

The Therapeutic Relationship in Counselling for Phobias

Working to conquer phobias has the flavour of a psychological treatment rather than counselling. While understanding fears and looking for cognitive change is helpful and necessary, the client needs also to go through a circumscribed programme – actively orchestrated by the counsellor – to treat their fears. Clients, by the nature of the case, find it hard to face up to phobias on their own, and a structured approach and an empathic and encouraging counsellor is required for the client to go the last mile. Working on phobias involves sensitively mixing the developing therapeutic relationship with the need to encourage the client to do specific tasks. I feel like a mildly bossy but empathic cheerleader when working with phobic clients, wanting to break into smiles and applause when they tackle ever greater fears, and not immediately giving up when they report that the next task is 'impossible'. The therapist has not only to be more directive and instructional but also more supportive and encouraging of the client. Some counsellors may find the directiveness necessary is at odds with their counselling philosophy and style; understanding phobias alone is not always enough to overcome them, and the evidence is that directing clients towards exposure is effective.

Stages of Counselling for Phobias

Counselling for phobias involves the following steps:

- Conceptualising the individual's phobia in terms of under-standing beliefs and predictions about the consequences of contact with the feared objects or situations and the nature of danger for the individual: costs, probabilities, coping and rescue factors.
- Developing a rationale for therapy and working out goals.
- Exposure to the phobia-triggers in order to conduct a series of experiments where the client can test out their specific fears and predictions.
- Encouraging the client to undertake continual, repeated experiments and lifestyle change to avoid avoidance and keep on testing their fears.

Conceptualisation and understanding meanings

One aim of assessment and conceptualisation for phobias is to work out with the client what they fear and why. Using guided discovery, we aim to discover specific meanings the individual gives to the phobic situation and object, and aim to find more realistic and helpful appraisals. When assessing and conceptualising phobias, it is important to clarify whether the presenting problem is related to other forms of phobia, or to general anxiety (Chapter 8). For example, phobias of flying may relate to many different fears, including heights, claustrophobia, or agoraphobia (Bor et al., 2000), and the phobia may be more pronounced because of other stresses in the individual's life which need addressing. However many different phobias the main problem appears to relate to, it is valuable to identify the central fears linking them. Fears of travelling on trains may relate to fears of lack of control of the train, or levels of anxiety symptoms; or to confinement and inability to escape should a crash occur.

Despite the effectiveness of exposure work alone, for some clients counselling can be enhanced by exploring the origins of phobias in order to not only understand where they come from, but also to enable the client to look at the meanings they gave to their fears. The aim of understanding is to help the client transform meanings into something more helpful. Clients may have meanings associated with being scared: feeling helpless, hopeless, out of control. These meanings may be related to fears not taken seriously early on in life. They may have meanings associated with particular situations, relating to earlier traumatic experiences. It is useful to ask clients to describe other times in their life that they remember similar feelings.

Perczel-Forintos and Hackmann (1999) describe a client with injection phobia, looking at meanings she gave to the start of the phobia, in order to provide an 'emotional bridge' between her present fears and the past, distorted meanings. Once these meanings of being out of control could be found and modified, the client was able to test out her beliefs about injections in behavioural experiments.

A client with vomit phobia made connections back to early experience of seeing her mother dying of cancer, leading to her interpretation that vomiting always means serious illness and terrible loss; once explored, she began to realise all the reasons for sickness, including a healthy response to eating toxins, or morning sickness heralding a much-wanted pregnancy.

For both these clients, their fears could be transformed from loss of control, illness or grief, to beliefs about the healthy side of injections or vomit, which could then be tested out in therapy.

As well as finding out the origins and meanings of the phobia, it is important to identify specific predictions about the phobic situation with which we then work during behavioural experiments. The following illustrates finding meanings and predictions with Lillian, a spider phobic.

Lillian: I just hate spiders – I can't stand them.

Counsellor: What is it about them you can't stand?

Lillian: They're big and hairy and move so fast, one minute there it is here, and then I don't know where it is.

Counsellor: What is it about these fast movements you don't like? What is the worst thing about it?

Lillian: It might attack me, bite me, I just don't know where it is. If it sees me first it will go for me.

Counsellor: And if it did . . .?

Lillian: I'd die of being bitten by a spider – I know that's daft but it's how I feel – or I'd die of shock.

Counsellor: That sounds bad – is that the worst of it?

Lillian: I think it's something about not knowing, it's all so unpredictable.

Counsellor: You describe not knowing, feeling things are unpredictable. How does it make you feel?

Lillian: Terrified, like something bad is round the corner and I've got no control.

Counsellor: Can you remember a time in your life when you first felt like this?

Lillian: I think I was always nervous of spiders, but didn't tell anyone since they didn't take me seriously. When I was quite young, I remember my brother had a huge rubber spider for Christmas. He stuck it on my chair and I sat on it, got a terrible shock, but then he plagued me with it – chased me round the house, waved it in my face, put it in my bed – I just had no idea where it would turn up next. Dad just laughed at me and joined in. I felt so out of control. Then every time he saw a spider he'd threaten to shove it in my face. It went on and on.

Lillian made a link between feeling out of control and a spider encounter. She also had specific fears and predictions about spider behaviour, that they would attack her if they saw her coming, and they are fast movers, generally towards the phobic victim. We discussed her specific fears, the client disentangling her sense of lack of control as a child and having more power as an adult, and discussed her fears about dying of shock. She looked up information about spider behaviour, and found out that spiders tend to run away if approached, are benign non-aggressive creatures, and eat wasps, which Lillian also hated. Guided discovery enabled some change in beliefs, which she then tested during exposure and behavioural experiments, described below.

Helping clients to understand how things work can be helpful. For example, people with flight phobia find it helpful to understand what the various sounds and sensations experienced during flight mean: a sudden lurch, for example, may mean the plane is going to crash to the ground, or may simply be the aircraft adjusting to turbulence (Palmer et al., 2000; Bor et al., 2001). Clients can feel more empowered by information which helps to modify beliefs, such as information on animal behaviour or the relative risks of particular situations. Although many people with phobias have been helpfully reassured, 'Don't worry, it will never happen', most phobias are of situations or objects that could carry some risk, however small. It is also possible that people with phobias have an increased likelihood of the worst happening. For example, wasp phobics seem to get stung more often than non-phobics, possibly because of their attempts to avoid being stung, such as flapping the wasp away, which puts the wasp on danger alert, rather than letting it quietly investigate for food. Reappraisal of the risks of events, and how to cope should the worst happen, is important – how to cope when a wasp lands on you, what to do with a sting, and how clutching the seat of an aeroplane or the hand of a fellow passenger is unlikely to avert an air crash. We need to look at the cost side of the argument: while travelling by car has risks, the costs of not driving are far greater, for example, in time, convenience or money.

Developing a rationale for therapy and negotiating goals
Many clients expect that therapy for phobias will involve some kind of shock exposure, being forced into a room full of wasps or spiders, or being made to look down a steep ravine. We need to find out and work with these fears, and explain that while being in contact with fears is a necessary part of therapy, the client is always in charge and in control. It is important to explain that getting very anxious is an important part of the therapy, and the only way of really identifying and testing predictions in order to learn something new. Many of the clients we see with phobias are catastrophising the effects of anxiety, fearing losing control, with dreadful consequences. Therapy is aiming to help the client find out whether their fears are true, or whether situations are much less harmful than feared. Therapy involves a careful balance between building up gradually – equipping clients with skills and confidence and exploring their fears before starting exposure – and getting on with the work of exposure experiments. Our balance is often to steer in the direction of getting going with the exposure experiments for clients who would prefer just to talk, being encouraging and supportive without agreeing with their fears. We remain neutral, stressing the importance of really testing things out.

We start by asking the client to identify a first step which feels manageable: in Lillian's case, looking at pictures of spiders. The counsellor always models each experiment before asking the client to do it, which emphasises the importance of us not sharing our clients' phobias. It can be helpful for the client to set up some kind of reward system for getting going ('If I start the exposure work today, I will buy myself a book or CD'); or to enlist help from a friend or family member. Most of the time, if the client gets to the counselling session, they are committed to making a start on their phobia treatment.

During therapy for phobias, the counsellor may have in mind goals that are different from those of the client, and which are deliberately not shared with the client at the beginning of therapy. For example, a valuable goal at the end of therapy for spider phobia may be for the client to have two spiders running over their hands and arms without significant anxiety on the client's part. If we were to share this with the client at the beginning of therapy, it is likely that we might never see the client again, or that they will be so distressed at thinking about this possibility that they are unable to concentrate on the simpler tasks. It is more helpful to explain general principles, and start off with a small manageable exposure task, before moving on to the next one, if necessary being vague about what is next. The client needs regular reassurance and support that they are in charge and we will spring no surprises. However, we must not collude with their fear of fear, stressing the importance of really finding out what happens in order to face the phobia. We may have mixed feelings about not being totally explicit about our goals, and question the ethics, but in clinical and research experience (Öst, 1997), clients have found this acceptable and indeed been pleased not to have to worry too much about what is ahead. Lillian reported, 'If you told me at the start you were aiming for me to have a huge spider on my hand, there is no way I would have started – but I now know I can do it.'

Behavioural Experiments involving Exposure to Fears

The aims of exposure in cognitive therapy are to enable the client to test out their thoughts, beliefs and ability to stay in the situation long enough for their anxiety to reduce by learning that nothing bad happens. One frequent prediction is that the client will be overwhelmed by anxiety and dreadful things will happen: the client needs to be able to stay in the situation long enough to test this prediction and see that anxiety does reduce over time.

The first step is to work out a plan for the exposure experiments and then work through the steps, as follows:

- Identify with the client a manageable phobic situation, which enables anxious predictions to be tested.
- Identify specific beliefs in the situation, and make predictions.
- Do the experiment, staying in contact for sufficient time for predictions to be tested, leading to a reduction in anxiety.
- Ensure that the client does not use any overt or subtle safety behaviours when exposed to their fears which may prevent the client from re-evaluating predictions.
- Move on to the next task, until phobic beliefs and predictions are changed.

Before each experiment, the therapist demonstrates what the client has to do. For example, when working with Lillian's spider phobia, the therapist freely discusses spiders and looks at pictures of them. The therapist models being comfortable holding a container with a spider in it, and shows how to touch a spider. The therapist demonstrates catching a spider with a glass, finally allowing a spider to walk over her without showing any fear.

Figure 9.3 shows an example of Lillian's experiments during treatment for spider phobia. Her predictions were about her ability to cope, the effects of anxiety, and about spider behaviour based on her fears – for example, 'Spiders run towards you if you get close to them'; 'They run very fast.' By looking at, talking about and eventually touching and catching spiders, Lillian learned that anxiety itself was not dangerous, that she could feel in control and deal with her fears, that spiders would tend to move away from danger, and that they do not move as fast as she predicted. Lillian would normally have 'coped' by safety behaviours, such as shutting her eyes, tensing up, getting as far away from the spider as possible, and breathing deeply to stop the anxiety overwhelming her. By not using any of these coping strategies and just staying with the situation and letting herself feel anxious, she could really see that her fears were unfounded. On her own she worked through other eventualities, such as dealing with jumping spiders and how to cope if a spider got on to her, by keeping as still as possible and catching it rather than killing it. Lillian also read books on spiders, and looked at different varieties in a zoo. Her fears about fear decreased and she was delighted with the increase in her confidence.

The aim of exposure experiments is not necessarily to get rid of the phobia immediately so the client feels no anxiety at all, but to

Task	Prediction to test	Outcome and what I learned
1. Saying the word 'spider'.	It will make me anxious and feel awful: I'll start sweating and have to run out of the room.	I repeated the word spider frequently until I got used to it. Felt very anxious, but I did not lose control, stayed with it and realised the word could not harm me. Felt better.
2. Looking at pictures of spiders.	I won't be able to do it – I'll throw the book across the room.	Unpleasant at first but got used to it – amazed at variety of spiders. I may not need to worry so much about losing control.
3. Watching spiders on video and talking about the spiders to my friend.	It will make me feel terrified: I'll burst into tears.	Unpleasant at first, not as bad as I thought. Interesting. Friend likes spiders, and told me about holding a tarantula and surviving. Terror becoming less terrifying.
4. Looking at a small spider in a jar.	It will see me and look at me. I can't do it.	Anxiety leapt up, but I didn't lose control. The spider didn't take much notice or move around much, and I coped fine.
5. Looking at a small spider in an open bowl.	It will jump out and run all over me. I'll be overwhelmed – so frightened I'll lose control of my bowels.	Spider moved around the bottom of the bowl, slowly. Could not jump out. Again, I felt scared but the fear did not hurt me, and no bowel problems!
6. Touching a small spider in an open bowl.	If I touch it it will run up my arm and get into my clothes, and I will die of fright.	The spider moved away as soon as it saw my finger coming. Kept on moving away from me. I leapt away and burst into tears, feeling so bad – but felt better over time and determined to overcome this.
7. Working with gradually increasing sizes of spider.	The bigger the spider, the worse they are. They are better at jumping up at me. The bigger the spider, the more I'll lose control.	Even big spiders move away from me, and although they scuttle, they are not that fast. Got interested in variety of spiders, and how small even the big ones are relative to me. Even if I lose control, nothing bad will happen – the feelings only last a few seconds now.
8. Catching a spider using a glass and a piece of paper.	It will go berserk, I will go mad having one near me, drop the glass and it will attack me.	Fairly easy to catch a spider by putting a glass over it and slipping paper underneath. I can do this!
9. Allowing a spider to walk on my hand, swapping from hand to hand.	I can't possibly touch it – it will run into my clothes.	I can move faster than the spider – I can predict what it will do and put my hand out to catch it.

However anxious I feel, it cannot harm me at all – the anxiety goes away much quicker if I stay with the feelings and stay in the situation. |

Figure 9.3   *Example of spider phobia experiments*

change anxious predictions, and equip the client with confidence and skills to then practise exposure and test predictions for the rest of his or her life. Having said that, if the client can find out that their fears of fear are unfounded, it is quite possible for a 30-year phobia to vanish after a single session. We are empowering the client to stay with their fears and prove that nothing bad will happen. This enables the client to reintroduce their feared objects as an integral part of life, thus continuing exposure work in more natural settings. For long-term work on phobias, clients can introduce regular exposure work into their lives – from the needle phobic becoming a regular blood donor or cat phobics getting a kitten, to the extremes of claustrophobics taking up caving or height phobics bungee jumping. The key point is for the phobic person not to allow themselves to slip back into avoidance, but make their feared object or situation part of their everyday lives, using each experience as an opportunity to test out their predictions and make cognitive shifts.

Finding exposure objects and situations
Working out exposure objects or situations requires imagination and therapeutic creativity. When working with animal phobias such as spiders, it is very helpful to have access to unusual or exotic creatures: for example, finding a source of friendly tarantulas at the local university, zoo or pet shop. Museums may be able to supply stuffed birds when working with bird or feather phobias. Minestrone soup with a few imaginative additions can be used for exposure work with vomit phobics, and the television provides a good source of gory sights for working with clients phobic of blood injury or vomit. A shopping centre or airport can be used for exposure to open spaces, escalators and staircases, lifts, or eating in public. There are also commercial videos and computer programmes available to simulate situations (Davey, 1997; Kahan et al., 2000; Palmer et al., 2000). The ultimate test, however, has to be the real thing.

A WORD ON KEEPING SAFE WHILE OVERCOMING THE PHOBIA   Although people with phobias consistently overestimate the likelihood and severity of danger connected to their phobias, some situations do carry dangers which need to be respected. Working with height phobias, people can experience loss of balance and their attempts to keep safe, such as tensing their legs, not moving or gripping on to something may increase the likelihood of a fall. People with driving phobias may inadvertently cope with the phobia in a way which makes them more dangerous drivers. They may be paying attention to their breathing, gripping the steering wheel and concentrating on not hitting the curb, all of which diverts attention from safe driving. Leaping out of the chair in the middle of dental treatment may help the person escape but may do more damage than remaining relaxed. Similarly, we need to find methods of exposure while ensuring safety. People with height phobia can experience heights by reverse viewing through binoculars or practising in glass lifts in shopping centres, or the London Eye, or braving Alton Towers. Driving phobics need extensive cognitive preparation about the risks of driving and safe driving methods before experimenting on the road; it can be helpful for people who have avoided driving, but need or want to drive, to take professional driving lessons.

Special Cases: Blood, Injury and Injection Phobias

When people feel anxious or panicky, they may feel very faint, but because of the raise in blood pressure fainting is extremely unlikely. For those who are phobic of blood, injuries involving bleeding, or injections, blood pressure and heart rate decrease on exposure, due to a parasympathetic collapse response. Over half of people with these phobias report that they have fainted at least once in response to blood, injury or injections (Öst and Hellström, 1997). More than half of people with blood injury phobias have a relative with the same phobia, possibly indicating an inherent susceptibility to lowered blood pressure. The sight of blood causes many people to feel squeamish or actually faint, a response which is adaptive, in that if we see we are injured, lowered blood pressure and collapse is likely to reduce bleeding. While many will accept that they are likely to feel faint, for others such a response can feed into a phobic reaction: the client may fear the consequences of fainting, or fear the feelings of being out of control.

Therapy for clients who tend to faint involves training to recognise the early signs of a drop in blood pressure and reduce the collapse response by using 'applied tension'. Applied tension is the opposite of the relaxation response, with clients deliberately tensing up as follows:

- Tense up the muscles of the legs, arms and body.
- Hold the tension for 10–15 seconds.
- Release and return to normal state of tension: but not to a state of relaxation.

Once the client has learned to tense and release in response to the feelings of low blood pressure, applied tension is practised during exposure to faint-provoking and gory situations, using pictures, videos, blood or injections. Öst and Sterner's (1987) original treatment culminates in taking the client to watch open heart or lung surgery. While being able to cope with such exposure produces total cure in both therapist and client, counsellors may be relieved to know it can be difficult to organise access to operating theatres. Brief therapy of one two-hour session, looking at slides of injuries, bloodstained bandages and having an injection, is equally effective (Öst, 1997).

The Effectiveness of Counselling for Phobias

The therapy described in this chapter has been shown to be highly effective with all sorts of specific phobias. At the moment, there is little difference between outcomes for purely behavioural therapy and cognitive therapy (Davey, 1997). For example, a comparison of one versus five sessions of behavioural exposure versus cognitive therapy showed no difference in the one-year outcome for clients with claustrophobia: around 80 per cent of clients offered treatment improved compared to only 18 per cent who had no treatment (Öst et al., 2001), indicating that both brief and five-session therapy can be effective. The treatment offered for phobias may well vary according to resources and therapeutic expertise available. With the current move away from purely behavioural therapies towards taking more account of meaning and belief changes, it is likely that we will see a move towards cognitive approaches. The active ingredient for therapy for phobias is no doubt empowering clients to make close contact with their fears and realise that they do survive the process. It is likely that cognitive processes play a large part in enabling clients to change. Although treatments for phobias have not emphasised the role of the therapeutic relationship, it is no doubt vital. Counsellors and therapists are providing clients with an environment where they can safely test out their fears, and a therapist who is on the client's side, cheering him or her on at all stages and not giving up when difficulties arise. While a good relationship is not sufficient for good outcome in phobia therapy, it is essential.

───────10───────

Social Anxiety

> The patient . . . through bashfulness, suspicion and timorousness will
> not be seen abroad, loves darkness as life and cannot endure the light,
> or to sit in lightsome places, his hat over his eyes, he will neither see
> nor be seen by his good will. . . . He dared not be in company for fear
> that he should be misused, disgraced, overshoot himself in gesture or
> speech, or be sick; he thinks every man observes him, aims at him,
> derides him, owes him malice. (Hippocrates, 2,400 years ago, cited in
> Saul, 2001: 26)

Many people experience a degree of anxiety in some social
situations. People who are apparently socially skilled and com-
petent fear giving a speech in public; accomplished actors report a
degree of stage fright; or people who are comfortable giving a
lecture to hundreds of people might find themselves nervous at
meeting new people. We are, first and foremost, social beings, and
the fear of being negatively evaluated or judged by others is
deeply ingrained. For many, anxiety is easily overcome,
rationalised, lived with and accepted. We may all have occasions
to be embarrassed, deeply regret what we have said or done in
front of other people, in line with Bridget Jones's famous gaffes.
For others, the fears of being with other people, looking a fool,
being judged, humiliated or rejected, are intolerable or overwhelming. We are self-conscious as well as socially conscious;
self-consciousness and belief in appearing, one way or another,
unacceptable to other people is a central feature of social anxiety.

In this chapter, we describe and define social anxiety and look
at new conceptual models in cognitive therapy. Within the model,
social anxiety is related to central fears of being evaluated
negatively by other people. The fears are maintained by a combination of the way which people try and cope with social fears,
with the central focus of attention being on themselves rather than
on the social situation. How the person feels is then taken as
evidence of how they are coming across to other people, which
maintains their fears. We look at how to adapt counselling for
social phobia, including using an experimental approach for

clients to reduce unhelpful coping strategies and self-focus, and using a range of ways for clients to reality test themselves in social situations.

Defining Social Anxiety

Phil was referred by his GP when he became very low and anxious after losing his job in a computer shop, having had difficulties dealing with customers. Phil described himself as always having been nervous around other people. He was shy as a child, and in awe of his older brother who seemed to sail through life and charm everyone. Phil's parents often compared the two, trying to get Phil to match up to his brother and do as well. Phil had coped by trying to keep himself to himself, avoiding social contact as much as possible. After leaving school, he completed a computing degree which he enjoyed. He then went from job to job, working in telesales and internet sales, becoming increasingly fearful of social situations and of dealing with the public in his various jobs. He lost several jobs through giving a bad impression, or by failing to come to work because he could not face other people. He had a small number of close friends with whom he felt comfortable, but was terrified of most other social situations. Phil felt he never matched up, and was terrified that people would see what a fool he was.

Beck and Emery (1985) describe social anxiety in terms of the following:

- fears of having one's inadequacies exposed to other people;
- high sensitivity to shame or the possibility of negative evaluation or rejection by others;
- doubts about having the skills necessary to win others' approval;
- exaggerating the consequences of failure;
- rigid rules about social performance.

DSM defines social phobia (Table 10.1) as 'a marked and persistent fear of social or performance situations in which embarrassment may occur'. The individual fears acting in an embarrassing or humiliating way in one or more social situations, or situations in which he has to 'perform' to other people. Whether they are in fact embarrassing or open to humiliation is not as important as the persistent fears of this happening. The person is invariably anxious when in the feared situation and can

Table 10.1   *Defining social anxiety*

The person experiences excessive fear of being humiliated and/or embarrassed in social or performance situations.

Their anxiety is provoked by being in such feared situations.

The individual avoids social or performance situations, or endures them with considerable distress and discomfort.

For some individuals, only a small number of specific performance situations cause anxiety, such as speaking or writing in public; for others, a wide range of social situations are feared and avoided.

Source: APA (2000)

recognise that the fear is out of proportion to the actual danger. In counselling practice, our clients may meet criteria for *DSM* social phobia, but we also see many clients who have anxieties about social situations, but do not meet strict criteria. We therefore prefer the more general terms of social anxiety, encompassing a range of anxiety problems related to social situations.

People with social anxieties will try as far as possible to avoid feared situations, either by totally avoiding getting into social interactions or avoiding specific events such as talking in meetings, or going out for meals. If unable to avoid these situations, the individual will endure them as ordeals to be put up with and to feel upset about afterwards. Social anxiety can be very disabling and distressing, since we live in and rely on a social environment. It can therefore cause loneliness, isolation, reduced self-esteem, and can impact on the person's working life. Although we are wired to be social beings, the developments of modern life are pushing us to a greater degree of social isolation. It is now possible to do much business and follow leisure interests on the Internet, which can be welcome for those who are socially anxious, or can cause further isolation. People with social anxieties may rely on alcohol or drugs to get by. Very often the individual very much wants to form relationships and be well thought of by others, but is phobic about the possibility of things going wrong. They can also feel a great sense of shame and badness for being so fearful of others, and blame themselves excessively for problems in social interactions.

Social anxiety is reported equally for men and women and, as mentioned in Chapter 1, may be one of the more acceptable fears for men to admit to. Many people report times of their lives when they were shy or awkward, particularly during childhood and adolescence. While many 'grow out of it', for some the anxiety persists and can spread to many areas of life. For others, social anxieties may begin or become more of a problem during times of transition: changing roles at home or work, or times when the costs of not making a good impression increase, such as moving to a more critical or competitive work environment, or moving house and meeting new people.

People with social anxiety describe many different fears. When talking to others, they may fear being seen to be stupid, incoherent, talking rubbish or coming out with unacceptable statements. They may fear others' perception of them: being seen to be anxious, or blushing. They may fear situations where they feel themselves to be watched by others, such as eating, signing a cheque, using a cashpoint machine. Social phobia can be highly specific, such as talking to an audience, eating a meal in public, writing a cheque. Fear of blushing is a common form of social anxiety (Edelmann, 1990; Mulkens et al., 1999). For others the fears are generalised to almost any social situations other than those where the individual feels in control or in which events are predictable. Shyness can also be a form of social phobia, particularly if it persists into adulthood, and gets in the way of meeting life's goals (Butler, 1999).

Conceptualising Social Phobia

Since Beck and Emery (1985) described and conceptualised social anxieties, newer models of understanding the problem have been developed. Two factors have been given more prominence:

- Safety behaviours used to cope with social situations, which can themselves cause social difficulties.
- A greater understanding of how social fears lead clients to focus on themselves and their own feelings of fear, and to use these as evidence of being socially incompetent (Clark and Wells, 1995; Chambless and Hope, 1996; Clark, 1997).

A conceptual model of social anxiety is shown in Figure 10.1. The model describes interlinking factors in understanding social phobia and how it is maintained:

- central fears of negative evaluation by others;
- physical and cognitive symptoms of anxiety and behaviours to keep safe in social situations;
- self-consciousness and preoccupation with the self;

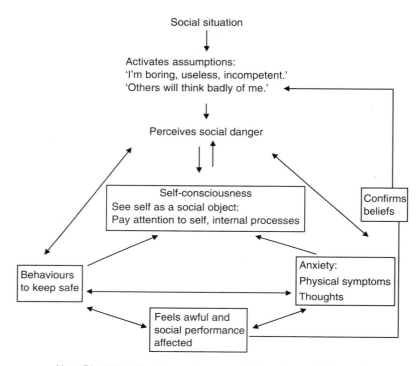

Note: Direction of arrows can be uni- or bi-directional: will depend on individual conceptualisation

Figure 10.1   *Model of social anxiety*

Source: Clark and Wells (1995)

- rumination and post-mortems;
- underlying assumptions and beliefs.

Fear of negative evaluation by others

Central to understanding social phobia is the fear of being evaluated in a negative way by other people. While most of us would
like to be thought well of most of the time, the complex nature of
interpersonal relationships means that we can never be totally
sure about what the majority of people are thinking all of the time,
or that we will never be judged, criticised or rejected. The authors
expect to make complete prats of themselves several times during
their lives, and, without the intention to deliberately offend or
hurt others, realise that occasional mistakes and errors of judgement do occur, as part of being social beings. These cause sadness,

upset, regret, and the need to sort out interpersonal relationships. For the socially phobic individual, the remotest possibility of being judged weird or offensive by others is unacceptable and to be avoided at all costs, including the cost of avoiding any inter-personal relationships. Appraisal that judgement or rejection had occurred would confirm their painful, low feelings about the self: for example in social situations Phil would hear his parents criticism of him in his mind: 'You'll never be good enough.' Individuals may also lack confidence of being able to handle another's judgement, criticism or rejection, and catastrophise the conse-quences of not being well thought of.

Symptoms of anxiety and safety behaviours
In social situations, the individual experiences somatic symptoms of anxiety, such as shaking, becoming hot, sweating, and experi-encing palpitations, a racing mind, or difficulty in thinking straight: the adrenal system goes into overdrive. The mind will switch into anxious thinking, the favourite styles being:

- Mind-reading and projecting own beliefs on to others: 'I know what other people are thinking of me; they are judging me as I am judging myself.'
- Fortune-telling: 'Any minute everyone is going to turn around and stare; I'm going to go bright red and everyone will notice; he will ask me about my job and I won't make sense.'
- Personalising: 'Everyone is looking at me; if I make one mistake, everyone will notice and think badly of me.'
- Judging and labelling: 'idiot', 'prat', 'hopeless'.
- Catastrophising: 'One blush and I've blown my chances of her ever wanting to speak to me again.'

Once anxiety is activated, people with social phobia have many methods of trying to cope with their fears and feelings and keep safe. These methods only compound the problem. Some of these include:

- avoiding eye contact, or having excessive eye contact to appear interested;
- mentally rehearsing what to say;
- watching every word they say;
- never expressing one's own opinion;
- trying to keep control of the conversation;
- wearing clothes to cover up sweating and/or other bodily signals;

- holding cup or glass very tightly to avoid spilling it;
- holding hands over face to avoid being seen blushing;
- laughing or talking too much; being the life and soul of the party;
- asking lots of questions;
- checking rooms before entering; always being first or last to arrive at social events;
- avoiding specific (meeting the boss) or general (meeting new people) social situations.

> Mike was very concerned about giving seminar presentations in college. He was nervous and thought that people would see him streaming with sweat. Someone had once commented on damp patches under the arms of his shirt. In order that people should not see his damp armpits, Mike would keep his arms pinned to his side like a guardsman. This, however, led him to walk around in a rather peculiar way so that people would be much more likely to pay attention to him.

People often use avoidance as a means of coping. They may avoid particular situations such as eating in public, or try to avoid social interactions as much as possible except those that feel safe, such as being with one or two close friends. Avoidance can be subtle, such as not looking at people, or finding out exact details of social situations beforehand.

The range of safety behaviours and avoidance can increase anxiety, increase the likelihood of something difficult happening, or make the individual come across as strange, different, bored or disinterested. People with social anxiety can appear socially unskilled or strange, and may not make the best public orators. Observer ratings of socially phobic clients for their social skills can be lower than ratings given to non-anxious individuals (Stopa and Clark, 1993, 2000). However, clients themselves will rate themselves much worse, and be far more critical of themselves than are other people. Going blank, not making sense or looking nervous may be noticed and commented on by others, but, for the client, these would feel like unacceptable catastrophes.

Preoccupation with the self

An important aspect of social anxiety is the high level of attention clients focus on themselves and their feelings of anxiety rather than being active participants in social situations (Mellings and

Alden, 2000). They use the information they collect about themselves as a basis for working out what other people think (Clark and Wells, 1995; Wells, 2000). In a social situation, the individual feels uncomfortable – hot, shaky, nervous or out of breath, and pays attention to their feelings. They take these feelings as evidence that other people think that they look anxious or stupid, or make other negative evaluations: 'I feel stupid, therefore others think I'm stupid'; 'I feel anxious, therefore I must look anxious.' The socially anxious individual will then try and control the symptoms, or control the self, which may make the problem worse. Such behaviours also increase the individual's focus on themselves rather than on the other person or the conversation. For example, a client with a fear of blushing tries to control blushes by paying attention to them, which makes the blushing worse, and increases their anxiety and self-focus (Bögels et al., 1997).

Anxious feelings can be accompanied by images which are interpreted as evidence of how the person is being perceived by others (Hackmann et al., 1998). These images are as though they are watching themselves through others' eyes; an observer perspective rather than a self-perspective (Wells et al., 1998; Wells and Papageorgiou, 1999). The client takes this mind's eye image as reality. Images are often related to specific memories of unpleasant social events around the time the social anxiety started. Images include experiences of being bullied, criticised for getting something wrong or looking anxious, and images of earlier feelings of self-consciousness and social discomfort (Hackmann et al., 2000). In present time, the images are not correct reflections of what is currently going on, but reflect the individual's fears rather than reality. Clients are often surprised when they see video evidence of how they do actually come across:

> Ruth had a terror of blushing when teaching. She had a horrid mental image of her bright red shiny face, which got bigger and redder the more nervous she became. She saw herself as looking ever hotter and more uncomfortable, and starting to shake. In her mind's eye she shone like a beacon, and her pupils would be staring and laughing at her. Ruth related her images to a painful experience of being ridiculed at school for blushing when she read out her homework. She did indeed blush frequently, particularly when stressed or anxious, but when she saw herself on video teaching a class, she was surprised how unnoticeable her blushes actually were, more a pinkness than tomato red, even when viewed from the first row of desks.

When paying attention to the self, it is difficult to notice what is going on externally, which in turn affects social behaviour. Self-focused attention means that the person is less likely to get feedback from others, thus making it hard to disconfirm their beliefs that others are being critical of them. For example, the individual may feel the centre of attention, but if they looked around carefully, they might see one person looking vaguely in their direction, with everyone else paying attention elsewhere. When giving a talk in public, it is difficult to gauge the audience's response, unless one pays attention to them as well as what one is saying. The client will also make interpretations of social interactions based on themselves and their own feelings. For example, during a conversation, the other person may look distracted, which could be interpreted as 'They have something on their mind, or other worries', or 'I'm being completely boring, he thinks badly of me . . . .' Many social situations are ambiguous, and without being a mind reader it can be difficult to know what is going on for other people.

The combination of internal focus of attention and coping strategies interact in a vicious cycle, which makes the problem worse. Phil, for example, described going to a friend's birthday party, an event which he would much rather have avoided, and which he had worried about in advance. His assumptions about himself were activated as he was introduced to other people, leading him to feel very anxious, switch attention on to himself, notice how anxious he was feeling and try and control the feelings. He was unable to pay attention to the other people, remember their names or be able to join in the conversation. This in turn confirmed his beliefs about being boring and socially useless.

Rumination and post mortems

While it is normal and human to think about social situations in advance and analyse them afterwards – particularly more challenging events or social difficulties – this process shifts into worry and rumination for people with social fears. Rather than going over things to gain a new perspective, find resolution and closure, or to learn to live with and even laugh at social gaffes, people with social anxiety get stuck in a loop of ever more catastrophic thinking. They tend to worry excessively in advance about social situations, going over possibilities in their minds or trying to rehearse what they will say. When giving a talk, it is very anxiety-provoking to try to plan every word or gesture in advance, whereas being able to rely, to some degree, on it being 'all right on

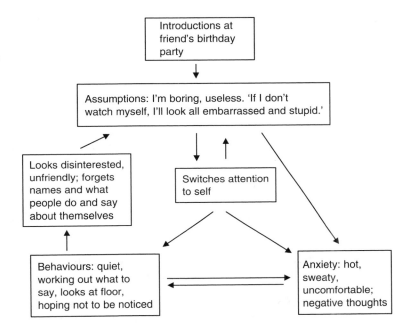

Figure 10.2   *Conceptualisation for Phil*

the night' reduces anxiety, and allows more spontaneity and a much better talk. The effect of worry is to increase anxiety and intrusive, anxiety-provoking images (Butler et al., 1995; Wells and Papageorgiou, 1995; Mellings and Alden, 2000). Socially anxious people often conduct thorough post mortems after social events, going over in their minds exactly what they said and how they came across to others: but as in Chinese whispers, the more the message is repeated, the more likely it is to be distorted, especially if it is based on negatively biased information.

Phil had to go to a job interview at a small computer shop. He was told this would be an informal chat with the owner. He agonised for the week before the interview, going over in his mind what he would say, rehearsing a speech about his previous job successes, working out that if he did not look too carefully at the interviewer he would be all right. He managed to do the interview, but afterwards came out feeling awful: he went over exactly how he had looked, what he said, all his answers to the various questions, convincing himself that he had said all the wrong things. As the post mortems became more detailed, the images became more florid and catastrophic: he thought he could remember laughing inappropriately, swearing, forgetting to tell the interviewer everything he'd done before, and looking hot and bothered. As we see later, his fears were not borne out by reality.

Assumptions and Beliefs

Clark and Wells (1995) summarise some of the rules, assumptions and beliefs about the self and social situations underlying social anxiety:

- Beliefs, often core and unconditional, about the self: 'I am strange, weird, boring, incompetent, unworthy.'
- Rigid rules about social situations: 'I must always get it right, any mistakes are intolerable, unacceptable; I must never look at all anxious.'
- Rules about responsibility for social situations: 'It is all my fault if a conversation goes badly; I have to be entertaining and interesting always otherwise no one will like me.'
- Meaning of social awkwardness or gaffes: 'If I stumble over my words, or make a mistake, people will think I'm incompetent; I'll be judged, humiliated, rejected.'
- Beliefs about others: 'People are totally judgemental; I am the centre of their attention; people always notice when other people look anxious; if they think something is different, they'll stare at me.'

Such beliefs form early on, and are related to core schema of the self. Clients with long-standing general social fears can have very poor opinions of themselves, based on early experiences of being judged, ridiculed and criticised. A significant number of clients with social anxieties have been bullied during childhood (Slee, 1994). They may have been brought up in situations where it is difficult to gain and practise social relationships, or where they felt different from other people. Very high standards about social interactions can contribute to the problem, as well as beliefs about other people being critical and judgemental.

Adapting Counselling for Social Anxiety

When working with clients with anxiety, we aim to collect evidence that disconfirms their fears. A client with panic, for example, may fear fainting, collapsing or dying when having a panic attack; but these have not happened. Clients with social phobia, in contrast, may have many examples in their lives when their fears come true: for example, blushing, shaking, not being able to hold a conversation, coming across as strange, bored or disinterested. They may have few friends and be socially isolated, causing other life difficulties. Unfortunately, the client's painful attempts to avoid the feared consequences of social interactions can come true, through a combination of unhelpful coping strategies and poorly developed social skills.

Our work within counselling is not necessarily to dispute the evidence that the client is socially awkward, embarrassed or cannot communicate well with others, but to look at the meaning and interpretation of social anxieties and awkwardness, and enable clients to develop more helpful means of relating to other people. This involves understanding the day-to-day conceptualisation of client's problems and how the client's safety behaviours and internal focus of attention lead to social difficulties, and looking at unhelpful or unrealistic beliefs and assumptions about themselves and other people.

When working with our clients with social fears, we are by definition interacting in a social context, and the therapeutic relationship can be a powerful stage upon which to act and learn. The relationship can be an arena in which clients feel accepted and understood, and provides an opportunity to test out beliefs about social fears. To make the therapy more dynamic and generalisable to other social situations, it can also be helpful to introduce other people into the therapy, by setting up social interactions, observing what happens and reviewing meanings. However, for many of our clients with general social fears this can be very threatening, and we need always to proceed at a pace that is comfortable for the client.

The stages of counselling for social anxiety are:

- Developing the individual conceptualisation.
- Helping clients to try things differently: working with safety behaviours.
- Workng with internal focus of attention: self-consciousness.
- Collecting evidence about social situations.
- Working on underlying assumptions and beliefs.
- Developing self-acceptance, confidence and finding the right environment.

Developing the individual conceptualisation
Assessing social anxiety involves using standard assessment methods as described in Chapter 5, working with detailed

examples to build up an individual conceptualisation. For socially anxious clients, one important aspect of the model is the concept of self-consciousness, and it is important to find out what this means for the individual client. We work together to build up a model of how the client believes they look to other people: collecting information about their thoughts, images and meanings. For example, a client may describe himself as looking terrified to others: we need to unpack this and see it through the client's eyes. Helpful questions to ask include:

- How do you look?
- Do you get an image in your mind? Describe the image.
- Act out how you think you comes across: for example, having a petrified expression, shaking, stuttering, going red and sweating.
- What does it mean if others see you as terrified?
- What might be going through others' minds when they observe you?

We then can build up a model of how the client sees what he is feeling, and use this as a basis for modifying self-consciousness through guided discovery and experimentation. For clients who avoid social interactions as much as possible, it may be helpful to set up social situations in the counselling time in which to collect information. Social situations can include asking a colleague to be present in the room, or asking the client to have a short conversation with the receptionist and report back.

Helping clients to try things differently: working with safety behaviours

Although it can feel like the most threatening and difficult arena to work on at an early stage of counselling, clients can make significant changes by beginning to practise behaving differently in social situations, finding out that their attempts to control situations may not work and may make matters worse, and trying out different strategies (Wells, 1997, 1998). Two examples of experiments are given below:

A client who fears spilling drink in front of other people made a specific prediction: 'If I don't hold the glass tightly then I'll spill it all over the place and everyone will stare at me.' The experiment involved first walking around the counselling room holding a full glass of water very tightly, trying not to spill a drop. Some slopped over the edge. Then she repeated the experiment, holding the glass normally and carrying on a conversation with the counsellor. She was less likely to spill any drink, and felt able to talk at the same time.

Mike, concerned about sweating, would wear a jacket regardless of the weather, keep his arms down by his side and try not to sweat. We discussed how these strategies might not be helpful and might even increase the sweating. He experimented with wearing a shirt most likely to show sweating, moving his arms around as normal regardless of sweaty armpits, and looking at other people to see whether he could notice signs of sweating. He found that not trying to control the sweating actually decreased it; he also noticed that others did show some signs of sweating, but were not at all bothered by it.

Clients need to feel safe as we encourage them to do things that might lead to distress, so it is important to look at ways clients can feel better should their anxiety increase – paying attention to other people and the external environment rather than to the self, using other distraction approaches to reduce distress, and using the counselling setting as a safe place to discuss and evaluate experiments. Post mortems and rumination increase distress, leading the client to focus on what might have gone wrong. Ask about the pros and cons of analysing social situations; how much is helpful and appropriate? When is it unhelpful? Worry-reduction strategies, discussed in Chapter 8, such as the worry decision tree (Butler and Hope, 1995) help reduce distress and rumination. Post mortems should only be allowed with other people, preferably understanding friends, who can help to see alternative, possibly humorous, perspectives.

Working with internal focus of attention: self-consciousness
Paying attention to internal feelings rather than to the external social situation means that the client gets a one-sided and dis-torted impression of what is going on. While the counselling ethos and methods often focus on helping clients to identify and get in touch with how they are feeling, clients with social anxiety may be too much in touch with their negative feelings about themselves, and use these as a basis for reality. Counselling for social anxiety aims to help the client examine the reality of situations, be aware that how we feel does not necessarily determine how we come across to other people, and discover ways of shifting the focus of attention externally. In this way, the client becomes more of a

social participant rather than an observer. We need to find out what the client believes will happen if she does not focus on herself, such as, 'If I don't keep an eye on everything I say, I won't make any sense, I may offend someone else.' We may use behavioural experiments to enable the client to collect evidence of the social realities and test out what happens when she pays attention externally rather than internally. Ask the client to describe their 'mental video' – how does the client believe they look to others? What would someone else see? Be as precise as possible about the client's predictions, such as exactly what colour they think they go when blushing (paint colour cards can be useful), how I would know that the client was looking stupid. Client and counsellor work together to find out if the mental images and predictions are true and what happens if the client focuses attention externally.

> We set up an experiment where Phil had a short conversation with a nurse in the practice, while being videoed. Each had to say something about themselves. We reviewed his predictions before the meeting: 'I will not be able to say anything; I'll be boring, stupid, unlikeable.' During the first meeting, Phil was asked to behave as he normally would: trying hard, paying attention to himself and trying to be liked. He was then asked to say how he felt he came across, and also to report back what the nurse had said. He felt he had been hopeless and looked stupid; and he was unable to remember much of what he had heard. In the second conversation, Phil had to stop doing all the things he did to keep safe, not try particularly hard, and focus more on the conversation. He was able to remember far more of what he had heard, and was interested to hear about the nurse's recent holiday. We had a discussion about Phil's and the nurse's observations, and watched the video. Phil could see that he came across as slightly more awkward in the first interaction, but was not as terrible as he thought. He learned that by not trying to keep safe, he felt better, more relaxed, and had a more interesting and human conversation.

Imagery techniques (Hackmann, 1997) can be used for clients who have strong internal images: for example, the client with a fear of blushing can first practise seeing her catastrophic image in her mind's eye. We can then use imagery to show the catastrophised colour of her face shading down to normal; or an image of shaking uncontrollably fading to calm.

Paying attention to other people and to the situation can be used as a means of reducing distress, as in the technique of distraction, but also enables the individual to collect information about what is going on socially, and work actively to disconfirm their fears (Wells et al., 1997; Wells and Papageorgiou, 1998). Mulkens et al. (1999), for example, describe a client with fears of blushing who learned to change her focus of attention externally, and found that self-consciousness, anxiety and blushing all decreased.

Collecting evidence about social situations
Many anxiety problems are characterised by fears of uncertainty, and for socially anxious clients the ambiguity and uncertainty in social situations are interpreted in a negative way. It is also particularly difficult for clients to look at a range of interpretations of situations when they are paying attention to themselves rather than collecting evidence about what is going on outside. As well as encouraging clients to reduce self-awareness and focus attention externally, counselling aims to explore with clients what range of interpretations can be given to social situations, particularly when the situation is ambiguous. For example, during a conversation we may notice that the other person looks distracted. One interpretation is that I am being extremely boring or offensive, and the person does not like me. Alternatively, the person may have just received bad news, or have something else on their mind. Using guided discovery, we can explore with clients the different possible interpretations of socially ambiguous situations, as shown in Figure 10.3.

Clients can collect evidence from other people about social situations, to find out if their predictions and fears are confirmed:

> Phil got the job in the computer shop, much to his surprise. His success enabled him to test his predictions and beliefs about the interview. After a few weeks, with the counsellor's encouragement, Phil asked the owner, Hanif, how he came across in the interview. Hanif said Phil and he had had a good chat and he thought he was a nice guy. Hanif was interested in Phil's previous experience, and liked the fact that he did not go on too much about it. He thought Phil was thoughtful and would try hard to do a good job, unlike the previous employee. Phil was able to ask Hanif if he looked anxious, and was surprised by his answer: 'I don't know, I was pretty anxious myself. I don't really know how to interview people, and I really hoped that you wanted the job.'

A diary for clients to record their observations and learning in social situations is shown in Figure 10.4.

1. Client reports noticing a woman staring at her outside a shop.

Possible interpretations:

They think I look stupid, ugly, incompetent.
I remind them of someone else.
I am looking nice, attractive.
They were looking at my scarf, since they want to buy one and are collecting ideas.
They were not looking really, but thinking about something else.
They may be concerned if I was looking upset.

Reality testing:

Do a survey to see how many people look at her when shopping. Smile if she sees someone looking at her. Finds out that most people do glance at others in passing, but generally look distracted and are thinking about other things.

2. Client reports that a work colleague walked past her in the street without saying hello.

Possible interpretations:

I have offended her.
She does not like me.
She was distracted, busy.
She has poor eyesight.
She has just had bad news.
She is socially anxious.

Reality testing:

Says to work colleague that she saw her, and finds out that she had been in a hurry and was distracted, but realised she had not said hello after walking by, and turned around to greet her.

Figure 10.3   *Interpretations and reality testing*

Part of reality testing can involve conducting surveys of other people. For example, a client believes that if people saw her looking anxious, they would think she was incompetent at her job. Both client and counsellor asked ten people the question 'If you saw someone looking anxious, what would you think of them?' They discovered a range of responses, including:

Date	Describe the social situation	What happened? What did I notice about other people?	What I learned

Figure 10.4   *Diary of social situations*

- I probably wouldn't notice: I'm not very observant of others.
- I'd wonder if they were OK.
- I'd think they had received bad news or were worried about something.
- I'd sympathise – I get anxious too.
- I'd wonder if they were unwell.

Working on underlying assumptions and beliefs

People with social anxiety can hold very rigid, global rules about themselves and social performance. In reality social performance is much more flexible, with different rules applying to different

situations; counselling aims to help clients explore their
assumptions and rules and find ones that can be more flexibly
adapted and applied to social situations.

Phil believed that he was a boring person, because of his interest
in computers. As a result he would keep very quiet about his skills
and knowledge. Using guided discovery, Phil looked first at how
to be a very boring person, and then at how to be a very interesting person, and worked out that much depended on the situation
and environment. For example, endlessly discussing new computer
programmes would be of great interest to those at a computer
conference, but perhaps less apt for a first date. Phil kept notes
of evidence to support or refute his belief. He also included in his
notes what he had learnt about picking up on social cues from
others, and how he had appraised other people when they had said
boring things. He also kept evidence about the different things
he talked about during the day, and found he had plenty of opinions
and knowledge to make interesting conversation. Phil revised his
belief to 'I can be really boring if I really try, but I've got lots to say
as well.'

Clients can hold confusing messages, such as having low self-
worth, and yet believe that they are the centre of other's attention.
They may believe: 'Everyone has to like me for me to be acceptable as a person' or 'If anyone criticises me it means I'm completely worthless', and yet have a range of feelings for other
people. Guided discovery can help clients to find out that social
relationships are complex and variable, and being liked or not
liked is not an absolute. We aim to help clients discriminate
between being judged for behaviour or attributes, and being
judged for personal worth. If someone does not like your shoes,
does that make you a bad person? Is wanting everyone to approve
and like you realistic? Whose opinion is important to the individual, and whose is not important? People can be judgemental
and prejudiced, but do we need to pay attention to their views?

Developing self-acceptance, confidence and finding the right environment

People with social anxieties can be much more judgemental of
themselves than they are of others, holding double standards for
social performance, and being very unaccepting of their difficulties. Counselling can help the client to develop a compassionate
non-judgemental self, using guided discovery to explore these

self-judgements, find out where inner critical voices come from and become aware of ways in which they are similar to or different from others (Fennell, 1999). Building self-confidence can be part of the counselling plan. However, clients may hold beliefs such as 'Only confident people are OK', or 'If I'm not confident I'm incompetent', which need to be examined rather than moving too early into skills such as confidence-building or assertiveness. A client was asked to compare two people they knew, one overtly confident individual and one quieter, shyer person, and describe their opinions and feelings for them. The client reported that she would rather get to know the quieter person, feeling rather put off by the confident one, but if she were marooned on a desert island, someone with lots of confidence about surviving would be very useful.

Confidence comes through practice, trying things out and observing others to see how confident people come across. Particular skills can be helpful, such as assertiveness and dealing with compliments or criticism (Butler, 1999). Butler points out that social skills are not about doing the 'right thing' in social situations, but about being flexible with a range of social skills and conventions, appropriate to the situation.

Clients with social phobias may be working or living in environments which exacerbate their problems. Phil thought he ought to be the life and soul of the party, based on comparisons with his extrovert, and more socially acceptable brother. We spent time in counselling looking at his strengths as a quiet, more introverted person: he was excellent at working with computers, and rather than being a 'computer nerd' as his brother had always called him, was skilled in a valuable area. He kept a diary of what he did have to offer: he was a loyal friend, valuing close friendships. He began the 'shame-attacking' approach of disclosing to his friends how difficult he found social situations, and found that people sympathised rather than judged, often sharing their difficulties. He felt more comfortable describing himself as a shy sort of person, and realised that this in many ways made him more interesting and attractive to others than the louder more confident members of society. He had experience of working in sales, which was all he felt he could do, but realised that the environment which would suit him best would be a small setting where he could get to know a limited number of people, and feel safer. He began to investigate other jobs that he might be more comfortable in and, by the time counselling ended, he had been offered a job as computer manager in a small voluntary organisation.

The Effectiveness of Counselling for Social Anxiety

There is emerging evidence that following the procedures described in this chapter is effective in helping clients to overcome social anxieties (Chambless and Hope, 1996). In preliminary analyses of a trial of 15 clients with social phobia, most improved substantially in relation to their social anxieties, including fears of being negatively evaluated by other people (Clark, 1999b), cognitive therapy being significantly more effective than medication or placebo with exposure. Cognitive therapy is more effective than supportive therapy (Cottraux et al., 2000). In a small case series (Wells and Papageorgiou, 2001), six clients improved following brief cognitive therapy, designed to help clients to modify self-focused attention and redirect such attention to the external environment. Clients were also helped to reduce worry before and after social situations. One of the active ingredients in therapy may be changing clients' subjective estimates of the probability of negative social events occurring (McManus et al., 2000) and shifting their internal focus to pay more attention to the outside social situation (Wells and Papageorgiou, 1998). If clients are not helped to change their predictions about difficult or negative things happening, or modify their tendency to pay attention internally, they may continue to hold on to their negative predictions and fears. Counselling therefore aims to help clients make and test out specific predictions, and, rather than focus on inner feelings, pay attention to external social events as a means of collecting more accurate information. Many of the clients we see with social phobia also have other difficulties, such as being extremely avoidant. They may live in environments with few social encounters and have long histories of social difficulties and isolation. The trials have tended to include clients who meet strict criteria for social phobia and exclude those with other major difficulties, whom we also see in clinical practice. We need to take into account other difficulties. However, as with much of counselling for anxiety described in this book, following the procedures which have been shown to be effective with social anxiety is a good place to start, venturing into longer-term issues only when the preparatory work has been done.

11

Health Anxiety

Tuesday
The nagging, stitch-like pain in the lower back persists, and I suspect that the kidney tumour has now grown to the size of a mango. Dr Sarah Jarvis disagrees, and thinks it is nothing more than backache, but says that if I am concerned I should give a urine sample for analysis. Ha ha, very droll. . . . The thing about giving samples is, you have no idea what they might find.

Thursday
This morning, the doctor's heroic patience evaporates further. 'If you are concerned about the kidney,' she says, extremely slowly, like a traffic cop directing an au pair newly arrived from Helsinki to Carnaby Street, 'come . . . in . . . and . . . do . . . a . . . urine . . . sample.' A silence ensues. 'What really gets to me is the boredom', says Dr Jarvis eventually. 'This is the seventh time in a fortnight you've asked about the same thing. It's the repetitiveness. Can't you come up with something new? You haven't presented anything new for years. Literally, years.' (Matthew Norman, 'Diary of a hypochondriac', *Guardian*, 23 May 2000)

A certain level of anxiety about our health is normal and helpful, keeping us alert to the possibility that all is not well, and enabling us to take early action if necessary. Taken to an extreme, however, as with all anxiety problems, too much anxiety and preoccupation with health matters is counterproductive, particularly in the absence of tangible evidence that there are problems that merit a large amount of anxiety. Health anxiety can seriously affect people's relationships with others, with their bodies and with the medical profession on whom they often rely for help. Health anxiety, in psychiatric diagnoses, is not even included as one of the anxiety disorders, but is classified as one of the somatoform disorders, which cover a range of problems including unexplained physical symptoms, somatisation, pain disorders, conversion disorder and body dysmorphism (APA, 2000; Sanders, 2000). However, more recent understandings of health anxiety and hypochondriasis have placed the problem firmly in the realm of the anxiety problems: as anxiety centred on health concerns, as its name implies.

Clients with health anxiety present particular challenges to counselling. One main issue is that these clients may not, at least initially, view their primary problem as one of anxiety, but more that the anxiety arises from the possibility of serious medical disease, particularly when the individual believes this has not yet been correctly diagnosed. They may wish to talk predominantly about medical problems, gain reassurance for their worries, or enlist the counsellor's help in obtaining better medical tests (Sanders, 1996). These clients can be reluctant to start counselling, which immediately means adapting the counselling relationship and methods to take into account their needs and understanding of the problem. They may come aiming to find out for sure that there is nothing wrong, a goal which may be unrealistic. In this chapter, we define and conceptualise health anxiety, and discuss ways to adapt counselling to engage and work with these clients.

Table 11.1   *Defining health anxiety*

Preoccupation with fears of having, or the idea that one has, a serious disease based on the person's misinterpretation of bodily symptoms.

The preoccupation persists despite appropriate medical evaluation and reassurance.

The preoccupation causes clinically significant distress or impairment in social, occupational, or other areas.

The problem has lasted at least six months, and the person's beliefs are not of delusional intensity.

Source: APA (2000)

People with health anxiety believe that they have, or may develop, a serious disease, a belief that is out of proportion to the evidence that the person has definite organic signs or risk factors. The belief persists, as the definition goes, 'despite medical reassurance', an interesting statement which we shall look at in more detail below.

Clients with health anxiety can be significantly disabled by their fears: they worry excessively about their health, and engage in many different activities to check their state of health or to prevent future problems which can impact on their lives. These include seeking medical reassurance and many medical tests to confirm and re-confirm negative results. They read up on information about health, and are preoccupied with the slightest signs or symptoms, as illustrated in the quote at the beginning of the chapter. On some level, people with health anxiety know that their fears and behaviour are 'over the top', and they would like to be able to stop worrying so much about their health. They may believe that the likelihood they really have the feared disease is very low. However, this is unlikely to be of much comfort, as we discuss below, since for these individuals, issues such as cost of illness and absence of rescue factors mean that the overall anxiety equation remains high. People with health anxiety often want total reassurance and certainty that there is nothing wrong, finding it very difficult to live with uncertainty; yet they may be convinced that there is something wrong, and are either waiting to have it confirmed by the 'right' doctor, or are terrified to be told 'the truth'.

> Daniel, a 24-year-old trainee teacher, had been worried about his health on and off for years. The problem had got much worse in the previous few months, coinciding with extra stresses from the training. He described himself as feeling really awful, exhausted and aching, and being woken at night with irregular heartbeats and pains in his legs. He was convinced that there was something seriously wrong with his heart, causing irregular beating and tiredness, and worried that the pains in his legs were caused by thromboses. He had also begun to worry that the strange feelings were evidence of multiple sclerosis. He had consulted his GP several times, and was annoyed with her for 'dismissing' his worries. He had also consulted several other GPs in the practice, and his mother had arranged a private consultation with a specialist in London. He regularly phoned his mother to report on his symptoms, and discussed them endlessly with his friends. He had read up on his various 'illnesses' in medical textbooks, and looked at lots of health sites on the Internet. When he came for counselling, he said he realised that it had all got out of proportion, but felt overwhelmed by his worries.

Health anxiety affects around eight per cent of the population, taking *DSM* as the criterion (Noyes, 2000). A large proportion of people attending GP surgeries and outpatient departments have symptoms which cannot be medically diagnosed, and will be linked with anxiety. Anxiety about health is a cause for people to use medical services more, see more doctors, have more tests and investigations and hospital admissions, and use more medication, but to be more dissatisfied with the care received. Interestingly, health anxiety follows trends, depending on publicity given to specific health issues and scares: for example, when media attention to HIV and AIDS was at its peak, the fears of people with health anxiety was around HIV infection; as other diseases such as CJD, or the risk of pulmonary embolism from long-term flights, take prominence, so those prone to anxiety about their health will focus more on these health problems. We write at the time of the anthrax outbreak in America, leading, understandably, to high levels of fear. It is not unusual for health anxiety to go hand in hand with other psychological difficulties, such as depression or general worry.

Health anxiety can occur when the client has a positive diagnosis of physical disease, but where their anxieties and fears and coping style are out of proportion to the 'objective' dangers of their physical problems. The client has to be the best judge of whether their fears are more problematic than they need to be, given the physical problems they are facing. People with health anxiety can be far more distressed and disabled than those with known and diagnosed physical disease, who are seen to have more legitimate cause for their difficulties and gain sympathy and help. Much of the literature on health anxiety describes how difficult the medical profession finds it to manage patients with health anxiety, who can use up a great deal of time and resources looking for medical reassurance or answers to their concerns (Sanders, 1996).

One of the central issues of health anxiety is the misinterpretation of 'normal' bodily signs and symptoms as evidence of disease, which has similarities to the definition of panic attacks (Chapter 7). People with health anxiety may suffer episodes of panic. However, the difference lies in the time-course of disaster: a panic attack signals immediate danger – 'I'm going to drop dead right now' – whereas people with health anxiety believe that something is wrong, but the danger is more in the future: 'It will get me in the end.'

Conceptualising Health Anxiety

The cognitive model of health anxiety (Warwick and Salkovskis, 1989; Salkovskis and Bass, 1997) is summarised in Figure 11.1.

The central theme of the model proposes that health anxiety arises from clients' misinterpretation of 'normal' bodily signs and symptoms, as evidence of serious disease. Physical signs and symptoms can arise from many different causes. Our bodies are complex, sophisticated systems, constantly busy, with all sorts of aches or pains, twinges, gurgles, rashes, lumps or bumps or strange sensations. Many of these are entirely normal and can be safely ignored; many are signs of unrest or illness, which require

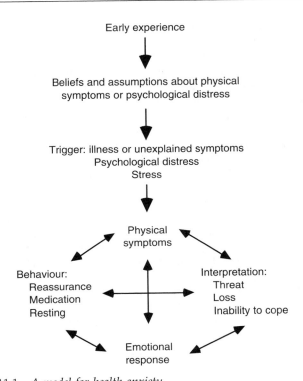

Figure 11.1   *A model for health anxiety*

Sources: Adapted from Sanders (1996); Salkovskis and Bass (1997)

looking at. Stress, physical tension, anxiety and depression can lead to symptoms. Regardless of the cause of the symptoms, how the individual interprets them, and consequently behaves, can lead to the complex cycle of health anxiety. If symptoms are interpreted as dangerous in some way, or as signs of disease or illness, the individual will feel anxious and concerned; this in turn can lead to further symptoms. The anxious individual will then start to cope with the symptoms by looking for reassurance or diagnosis, trying to get rid of the symptoms, acting as an ill person, and other behaviours described below.

Cognitive processes in health anxiety

Once attention beams in on health issues, the cognitive spotlight is on the symptoms or areas of concern to the individual. The person's thoughts centre on the possibility of illness, and evidence of illness, paying no attention to other possibilities. The thinking style runs along the lines of 'It must be serious; this is not normal; if it is a sign of cancer/heart disease then it will be completely awful, I'll never cope, no one will help.' Evidence or information which challenges their beliefs is discounted: a headache may be seen as evidence of a brain tumour, and alternative, benign explanations such as tiredness or tension will be overlooked. Clients often discount medical tests and reassurance, thinking that something must have been missed and that doctors cannot be trusted, and holding other beliefs about the medical profession. It is as though an anxious switch has been turned on, and the individual is unable to switch off their anxious thoughts and behaviours (Beck et al., 1985)

Many clients with health anxiety have some good reasons for thinking the way that they do: they, or friends and family, may in the past not have been correctly diagnosed, or may have been told that there was something wrong which turned out later not to be the case. We all hear terrible stories in the media about medical mismanagement and mis-diagnosis. While medicine and medics are fallible, and mistakes *are* made, people with health anxiety selectively attend to information which shows that medicine is not to be trusted, and ignore statistics and evidence of medical treatments being effective. They may have very high expectations of their doctors – that they should be able to diagnose and treat everything with 100 per cent accuracy – rather than using doctors as a resource with which to help themselves.

Behaviour and safety behaviours

People who are concerned about their health will try to find answers about what is causing the symptoms and what they need to do to cure the problem – behaviour that is very understandable. In health anxiety, the way the individual tries to cope is very much part of the problem and includes:

- seeking medical reassurance
- repeated checking
- avoiding tackling the problems
- trying to keep safe.

SEEKING MEDICAL REASSURANCE   One of the main coping strategies is to gain reassurance from the medical profession, complementary practitioners, friends and family: reassurance that there is nothing seriously wrong. The client may repeatedly consult to obtain answers, and may have many tests and investigations. Although they are reassured by their discussions for a short time, the reassurance fails to last: for one client, doubts would start in his mind 20 minutes after a consultation in which the GP had reported negative test results (Warwick and Salkovskis, 1985). Medical information may be discounted or distorted by thought processes such as 'Did I tell the doctor all my symptoms?'; 'She looked tired and distracted, she may have missed something'; 'There may be something wrong with the ECG machine'; 'Doctors do get it wrong'; 'I'm sure they muddled up my test results with someone else.'

Part of the problem is that the client is continuing to get symptoms, and although told what is *not* causing the problem, he or she has not had a convincing explanation for what might cause such symptoms. Medical reassurance may be phrased in a way which is ambiguous or contradictory, particularly when the patient consults several GPs with different styles and attitudes to testing and referring to specialists. When the individual returns to the doctor with the same symptoms, over and over again, the GP may doubt the diagnosis, and ask for further tests. This serves to keep the patient's mind firmly focused on the symptoms and the possibility of illness; and further tests may themselves carry some risks or contribute to symptoms. Repeated visits can also lead the doctor to feel frustrated, annoyed or helpless, responses which the patient may well pick up, and themselves feel misunderstood and helpless.

CHECKING   A second coping method is to repeatedly check the symptoms. A spotlight is turned on the area of concern, taking up the client's focus of attention (Barsky and Wyshak, 1990; Papageorgiou and Wells, 1998). When we pay attention for any length of time to any part of our bodies, we become aware of sensations which may be perfectly normal but which are usually out of our range of consciousness: for example, try focusing all your attention on your left foot, and notice what you can feel. It is likely that you may notice warmth, tingling, pins and needles, numbness or other sensations, which may be open to a range of interpretations.

Clients make symptoms worse by poking, rubbing or checking. Daniel, for example, would press his leg several times a day, to check for thrombosis, an action which led to soreness and bruising, which he then interpreted as a problem with blood clotting. Another client concerned about breast cancer checked her breasts thoroughly many times a day, with vigorous attention to normal fibrous tissue, which itself caused breast soreness and tenderness. A client concerned about choking sensations may repeatedly swallow, thus inhibiting the normal swallowing reflex and causing throat tightness. Thus, the solution becomes part of the problem, producing further symptoms to be worried about.

AVOIDANCE AND KEEPING SAFE   Other clients may use the coping strategy of avoidance – avoiding looking in the mirror or touching their bodies, avoiding medical information or medical programmes on television, and avoiding going to seek medical help for problems, even for obvious symptoms, being too fearful of something more sinister being found. They may try to stop worrying about their health, a process which increases worrying thoughts. The individual may avoid doing anything that might be risky, such as too much exercise or breathing too quickly. By taking active steps to avoid thinking about health issues and avoid exposure to medical information, the client inadvertently becomes more concerned and preoccupied: their fears cannot be actively looked at and resolved.

Clients use all sorts of other safety behaviours to cope: resting excessively, behaving as though they are ill, taking various remedies, vitamins or supplements, which might go beyond looking after themselves well. One client was convinced that he was developing multiple sclerosis, and had spent a great deal of money on herbal remedies which claimed to allay the symptoms.

Background, assumptions and beliefs

The individual's personal and family histories of illness and illness behaviours help to explain patients' assumptions and beliefs regarding their health, the medical profession and their personal vulnerability, all of which contribute to both development and maintenance of health anxiety (Warwick and Salkovskis, 1989). Illness during childhood correlates with levels of health anxiety in later life, contributing to the individual's sense of vulnerability to disease or harm. Parental attitudes to illness may be relevant, such as how episodes of minor or major illness are managed within the family, and whether children are over-protected, or rewarded overtly or implicitly for being ill (Mechanic, 1986; Stuart and Noyes, 1999). The person may have experienced illness or death of other family members or close friends, which understandably increases concern and vulnerability. Stressful life events, including illnesses, can also trigger episodes of health anxiety in individuals who may be vulnerable. Such backgrounds can lead to specific assumptions, such as:

- My body should always function perfectly.
- Any symptoms must mean something is seriously wrong.
- If I have symptoms the doctors should always be able to explain and treat them.
- My health is the doctor's responsibility.
- I am weak and vulnerable to physical illness or unable to cope on my own. (Warwick and Salkovskis, 1989)

Wells and Hackmann (1993), in a study of ten clients with hypochondriasis, found specific beliefs about the nature and consequences of illness or death. The clients viewed death as meaning being alone, trapped and punished for ever, and illness as representing weakness, inadequacy and being abandoned. All had some kind of metaphysical or superstitious beliefs about death or illness. Some clients with health anxiety and other somatic problems report histories of difficult childhood environments, childhood sexual abuse, physical abuse and family upheavals, which contribute to their beliefs and schemata (Barsky et al., 1994).

Adapting Counselling for Health-Anxious Clients

There are several ways in which it is necessary to adapt general counselling approaches to working with clients with health anxiety:

- engaging the client in counselling;
- adapting the therapeutic relationship;
- looking for alternative explanations of symptoms;
- dealing with unhelpful coping strategies.

Engagement in counselling

Clients with health anxiety are a varied group in terms of how relevant they see psychological approaches and counselling to their particular problems. Some realise that they are over-anxious, but are unable to control their anxieties or stop their various behaviours and thoughts contributing to the anxiety: these clients may self-refer for counselling and be relatively easy to engage. Others may be very reluctant, feeling that their real, primarily physical problems have been unhelpfully managed by the medical profession, and that they have been pushed into counselling as a way of the doctor getting rid of them. These clients may not have requested counselling and may not see its relevance; they may acknowledge that they are psychologically distressed but see this as secondary to their real physical problems.

An important challenge for the counsellor is actively to engage the client in counselling in a way which works with, rather than threatens, their views of their problems, and offers an understanding of the client's difficulties without either agreeing or disagreeing with them. It is probably the case that when the client with health anxiety is engaged in counselling a large part of the work has been done.

One of the most important means of engaging clients is for the therapist to remain open-minded and impartial or neutral about what might be causing the symptoms, but to focus on what might be keeping the client's worry in place. This avoids polarising between physical or psychological explanations, and begins the debate about possible other causes and maintaining factors. In the initial meeting it is helpful to focus on the client's symptoms and explanations, and give them sufficient time to feel that these have been heard and understood. The therapist can offer an empathic understanding of how difficult it must be for the client, and begin an exploration of emotional factors. One way of engaging is to offer the client the possibility of two hypotheses:

- One hypothesis is that the client is indeed ill, and has serious problems so far undetected.
- The second hypothesis is that the client is worried and concerned about illness, and, regardless of whether their symptoms are caused by illness, the worry and concern is a major problem which can be helped by psychological approaches (Salkovskis and Bass, 1997).

Client and counsellor can review what the client has so far done to test each hypothesis: many clients realise that they have focused on hypothesis one to the exclusion of hypothesis two, and their search so far has not been useful or helpful.

Daniel was initially very reluctant to see me in the GP surgery, feeling that he had been fobbed off by the doctor. He talked about his frustration with the doctors who had 'not taken me seriously', and I gave him time to describe all his symptoms and worries about underlying illness. He began to talk more about the fears and stresses in his life, and could begin to acknowledge that his fears might be out of proportion, but was concerned that accepting counselling meant that he had to accept that there was 'nothing wrong'. He had felt pushed into looking for an answer to his physical symptoms: since had he told his GP about his worries and feelings he was afraid she might have put it all down to stress, a model which Daniel could not accept. We began to draw up an initial formulation of his difficulties, and Daniel could see that there might be a 50:50 split between his anxiety about the symptoms and the real possibility of illness. He could understand how seeking reassurance and checking his symptoms all the time probably was not helpful, but it made sense in terms of fitting in with the illness beliefs. We both agreed to keep an open mind about his problems, and not focus on what was causing the symptoms, but start to work on reducing the 50 per cent anxiety.

A very important goal for the engagement phase is for client and counsellor to draw up a shared conceptualisation of the client's difficulties, with a model for how the problems developed and the various cognitive, affective, behavioural and physiological factors which keep the problem going. As for assessing and conceptualising all anxiety problems, working with specific concrete examples enables the client and counsellor to understand what happens in practice to maintain the client's problems. Client and counsellor can then discuss what the goals of therapy may be, taking an experimental and curious stance to test out whether such a conceptualisation fits, and whether changing the maintaining factors can reduce the client's health anxieties.

Negotiating goals for counselling

Many health-anxious clients may have unrealistic and unhelpful goals, such as to have their minds put totally at rest that there is nothing wrong, or for them never to have to worry about their health again. No form of medical tests or therapy can offer reassurance that there is nothing at all wrong: most of medicine is a process of elimination or positive diagnosis. We discussed what, in Daniel's case, would give him total reassurance that there was nothing seriously wrong. He wryly identified that in order to prove this, someone would have to look at and test everything in his body, inside and out, in order to be sure: in other words, a post mortem. (I offered to arrange one for him but he declined.) Similarly, absence of anxiety is an unrealistic outcome, given that anxiety is part of our lives and some level of health anxiety may be necessary in looking after ourselves. The client may well have the same level of physical symptoms at the end of therapy, but be less worried, focused on and disabled by the symptoms.

Discussing alternative explanations of symptoms

In line with the two-hypothesis model, one of the aims of coun-selling is for clients to look for alternatives to disease explanations for their symptoms. Physical symptoms can have many causes, and the client can be encouraged to think about alternatives, such as levels of stress, anxiety and tension. In addition, focusing on symptoms makes them seem larger, and scanning and checking the body can cause us to notice normal bodily changes. The client and counsellor can do mini-experiments in sessions, the client perhaps being asked to focus excessively on their left knee and describe sensations, such as numbness or tingling, which they had previously not noticed. This might lead to a discussion of how focus of attention and interpretation plays a major role: for example numbness and tingling may be normal, or an early sign of neurological problems, depending on our mind-set at the time. Other experiments include the client repeatedly checking, by rubbing a sore area for example, and noticing how this exacer-bates pain, or holding their arm very tense for five minutes and experiencing pain sensations. A pie chart can be helpful in identi-fying causes of symptoms, as illustrated in Figure 11.2. The client is asked to brainstorm all the possible causes of a particular symptom, for example a headache, and assign each cause a prob-ability rating. Often the most catastrophic cause is the one rated the least likely, and may even be left out of the client's brainstorm when thinking more objectively, despite it being the one that springs to mind when anxious. Clients with health anxiety tend to focus on the one most catastrophic interpretation, and learning to look at the bigger picture can help them to work out other possible causes and likelihoods.

While such discussion and experiments can be helpful in exploring options, it is important to avoid too much focus on single causes of symptoms, by implying that the symptoms may *only* be caused by behaviours or worry: this may lead the client to revert to their model of physical illness. Instead, the discussion is in the spirit of curiosity and finding things out, and of looking at all the options rather than at a unitary disease model.

Dealing with maintaining factors

Depending on the particular maintaining factors that arise from a detailed assessment and conceptualisation for each individual client, the client can be encouraged to reduce their level of checking or seeking medical reassurance or stop them altogether (Warwick, 1992). This can feel very threatening to the client, and

- Ask client to brainstorm causes (e.g. stress and tension, eye strain, tiredness, flu, alcohol, etc.).
- Give each cause a probability rating.
- Draw up a 'pie' to show causes.

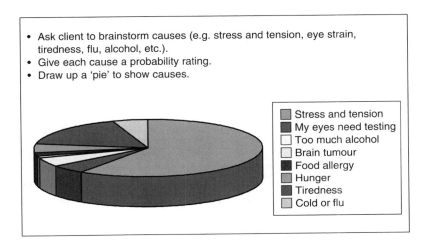

Stress and tension
My eyes need testing
Too much alcohol
Brain tumour
Food allergy
Hunger
Tiredness
Cold or flu

Figure 11.2   *Pie chart of causes of headaches*

activate thoughts and beliefs such as 'If I don't check then I may miss something and it will be too late.' While it is no doubt better to catch medical problems at an early stage, most people with health anxiety can see that their level of checking or asking for reassurance is over the top. In order to change this they can conduct experiments. A client can be asked to monitor their anxiety level after medical reassurance, and then when they have wanted reassurance but have not allowed themselves to make an appointment. Often clients find that the reassurance reduces anxiety in the short term, but some time afterwards the anxiety levels rise again; not asking for reassurance makes the person feel very panicky and anxious in the short term, but with time the anxiety reduces, and the person no longer feels the urge to get reassurance.

For clients who are persistent attenders at their doctors, and perhaps consult many different doctors or complementary practitioners, it can be helpful to work out a contract so that the client reduces or stops their attendances for a specified time in order to give counselling a proper try and not muddy the waters with a range of different treatments at the same time. However, just because a person has health anxiety does not mean that they never get ill: so we have to be sensible in negotiating reduced levels of help-seeking, which may be appropriate for new symptoms.

People with health anxiety can be very skilled at gaining reassurance from many people, including their therapist.

At the beginning of therapy, Daniel asked many questions about my knowledge of cardiology and neurology, and would describe a new symptom and look carefully to see if I looked worried. When we both got wise to his covert use of reassurance, I was able to ask whether such questions or showing me his symptoms was useful, what might happen if I did not give him reassurance, and thereby test out reducing his level of covert reassurance. Daniel found this very helpful in enabling him to become more independent of others about his health, and gain confidence in his ability to make decisions about his health rather than relying on me.

Part of dealing with maintaining factors is to enable the client to reduce their safety behaviours and test out the impact on their health. Some clients may be encouraged to gradually do more exercise; others may be very over-protective of their health in ways that are not helpful. A client who repeatedly checked her breasts for lumps was encouraged first to check several times a day to monitor pain or lumpiness, and then to check only once a month and see if there was a difference. The result was that lumps and soreness she found when she checked several times a day had disappeared when she did not check for several weeks. This helped her to work out a sensible level of checking in order to look after herself, without increasing her anxiety. Other ways of reducing safety behaviours are described in Sanders (1996), Wells (1997) and Salkovskis and Bass (1997).

Working with underlying assumptions and beliefs
Using downward arrow approaches and imagery helps the client to look at the beliefs and assumptions underneath their fears, and assess their reality.

Underlying Daniel's fears was the fear of being left all alone, of not being able to cope and of being abandoned by all his friends. Daniel would get an image of himself sitting at home, having been told that there was something seriously wrong with his heart, being all alone and feeling unable to cope. The image always stopped at this point, with him feeling awful. We used imagery to push this scenario on to its completion: first he saw himself wasting away, becoming more and more disabled, taking medication and eventually dying painfully of a heart attack. After discussing the image, he could then substitute a more realistic one: being told that there is effective treatment, family and friends offering support, going for surgery which would be difficult but he would be able to cope, then getting back to health and seeing himself working out at the gym.

When we talk to our clients who fear death, it makes sense for us to assume that their fear of death is normal and justified, but such an assumption can miss valuable understandings of the client. While 'What is so bad about dying?' may sound a strange or insulting question to ask, it is always worth asking, in an empathic and tactful way, since many clients have idiosyncratic and often terrifying views about death which make it too terrible to contemplate. They may see death as a permanent stage of immobility, being conscious but unable to move, being trapped in a dead body, or going to hell: 'When you are buried the worms and insects get into your coffin and eat your body. It's horrible. I might be able to feel the insects and know what is going on' (Wells, 1997: 161). People often avoid thinking about death, enabling such fears to rumble away in the background and generate chronic fears without the person being clear about what their fears are. So, enabling the client to articulate their underlying fears helps them to evaluate them. Some may be based on misunderstandings of physical processes: in the example above, Wells (1997) helpfully discusses with the client how the body decomposes before the coffin rots and lets insects in. This may of course then lead on to a discussion about the horrors of decomposition for the client.

Whatever the individual's fears, much of the time no one can answer them with any certainty. Sometimes, understanding the processes of death can be helpful – learning that we can only be conscious with brain activity, which ceases upon death (although I recently discovered that for those poor souls who died by guillotine it was likely that they remained conscious long enough to realise that their head had been severed from their body: a fact to be kept secret from our clients with health anxiety). It can be striking sometimes how much time people spend worrying about death and the afterlife and neglect paying attention to their lives. A useful question can be 'Say you only had one year to live, would you want to spend the year worrying about your death, or would you focus on other things?' Oscar Wilde pointed out that there was nothing like the threat of execution to clarify the mind. Most clients I have asked reported that they would want to make the most of their lives and let their deaths take care of themselves, which led to an evaluation of what is important in the here and now.

The Effectiveness of Counselling in Health Anxiety

One of the first studies of effective psychological therapy for health anxiety focused on helping the client to seek less reassurance and become less anxious about physical symptoms, and also assist the client's family and doctors to reduce their reassurance. The work was behavioural rather than cognitive, and most of the 17 clients in the study remained well five years later (Warwick and Marks, 1988). Later studies have been more cognitive in focus and have shown very good results (Warwick et al., 1996; Bouman and Visser, 1998; Clark et al., 1998). Cognitive therapy for health anxiety has been shown to be helpful in group therapy format (Stern and Fernandez, 1991). In a small study, three clients with health anxiety found attention training helpful in improving their mood and reducing their preoccupation with illness (Papageorgiou and Wells, 1998), a finding which will be studied more in larger trials. Psychodynamic therapy also has an important place in working with clients with long-term health anxiety issues (Guthrie, 1995).

Overall, it seems that clients with health anxiety can be significantly helped by psychological approaches focused on their worries and illness behaviours. It is likely that the active ingredients include helping clients to re-evaluate the meaning of their symptoms and shift away from a disease model towards a greater understanding of the role of worry and anxiety. Clients are thus enabled to work actively to cope with the worry rather than seeing themselves as patients with undiagnosed medical problems. As for many forms of psychological therapy, the findings that different forms of intervention are helpful, both structured cognitive therapy and more behavioural stress management, show the potential importance of 'non-specific' factors in therapy: time, understanding, the attitudes of the therapist and the therapeutic relationship. Time is something that many people with health anxiety believe they never get enough of from their doctors, time in which to construct alternative models of their problems.

———— 12 ————

Obsessive Compulsive Disorder

Will all great Neptune's ocean wash this blood
Clean from my hand? No; this my hand will rather
The multitudinous seas incarnadine,
Making the green one red. (Macbeth)

Out, damned spot! Out, I say! . . . What! Will these hands ne'er be
clean? . . . all the perfumes of Arabia will not sweeten this little hand.
(Lady Macbeth)

Obsessive compulsive disorder (OCD) is one of the more complex
and most misunderstood of anxiety disorders. The problems of
OCD are dominated by seemingly strange behaviours such as
repetitive washing, checking and a variety of rituals. Such behaviours may become so much the focus of concern that it is difficult
to remember that OCD is a variety of anxiety. Clients with
obsessive compulsive disorder can be difficult to work with. They
may feel deeply misunderstood and may have taken many years
to come to terms with what is happening to them. The obsessive
nature of rituals means that clients can be experienced as going on
and on about the same problems, or continually seeking reassurance while at the same time being hard to reassure. Their rituals
can close them off in an isolated world. Exactly why people
engage in their strange and elaborate rituals can be incompre-
hensible to others. People often want to give commonsense advice
that actually turns out to be unhelpful to the client. Clients may
know that checking the locks 'just one more time' is illogical yet
still have to do it. The incomprehension of others is more than
matched by the clients' incomprehension of their own experience,
leading to strong feelings of being alone and unheard. By its
nature, OCD is a downward spiral, one problem triggering off
another.

Traditional treatment approaches have been behavioural,
focusing on exposing the client to their fears and anxious feelings,
and preventing them from engaging in ritualistic behaviour in
response to their anxious thoughts. This treatment has involved

direct exposure to what the client fears most, for example, contamination by dirt. While it is an effective intervention for many clients, the drop-out rate is quite high. Newer models of OCD have placed the problem firmly in the arena of the anxiety disorders, enabling more sophisticated conceptualisations to be developed by focusing on the role of thoughts and beliefs, rather than on overt behaviours alone. Therapy is now more targeted at the client's central concerns rather than getting sidetracked into the complexities of behaviours. Better therapies are now available for the clients with predominantly obsessive thoughts and rumination who were harder to help with purely behavioural models of therapy. Such therapy is more acceptable to clients, and we are beginning to see good success rates from trials.

Despite the fact that OCD clients are often seen as belonging to the domain of clinical psychologists and psychiatrists, we feel that counsellors are in an excellent position to work effectively in this area. Key skills involve being able to see the wood for the trees, and to understand what really underlies the client's difficulties. Even when implementing a highly focused programme for obsessive compulsive problems, the use of counselling and listening skills is absolutely crucial (Baines and Wills, 2001). These skills can help to overcome the sense clients often have of not being listened to or understood.

In this chapter we offer an overview of the conceptualisation for OCD and of therapy methods based on the new cognitive models. We look at how conceptualisation needs to take into account underlying beliefs and meanings while focusing on maintenance cycles. This enables the therapist and client to work with key issues rather than getting too narrowly focused on behaviours. We describe how traditional behavioural methods of exposure and relapse have been woven into newer cognitive approaches. We also look at some of the issues and difficulties that arise for counsellors and therapists when they are working with OCD clients.

Defining Obsessive Compulsive Disorder

The definition of OCD is shown in Table 12.1.

Obsessive compulsive disorder consists of two main features – obsessions and compulsions – which combine in different ways and in different strengths for individual clients.

Obsessive thoughts in OCD have typically negative and worrying themes. The main themes are fears of such things as contamination or illness, and of impulses to do harm to others. These

Table 12.1   *Defining obsessive compulsive disorder*

Obsessions: recurrent and persistent thoughts, impulses or images, experienced as intrusive and inappropriate. These thoughts and images are not excessive worries about real-life problems, and cause the person marked distress and anxiety.

The person attempts to ignore and suppress the obsessions, or neutralise them with thoughts or actions.

Compulsions: repetitive behaviours or mental acts such as hand-washing, ordering, checking, praying, counting, repeating words silently, that the person feels driven to do in response to an obsession, or according to rules that must be rigidly applied.

The compulsions are a means of preventing or reducing distress or preventing some dreaded event or situation.

The obsessions and compulsions are time-consuming, cause great distress and interfere significantly with normal functioning.

Source: APA (2000)

thoughts seem to be characterised by an inflated sense of responsibility for self and/or others, and an overestimation of danger in many of these events should they occur. The thoughts may be experienced verbally or as images of something terrible happening. When obsessive thoughts predominate, people can be described as 'ruminators'.

Compulsive behaviours are acts that the person feels compelled to do. These behaviours are directly related to obsessive thoughts, although for some clients it may initially be difficult to identify the thoughts or images preceding the behaviour. For example, a person who fears that she has been contaminated will wash her hands repeatedly. A person who fears that he will harm another, will go out of his way to avoid the person. Sometimes these behaviours are covert or private behaviours, such as saying a silent prayer to oneself to ward off harm. Such behaviours may not be visible to others and may have become so automatic that the person himself is barely aware of them. They can therefore become ritualistic. It used to be considered that these behaviours were problems in themselves, but it is now understood that thoughts and beliefs drive these behaviours. Where behaviours predominate, the person can be described as a 'ritualiser'.

> Sally is a 40-year-old secretary. Years before the current referral, she had an accident at work and a wound had subsequently become infected. Her problems began as simple worries about this infection. Over the years, however, these worries increased in number and became more and more complicated. Sally now gets very worried

about contamination, mainly from household dirt. She either tries to avoid thinking worrying thoughts about dirt or contamination, or works herself up to deal with them by wearing rubber gloves and afterwards repeatedly washing her hands. She finds that she cannot relax at home when she gets into these states. She is concerned that situations might arise at work that would expose her problems. Recently, she became concerned about some chemical cleaners in her house. She was not able to deal with this because she could not work out a way to move these chemicals without touching them herself or by asking someone else to help to deal with them. Not only would this person then realise that she had a problem, but he or she might also go on to touch her or objects in her house, risking further contamination and serious danger to herself and others.

Themes for obsessive thoughts and compulsive behaviours are shown in Table 12.2 (Obsessive Compulsive Cognitions Working Group, 1997). These themes can be highly idiosyncratic to individual clients. It is also important to remember that sometimes obsessions can appear without readily identifiable compulsions. This might mean that the compulsions are actually absent or, more likely, that they are well hidden and covert, such as mentally trying to ward off a thought, thinking a number after a thought to 'neutralise' the obsessive thought, or lifting up one particular finger in response to a thought. Listening skills and careful observation of non-verbal behaviours greatly help to pick up these subtle individual variations.

If we are honest, most of us experience occasional obsessions and compulsions. Indeed, research (Rachman and de Silva, 1978; Salkovskis and Harrison, 1984) supports the idea that the vast majority of people do have thoughts similar in content to those of OCD sufferers. 'Normalisation' of the content of OCD thoughts is therefore an important aspect of therapy. The difference between sufferers and non-sufferers lies not in the content of the thoughts but in the way that the thoughts are dealt with. OCD clients seem to find it difficult to put the thoughts aside because they make an appraisal of them that non-sufferers do not, seeing *having* the thoughts as meaning that the client is effectively *responsible* for the potential occurrence of the content of the thought occurring. To the OCD sufferer, having these thoughts means that they are highly likely to do something that will cause harm to themselves or to others. For example we may get frightening images of something bad, such as being dropped, happening to a baby while we are holding it. For the OCD sufferer, the image means that they are wanting to throw the baby on the floor, or that they are

Table 12.2 *Common themes in obsessive thoughts and compulsive behaviours*

Obsessive thoughts
- excessive responsibility
- over-estimation of threat and lack of tolerance of uncertainty
- over-importance of thoughts and the need to control them
- perfectionism
- intolerance of emotional discomfort

Compulsive behaviours
- excessive washing or cleaning
- checking
- repeating actions
- hoarding or saving things
- putting objects in a set pattern

Source: Obsessive Compulsive Cognitions Working Group (1997)

going to make it happen. For people without OCD, such thoughts and images are simply warnings to take extra care when holding a baby. Not surprisingly, the person with OCD believes they must take action to keep the baby safe, such as saying a prayer numerous times, or washing their hands and clothes to get rid of bad thoughts. The difference between 'normal' and 'problematic' obsessive thoughts is shown in Figure 12.1. We can see that, as a result of viewing the thought as having more meaning, the individual needs to take action to prevent feared outcomes, a process known as 'neutralising' the thoughts, which then sets up a vicious cycle.

Clients may try so hard to suppress intrusive thoughts that the thoughts are strengthened by some kind of 'rebound' effect. The process of trying not to think about something usually means that the thought is more likely to occur (Wegner, 1989).

Compulsive behaviours can be seen as a way of dealing with these troubling thoughts. For most OCD clients, the compulsive behaviours reduce anxiety and seem to 'work' – that is, they seem to 'ward off' or neutralise the feared disaster. By linking the non-occurrence of something with the compulsive behaviour, the client is unable to change the mistaken belief that such feared disasters are likely to happen. This way of dealing with intrusions, therefore, only results in an accelerating vicious cycle. The thoughts and the emotions that go with compulsive behaviours can be highly disturbing to the client. The behaviours themselves can become extreme and counterproductive. For example, some people will wash their hands so often that they become red, raw and very painful. Others have to get up before dawn to begin the

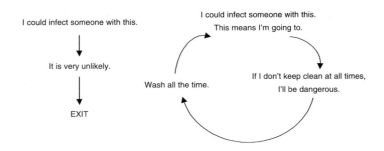

Figure 12.1   *Cycles of normal and problematic obsessive thoughts*

preparations to get to work over four hours later. The cumulative effects of these troubling thoughts, emotions and unhelpful behaviours can begin to disrupt normal functioning to the point where an OCD sufferer can seem, both to himself and to others, on occasions close to madness, which can further confirm his fears and interpretations.

Conceptualising Obsessive Compulsive Problems

Originally, the psychological therapy approach to obsessive compulsive problems was dominated by the behavioural perspective. This began with the work of Meyer (1966) who conceptualised obsessive compulsive problems in behavioural terms and also devised an exposure-based treatment method for them. A cognitive perspective has emerged more recently and in some trials this has produced a superior effect to exposure and relapse-prevention treatment (Abramowitz, 1997). In the cognitive models, themes of danger and responsibility are seen as central to OCD, with therapy working to test out such themes through cognitive change and experiments. The cognitive conceptualisation of OCD is shown in Figure 12.2.

At the core of the conceptual model lies the client's interpretation of thoughts and images, which sets up vicious cycles of anxiety, and neutralising and safety behaviours, which increase the occurrence and likelihood of obsessive thoughts, leading to greater need to neutralise and greater distress.

OCD cognitions and beliefs

The cognitive model has been developed primarily by Salkovskis (1989; Salkovskis and Kirk, 1997). It has been built from the finding that the majority of people appear to have thoughts

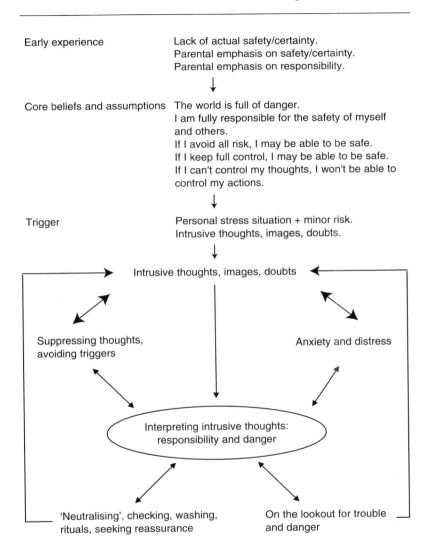

Figure 12.2   *Conceptualising OCD*

Sources: Adapted from Salkovskis et al. (1998); Wells (1997)

similar to those that trouble OCD clients. What distinguishes people who go on to develop obsessive compulsive problems is the way that they evaluate and pay attention to these thoughts. A number of cognitive distortions are evident in these evaluations, showing overestimates of:

212 Counselling for Specific Anxiety Problems

- the degree of personal responsibility for bad events;
- the consequences of being held responsible for these events;
- the likelihood of bad events happening;
- the degree of damage resulting from such events.

Foa and Kozak (1991) conclude that these appraisals result in a number of characteristic ways of interpreting events: for example, by defining the absence of guaranteed safety as equalling danger. Guidano and Liotti (1983) make a similar point when they suggest that people with obsessive problems require a greater degree of certainty and safety than is likely to be available in most situations. This leads to the problems in disconfirming the likelihood of bad things happening. For someone without OCD, disconfirmation means, 'This is unlikely to happen, I can forget about it.' The individual with OCD, in contrast, is likely to discount such disconfirmation by saying, 'How can I be sure? It hasn't happened yet, but it might.' One of the major problems is that while it is possible to prove beyond doubt that something has happened, it is impossible to be absolutely certain that something will never happen. Most of us find ways of living with this uncertainty: for clients with OCD, in common with clients with health anxiety, any level of uncertainty about their particular fears is intolerable.

The common themes that run through these distortions relate to central beliefs and assumptions, linked to responsibility or danger (Leahy and Holland, 2000).

- I am the only one that I can truly count on.
- I'm inherently irresponsible unless I try very hard.
- If a bad thing happens and I could have prevented it, then I am 100 per cent responsible.
- If you think something, it means you are responsible for it happening.
- The world is full of dangers.
- The probability of something bad happening is high.
- I'm a bad person with dangerous impulses.
- If a bad thing can happen, it will happen.

There is general support for linking these beliefs with childhood or other early experience. Some OCD clients describe histories where there was a strict form of religion or other value (emphasising extreme safety or cleanliness) system prevailing in their home. Beliefs linked to unrelenting standards may be evident. Salkovskis et al. (1998) identify five characteristic patterns of prior

experience associated with the development of inflated responsibility beliefs:

1. Having excessive responsibility foisted on them at an early
    age.
2. People who have been over-protected.
3. People who have had an experience where they mistakenly
    believed themselves responsible for causing serious harm.
4. Actually, but inadvertently, contributing to serious harm.
5. People who have been exposed to rigid and extreme codes of
    conduct and duty.

As counsellors, we have found that it is often helpful to include
exploration of such experiences when working with clients with
obsessive compulsive problems. Interesting, if not perhaps con-
clusive, links with early experience can be made. This in itself can
add to the general pattern of insight that develops during the
therapy, and, perhaps more importantly, helps the client to tell his
full story and to feel more fully understood. The following
illustrates how a generalised belief related to history arose during
counselling with Sally.

> Sally was doing a programme of behavioural experiments involving
> exposure to normal levels of dirt. The session was taking place in her
> home. When the counsellor arrived, Sally said 'Things are working
> against this therapy.' She explained that she had found a male
> intruder in the female toilets at work. She had talked it over with her
> manager, who sent Sally home and told her to 'take it easy'. Sally
> was resting at home when the therapist arrived for the therapy
> session. She found the sessions very physically and emotionally
> draining and thought that, having already been through a very dis-
> turbing experience, she could not go through with any behavioural
> experiments that day. We agreed to change the agenda and discuss
> some of the beliefs connected with her worries. One clear belief was
> '(Bad) Things happen to me.' This belief first emerged when we had
> discussed the event to which she traced the origins of her problems:
> a very traumatic accident 10 years before. Even this event, however,
> had many echoes in her earlier life experiences, where she and her
> family seemed to encounter many difficulties.

Metacognition and OCD

Wells (1997, 2000) advances several major arguments for regarding metacognitive beliefs as being very important in the conceptualisation and treatment of OCD. Metacognitions are thoughts

about thoughts, for example, 'Thinking this way is going to drive me crazy', and 'If I think opposite thoughts to those nasty ones, I will not become a bad person.' Clients' appraisals of their thoughts play a key role in the maintenance of OCD. For example, thoughts about going crazy are present in other anxiety problems such as panic disorder and are naturally associated with stress and anxiety. Anyone who had a thought like that and actually believed it would be bound to feel anxious. Anxiety feelings, however, normally motivate the individual to try to achieve alleviation of this feeling. Thus a person often follows the anxiety thought with a thought like 'Well this is an uncomfortable thought but it probably will not drive me mad. Perhaps other people have thoughts like this without going mad.' An OCD client, however, might think 'Unless I can force this thought out of my mind, it will drive me mad.' Forcing thoughts away, however, leads only to temporary relief because it does not undermine the idea that such a thought is actually capable of driving a person mad. Rather it implies that such a thought has this capacity but the possibility is circumvented by the client's distraction tactic. This type of thinking is like a form of safety behaviour. In this case, the behaviour is actually a thinking and metacognitive process.

The metacognitive perspective on OCD resonates nicely with many of the cognitive distortions associated with obsessional thinking. One such concept is that of thought–action fusion (TAF). TAF occurs when a client believes that if he thinks about doing something then that means either that he has done it or that thinking it is as bad as doing it. Such beliefs includes a chain of thoughts from 'What if I did X?' to 'I may have done X' to 'I *have* done X.' This often causes strong guilt feelings and an inflated sense of responsibility for clients with OCD. If a client concerned about contamination has the thought, 'I must have passed on disease when I shook his hand', then he begins to believe that he did actually do this. The theme running through all these types of metacognitions is a lack of a sense of absolute certainty, and extreme tolerance of uncertainty (Tallis, 1995). There seems to be what one could regard almost as atrophy of a sense of being able to know things for sure. Indeed, striving for 100 per cent certainty only increases the sense of doubt. While many of the metacognitions linked to OCD are somewhat similar to those associated with Generalised Anxiety Disorder (GAD), the underlying theme of uncertainty particularly points towards OCD. Wells (1997, 2000) has developed a metacognitions questionnaire and this may be used in therapy to help identify such beliefs.

Counselling for Obsessive Compulsive Problems

The main aims of therapy for OCD are to help the client identify their beliefs, and to help them work out less threatening alternatives. Client and counsellor work together to develop a conceptualisation of the client's problems, particularly focusing on the central interpretations clients make of intrusive thoughts, images and doubts, and the overt and covert safety behaviours and neutralising that prevents the client disconfirming their beliefs. Challenging thoughts involves discussing and looking for alternatives, and for behavioural experiments to test out alternative interpretations. The experimental stage of therapy mainly involves exposure to the client's fears, without allowing them to do the compulsive rituals to neutralise their fears. This way, the client is able to discover that their interpretations of danger and responsibility are distorted and unhelpful, and begin to construct more helpful interpretations and rules for living, particularly living with uncertainty. Most importantly, the client can separate out the occurrence of intrusive thoughts from meanings of responsibility and harm, seeing thoughts as irrelevant for further action, including paying them any further attention. Thus, the individual with OCD is able to observe the stream of obsessive thoughts without needing to neutralise them; the obsessive checker is able to ignore their thoughts 'Did I really lock the door?' as irrelevant, so breaking the cycle of obsessions and compulsions.

The therapeutic relationship

Therapists working with clients with OCD may well find that they can sometimes experience a variety of negative reactions to the client and/or his material. These reactions may include incomprehension and frustration, difficult feelings for any aspiring helper. We may get the feeling of going round in circles and of being pulled into and lost in the client's obsessive thinking. Counsellors with awareness of process issues and tools for working on the relationship will be able to stay with and manage the inevitable difficulties of such therapy. Clients with OCD may take up a disproportionate time in supervision. As counsellors and therapists, we need time and space to process our own reactions to our clients, as well as time to think through the complexities of their material.

When working with clients with obsessive compulsive problems, the use of counselling and listening skills is absolutely crucial (Baines and Wills, 2001). Many clients with obsessive compulsive problems have been in situations where they have not been well listened to or where their problems have been trivialised. This may be compounded by the fact that they can be difficult to listen to. Clients with obsessive compulsive problems may speak very rapidly, so that it is sometimes difficult for therapists to follow everything they say. A certain kind of attention seems to work well with clients with obsessive compulsive problems. This is developed from the concept of 'mindfulness' (Kabat-Zinn, 1990, 1994, 1995), where we observe and experience what is going on without being involved. Interestingly, it has been suggested that this type of attention is also useful for OCD clients (Wells, 1997), allowing them to regard their obsessive thoughts in a more detached way. As a counsellor, one can try to listen out for key information on the client's thoughts, feelings, behaviours, triggers and physiological reactions that occur during obsessive compulsive episodes, and let the less relevant material 'float on by'.

Developing a conceptualisation

During the initial stages of counselling, client and counsellor work together to construct a map of the client's specific problems. Having a clearly defined and written conceptualisation is extremely important when working with clients with OCD, to prevent client or counsellor becoming lost in the complexities of the client's material and to allow insights reached during counselling to be remembered and woven into the overall model. Here-and-now examples can really help with developing a model: talking about the symptoms can sometimes bring them on in the session, precipitating client and therapist into a here-and-now situation. It is extremely helpful to conduct at least one session in the client's home, so that we can observe exactly what the problems are (Salkovskis et al., 1998). When Sally was showing the counsellor an 'unclean' area of her house, he noticed that she sat on a chair and lifted her feet from the ground. We established that this was to avoid contact with dirt on the floor in that area. We were then able to build this small incident into the larger conceptualisation in Figure 12.3. The conceptualisation below was constructed for Sally. It followed some of the factors shown in the model offered by Salkovskis et al. (1998) but was adapted to Sally herself.

Sally's main presenting problem is the way that her obsessional fears interfere with her life. Looking at her conceptualisation, we can see that problems come from the interaction between her beliefs, such as those influenced by her previous experiences, and more immediate triggers in her environment. From the

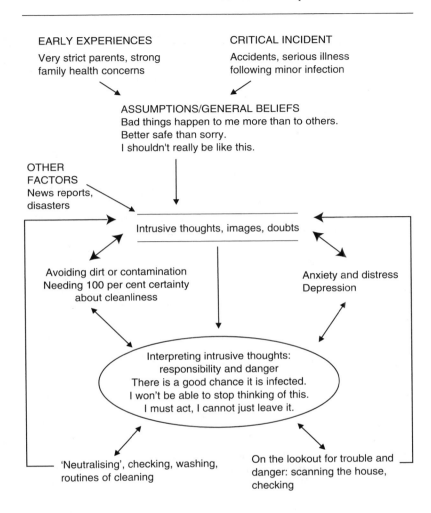

Figure 12.3 *Sally's conceptualisation*

conceptualisation, we are able to develop a plan for therapy, often beginning with current symptoms. Sally's current symptoms are dominated by the fact that she has to make frequent contact with her feared environment, as it is her home. This suggests that exposure to this environment is a potential key to therapy.

Ways of challenging OCD beliefs
It is generally agreed that there is no real point in challenging the content of OCD thoughts themselves, but rather the target should

be the interpretation or misinterpretation that lies within them (Steketee, 1999a). A wide range of cognitive techniques has been found to be useful in working on loosening these distortions. The main methods involve discussion and verbal challenging, and behavioural experiments to test out old beliefs and construct new ones.

VERBAL CHALLENGING   It is useful to think about matching up different types of cognitive interventions with the different themes of OCD. As there are quite a few variations and possibilities for each type of OCD thought, it is proposed to review the main themes revealed by the research of the international Obsessive Compulsive Cognitions Working Group, and describe one main method that links to each theme. These methods can be used either by themselves or as tied to behavioural experiments. It may be helpful to generate a list of situations the client would avoid, or believe to be dangerous in some way. Taking an item on the list, such as touching floors (see Figure 12.4) then the client is usually able to identify a belief such as 'If I touch the floor, I will get a disease and then be responsible for spreading it round.' We then aim to use Socratic questioning and guided discovery to explore the belief and begin to construct alternatives. Salkovskis et al. (1998) point out that it is very difficult to disconfirm completely a belief such as 'I might get a disease or spread it around', because the anticipated disaster may only emerge in the long term or not at all. When a counsellor gets trapped into trying such disconfirmation, he usually succeeds only in initiating a further cycle of doubt and reassurance. It can be helpful to point out this cycle to clients and to ask them how they might respond if a friend was disclosing similar worries. The counsellor concludes this discussion with an agreement that, while worries about the future can never be completely eliminated, keeping the doubt and reassurance cycle going is very likely to result in the persistence of obsessional compulsive problems.

The ideal base from which the client can be helped to get over these problems is the enhancement of their ability to recognise two possible explanations of their problems:

1. They really are in danger and must take all steps to avert it.
2. Their problems result from their anxious preoccupation with danger, rather than from the danger itself.

The things that clients fear are things that are rightly feared by all of us, such as cancer, disease, or mental illness. A key issue for everyone is how to manage such fears. How much attention should we give to them? How many times should we check things? How much worry is 'good' worry and when does 'bad' worry begin? There is obviously no right way of dealing with these issues and it is helpful for the counsellor to invite the client to, as it were, join the rest of humanity in considering the pros and cons of the various balances that are possible. Salkovskis et al. (1998) suggest a useful analogy that can be offered to clients: what is the price at which the cost of the insurance premium exceeds the risk being insured against? A client might argue that washing one's hands for half an hour is a price worth paying to eliminate the possibility of a life-threatening disease or illness. This is not, however, the full price, because the hand-washing is only one small part of a whole pattern and history of response that is actually very dysfunctional and detrimental to the achievement of the client's major life goals.

The cognitive methods described below are aimed at loosening rather than eliminating the specific beliefs that they challenge. The larger intention is always to strengthen the possibility that the client will move to seeing that their overall problems are their responses to perceived threats rather than the perceived threats themselves.

EXCESSIVE RESPONSIBILITY *Example* – 'I will be responsible for making my colleagues ill by infecting them.'

Possible method – Responsibility pie-chart. Here the therapist asks the client to brainstorm all the possible reasons why his colleagues might get ill and ask the client to make an estimate of the percentage risk for these factors. These risks can be reproduced as a pie-chart. Towards the end of the construction of the pie-chart, the therapist asks the client to estimate his own percentage of responsibility. By this time, only relative small percentages should be available. It is hoped that this will allow the client to see his degree of responsibility in much more relative terms.

LOGICAL ERRORS AND MISINTERPRETATIONS *Example* – 'Someone like me should not have a problem like this.'

Possible method – The cognitive distortion here is a 'should statement' (Burns, 1999). One possible way of countering this kind of distortion might be to ask the client to review the advantages and disadvantages of holding this view. The advantages might include keeping to high standards of conduct but the disadvantages might include pushing oneself too hard and courting stress.

The aim here is to get the client to take a 'more rounded view', rather than to achieve a total change.

OVER-IMPORTANCE OF THOUGHTS AND THE NEED TO CONTROL THOUGHTS
Example – 'The fact that I am having these impulses means that I am a bad person.'

Possible method – Ask the client to place herself on a continuum of, at one end, very moral people, and, at the other, very immoral people. This can help the client by stretching her constructs to take in the fact that there is a big difference between having the thought of doing something and actually doing it. The survey method might also help the client to realise that many other people might have this thought from time to time (Padesky, 1994).

DANGER AND ANXIETY *Example* – 'Because I got a letter from a government department, I will probably get anthrax from it.'

Possible method – Calculation of probability of risk. Clients often make the error of thinking that any chance of something happening means that it will happen. They ignore the fact that an event is an accumulation of risks. The odds greatly lengthen against any event when various other events in a particular sequence must precede it. In this case, the feared event (receiving a letter infected by anthrax) would have to have been preceded by something like the following sequence of events:

1. an attack on a British* government office;
2. an attack on the particular office sending this letter;
3. the attack would have to have involved this particular letter in some way;
4. the attack would have to have gone undetected;
5. this attack would have to be one of the comparatively few that cause harm.

The more events it takes to make an end event happen, the longer become the odds that the end event will happen. Because each of the above factors made the overall odds longer, the therapist and client were eventually able to calculate this risk as a 1 in 2 million chance, and this was probably a conservatively high estimate.

---

* A client reported this thought at the time of the anthrax postal attacks in the USA. There had not been, and at the time of writing has not been, an attack in Britain.

Situation	Belief and belief rating
Touching floors	I will pick up a disease. (40%)
Touching doorknobs	I will pick up a disease. (50%)
Using the toilet at work	I will get a sexually transmitted disease. (60%)
Touching clothes after using toilet at work	I will spread infection around the house and be responsible for other people getting infected. (70%)
Touching household chemicals	I will poison myself. (80%)
Dealing with a dead animal in the garden	I will contract a deadly illness, and pass it on to other people. I'll be a killer myself. (90%)

Figure 12.4 *Sally's feared situations and predictions*

CERTAINTY AND PERFECTIONISM   *Example* – 'There must be an absolute answer on why I failed in that business.'

Possible method – Continuum with a mid-point standard. The client can be asked to imagine what a perfect answer, an imperfect answer and a mid-point ('good-enough') answer might be. The latter answer could be explored as one that could be tolerable. Other methods include discussion of the pros and cons of absolute certainty.

BEHAVIOURAL EXPERIMENTS   Behavioural experiments are the most powerful way of disconfirming clients beliefs, and provide immediate experiential disconfirmation, allowing for 'gut-level' change. Behavioural experiments can be devised for any of the above situations (Wells, 1997). Clients can, for example, be encouraged to find out whether, if they don't check doors, it means that they will leave them open. One frequently used experiment is to encourage the client to increase the number of OCD thoughts to see if it really does result in the predicted catastrophe such as going mad or losing control. Another experiment is for the client simply to watch their thoughts, or count them, without getting caught up in the content: a kind of mindful awareness. Given that clients with OCD feel compelled to act on every thought, they can be asked to see whether many intrusive thoughts are actually fairly irrelevant to action.

Experiments are generally held to be more effective than the standard cognitive restructuring approaches with OCD. This may be because OCD clients often favour list-making and writing things down in a detailed and obsessive way, and therefore cognitive techniques such as keeping thought records may themselves become obsessional compulsive behaviours. Using imagery to explore client meanings may be more effective than writing things down, perhaps because imagery work is closer in spirit to the idea of mindfulness, mentioned earlier.

COMBINING EXPOSURE WITH BEHAVIOURAL EXPERIMENTS   In traditional behavioural exposure work, the client would generate a list of feared situations and be progressively exposed to these fears. The treatment would have the flavour of a pre-set programme. Counsellors frequently baulk at the idea of implementing a 'programme of treatment', probably because they rightly pride themselves on being extremely responsive to the needs of individual clients and do not like the idea of 'pre-programmed' interventions. While we share some of these reservations, we also see some benefits in having a list of feared situations that can act as an action plan. Client and counsellor can keep returning to the map to avoid getting lost. When confronting the very strong fears that arise in obsessive compulsive problems, it can be helpful to 'stay with the process' when it comes to facing up to fear by repeated exposure. Facing up to fears is scary and clients will sometimes divert themselves and the therapist away from this exposure activity if given much opportunity to do so.

When the client wishes to proceed, the counsellor begins by getting her to brainstorm different kinds of situation in which she becomes distressed. Client and counsellor can begin to pick out situations particularly associated with distress and those that might be avoided. For each situation, they should be able to identify a specific negative belief, usually in the form of a prediction, such as 'I will be responsible for giving food poisoning to my entire family.' The experiment is not usually devised to test a particular prediction because the outcome is likely to be too far in the future to be known helpfully now. The aim of the experiment is to test whether the person's way of dealing with that thought is contributing to a vicious cycle of reassurance and doubt. Sally's list is shown in Figure 12.4.

Experiments can proceed during the session or as homework tasks. Initially, it is usually helpful for the counsellor to be present until the client has really got the hang of things. When the initial experiments begin and the client makes contact with, for example, touching the floor, the counsellor should observe closely and ask questions such as:

- What are you feeling now?
- How strong are the feelings?
- What is going through your mind?
- What do you feel like doing now?
- What are the options?

The counsellor should be careful not to provide a distraction for the client as this could undermine the process of the experiment. The aim at this stage is to build up understanding of the client's reaction patterns. The counsellor should particularly listen and watch out for subtle avoidance and covert rituals, and encourage the client to drop their neutralising and safety behaviours, in line with the rationale of the experiment.

Experiments can also use imagery exercises rather than real-life situations. The therapist gets the client to bring images of the feared situations into her mind and to imagine, for example, touching the floors or not wiping down surfaces a second time, or checking the gas oven more than once. This can be particularly helpful when situations might be hard either to visit or to reproduce in sessions. Thought also needs to be given as to how the client will continue doing experiments as homework tasks. Merely doing exposures once or even twice a week with the counsellor is unlikely to be enough to secure change. Tape-recordings of imagery situations and looped (self-repeating) audio tapes that replay intrusive thoughts can be useful additions to homework tasks.

The main benefit from such experiments, however, comes from testing obsessional compulsive beliefs and from the reduction of anxiety that usually follows 'staying with' the repetition of the feared tasks. The counsellor needs to persuade the client to keep dropping their neutralising safety behaviours during the experiments. If safety behaviours are retained, then the client may attribute any reduction of anxiety or neutral outcome to having carried out the safety behaviour. The counsellor needs to be quite vigilant as these safety behaviours can be very subtle and covert. Once spotted, they can be identified to the client and their likely effect can be described. If the client articulates concern about dropping them, then it may be possible to mount a 'once with, once without' experiment.

Although we agree with the CBT textbooks that say the counsellor needs to actively keep the client to task, it is also important to 'negotiate' tasks. Some interesting issues can arise during this work. Sally, for example, sometimes wanted to wash her hands after a particular cleaning up activity and it would have been what anyone might have done in the same situation. This led to a discussion about whether she wanted to clean her hands because they were obviously dirty or whether she wanted to wash them because they were likely to spread disease or contamination. The attribution of meaning makes all the difference. Another point that arose was whether, if she worked too hard in a session, it might result in some 'rebound' effect on the following day. This indeed seemed to happen and the likelihood of such a rebound was taken into account in session planning.

The counsellor should try to stay with the client in the situation until she reports changes in belief ratings. Bearing in mind that belief ratings sometimes go up during sessions, this can take some time. This argues for relatively conservative targets for each session. It is also useful to prepare the client for the fact that the counsellor may not always be able to stay with the client until they have become completely calm. Such a discussion can include strategies that the client might employ if this happens. Each experiment should be followed by a discussion about the extent to which the client continues to hold OCD beliefs.

It is important that the counsellor encourages the client to keep working on these situations between sessions. Marking out specific tasks can make very pertinent homework assignments, though both parties should bear in mind that doing the tasks with a counsellor present as a 'safety factor' is usually easier than doing them alone. Another possibility is to work using a 'buddy' to help. The counsellor may agree to see such a 'buddy' to explain various aspects of counselling and to try to ensure that everyone is working to the same script. It is also important not to get drawn into over-ambitious goals. The aim should not be to eliminate all problems but to foster a more self-efficacious way of dealing with these problems. From this perspective, it is unlikely that all the situations on the list will be mastered. It is hard, for example, to imagine feeling cool about handling a dead animal!

It might be helpful for counsellors to admit that we sometimes find it difficult to stay with some of the experiments. As Steketee (1999a) also admits, this work can be hard and quite boring at times, and sometimes clients will feel that we enjoy watching them suffer. The therapist has to walk a careful line between holding the client to task and insisting on effort, and respecting the client's right to do it at his or her own speed.

Mindfulness and attentional strategies

As well as behavioural experiments, cognitive restructuring and exposure methods, attentional strategies have proved helpful to many OCD clients. Wells (1997) has produced consistent work pointing out that changing the attention paid to negative cognitions can be as fruitful as changing the content of them. Intrusive worries, such as those occurring in OCD, can be helped by mindfulness strategies (Kabat-Zinn, 1990, 1994). This involves trying to develop detached contemplation of one's thoughts, somewhat like that of meditation. This may involve developing a more relaxed state of mind and using metaphorical ways of processing thoughts, such as regarding them as leaves floating by on a river. Wells has described this as both a worry postponement strategy and as a 'letting go' of the ruminative element of worry. The client is encouraged to 'allow the intrusions to occupy their own space without engaging with them' (1997: 250). A more consciously intentional strategy is that of the worry decision tree, (Butler and Hope, 1995) described in relation to GAD in Chapter 8. It can also be similarly used with OCD intrusions. In response to each obsessive thought, the client is asked to consider two alternatives with different outcomes (Norma Morrison, personal communication) and make an active choice between the two.

When I have an intrusive thought, 'Have I really locked the doors?':

1. I can choose to act on it, by going to check one more time: this will lead to short-term lowering of anxiety, but a long-term increase in anxiety: I am just responding to the anxiety which keeps my OCD going.
2. I can choose to ignore the thought by letting it go. This will mean I will feel very anxious for a short time, and many more anxious thoughts and doubts will creep into my mind, but in the long term my anxiety will go down and help to overcome my OCD. I can also test to see whether it matters if I checked the locks again.

This way, the client is taking active control over the thoughts, and making a choice about how to respond, rather than automatically responding in a compulsive way.

Dealing with other life factors

Some of the key distortions in OCD are linked to the likelihood of bad things happening and the personal sense of responsibility for those bad things. Any kind of life change or stress is likely to be part of the general precipitating conditions that bring on OCD symptoms. It is therefore often helpful when all these themes can be woven together.

Sally was a single woman who, from time to time, struggled with feeling alone. Some of her friends had gone to live with partners and this resulted in her seeing less of them. One of the distressing feelings that she had was of being 'left without support and alone with her obsessions'. This feeling was sometimes sharpened by the fact that the therapist visited her at home for some of the sessions. This issue needed to be acknowledged and worked through because of both its transferential effect on the therapeutic relationship and the therapeutic need to explore potential sources of social support.

Many clients with OCD have spent years locked into their compulsions to the exclusion of other aspects of life. OCD can become a full-time occupation. For clients with severe OCD, their time may be dominated by the need to collect litter off the streets, clean their houses for ten hours a day, or never have contact with other people in case of contamination. It can be helpful for the client to begin to develop ideas about what life would be like without the OCD and how they would fill their time when without their compulsions. The client then sets small manageable goals towards developing a different life (Salkovskis et al., 1998). For some clients, OCD may evolve as a way of avoiding tackling other difficulties in life, and without the compulsions the client may find other significant problems emerging. Working with clients with OCD is often a long process, involving re-formulation of the problems as counselling proceeds. We may need to use other treatment and support services to encourage clients back into life.

Effectiveness of Counselling with Obsessive Compulsive Problems

There are several measures with which the effectiveness of counselling with OCD can be assessed. The Yale-Brown Obsessive Compulsive Scale (Y-BOCS) measures all the main dimensions of OCD and has been shown to be valid and reliable. A useable copy is available in Steketee's client manual (Steketee, 1999b). For some measures used in cognitive therapy, such as the Beck Depression Inventory, it is recommended that the measure is taken regularly at every session. With OCD, repeated measures can become a source of obsessions, and Steketee (1999a) recommends that Y-BOCS be used only at the start and end of therapy. A reasonable therapeutic aim would be to try to halve the scores during 12–20 sessions of counselling.

Several research reviews have been completed on the effectiveness of therapy with OCD (van Balkom et al., 1994; Abramowitz, 1997). These studies indicate that exposure-based treatment is effective with OCD, not only in reducing symptoms but in ensuring that gains in therapy are maintained up to two years later. However, Salkovskis and Kirk (1997) point out that when refusal and drop-out is taken into account, the average rate of positive outcome drops to about 50 per cent. Some studies (Emmelkamp and Beens, 1991; Freeston et al., 1997) have found that cognitive therapy is also effective with OCD. However, cognitive models of OCD are still developing and there is emerging evidence that the newer models based on countering responsibility beliefs and metacognitive aspects of OCD will prove to be even more effective (Salkovskis et al., 1998; Freeston and Ladouceur, 1999; Salkovskis, 1999; Whittal and McLean, 1999).

Appendix
Books and Self-Help Organisations

Books

Flying? No fear! by Adrian Akers-Douglas and George Georgiou. Published by Summersdale, 2000.

Living with Fear by Isaac M. Marks. Published by McGraw-Hill, New Edition, 2001.

Manage your Mind by Gillian Butler and Tony Hope. Published by Oxford University Press, 1995.

Mind over Mood. A Cognitive Therapy Treatment Manual by Dennis Greenberger and Christine Padesky. Published by Guilford Press, 1995.

Overcoming Anxiety by Helen Kennerley. Published by Robinson, 1997.

Overcoming Depression by Paul Gilbert. Published by Robinson, 2000.

Overcoming Depression: A Five Areas Approach by Christopher Williams. Published by Arnold, 2001.

Overcoming Low Self Esteem by Melanie Fennell. Published by Robinson, 1999.

Overcoming Panic by Derrick Silove and Vijaya Manicavasagar. Published by Robinson, 1997.

Overcoming Shyness and Social Phobia: A Step by Step Guide by Ronald M. Rapee. Published by Jason Aronson, 1998.

Overcoming Social Anxiety and Shyness by Gillian Butler. Published by Robinson, 1999.

Overcoming Traumatic Stress by Claudia Herbert and Ann Wetmore. Published by Robinson, 1999.

Phobias: Fighting the Fear by Helen Saul. Published by Harper Collins, 2001.

Take the Fear out of Flying by Maurice Yeffé. Published by Robinson Publications, 2000.

The Feeling Good Handbook (revised edition) by David Burns. Published by Penguin, 1999.

Booklets published by Oxford Cognitive Therapy Centre

- *Managing Anxiety: A Users' Manual*
- *Overcoming Social Anxiety*
- *Understanding Panic*
- *Understanding Health Anxiety*
- *Obsessive Compulsive Disorder*
- *Managing Depression*

- *How to Relax*
- *Understanding your Reactions to Trauma*
- *Overcoming Phobias*

These booklets are available from OCTC, Department of Psychology, Warneford Hospital, Headington, Oxford OX3 7JX.
Tel: 01865 223986
Web site: www.octc.co.uk

Self-Help Organisations

No Panic: self-help organisation for anxiety, including panic, OCD and phobias.
Address: 93 Brands Farm Way, Randlay, Telford, Shropshire, TF3 2JQ.
Tel: 01952 590545
Fax: 01952 270962
Web site: www.no-panic.co.uk

Triumph Over Phobia: a network of self-help groups using behaviour therapy to help overcome phobias.
Address: TOP U.K., PO Box 1831, Bath BA2 4YW
Tel: 01225 330353
Web site: www.triumphoverphobia.com

National Phobics Society: help for many forms of anxiety and phobias.
Address: Zion Community Resource Centre, 339 Stretford Road, Hulme, Manchester, M15 4ZY
Tel: 0870 7700456 e-mail: natphob.soc@good.co.uk
Web site: www.phobics-society.org.uk

Dental anxiety web sites

www.dentalphobia.co.uk
www.beyondfear.org

Fear of flying web site

www.flywithoutfear.co.uk

References

Abramowitz, F.S. (1997) 'Effectiveness of psychological and pharmacological treatments for obsessive compulsive disorder: a quantitative review', *Journal of Consulting and Clinical Psychology*, 65: 44–52.

Alford, B.A. and Beck, A.T. (1997) *The Integrative Power of Cognitive Therapy*. New York: Guilford Press.

Antony, M.M. and Barlow, D. (1998) 'Specific phobia', in V.E. Caballo (ed.), *International Handbook of Cognitive Behavioural Treatments for Psychological Disorders*. Oxford: Pergamon/Elsevier Science Ltd, pp. 1–22.

APA (2000) *Diagnostic and Statistical Manual of Mental Disorders: 4th edition text revision*. Washington, DC: American Psychiatric Association.

Arnz, A. and van de Hout, M. (1996) 'Psychological treatment of panic disorder without agoraphobia: cognitive therapy versus applied relaxation', *Behaviour Research and Therapy*, 34: 113–21.

Astin, J.A. (1997) 'Stress reduction through mindfulness mediation. Effects on psychological symptomatology, sense of control and spiritual experiences', *Psychotherapy and Psychosomatics*, 66 (2): 97–106.

Baines, K.M. and Wills, F.R. (2001) 'Challenging obsessive thoughts and compulsive behaviours within a collaborative counselling relationship'. Paper presented at the British Association for Counselling and Psychotherapy Research Conference, Bristol, 19 May.

Barlow, D.H., Esler, J.L. and Vitali, B.A. (1997) 'Psychosocial treatments for panic disorder, phobias and generalised anxiety disorder', in P.E. Nathan and J.M. Gormon (eds), *A Guide to Treatments that Work*. New York: Oxford University Press, pp. 288–318.

Barsky, A.J. and Wyshak, G. (1990) 'Hypochondriasis and somatosensory amplification', *British Journal of Psychiatry*, 157: 404–409.

Barsky, A.J., Wool, C., Barnett, M.C. and Cleart, P.D. (1994) 'Histories of childhood trauma in adult hypochondriacal patients', *American Journal of Psychiatry*, 151: 397–401.

Bateman, A.W. (2000) 'Integration in psychotherapy: an evolving reality in personality disorder', *British Journal of Psychotherapy*, 17 (2): 147–56.

Beck, A.T. (1976) *Cognitive Therapy and the Emotional Disorders*. New York: International Universities Press.

Beck, A.T. (1991) 'Cognitive therapy: a 30-year retrospective', *American Psychologist* (April): 368–75.

Beck, A.T. and Steer, R.A. (1987) *Manual for the Revised Beck Depression Inventory*. San Antonio, TX: Psychological Corporation.

Beck, A.T., Emery, G. with Greenberg, R.L. (1985) *Anxiety Disorders and Phobias. A Cognitive Perspective.* New York: Basic Books.

Beck, A.T., Freeman, A. and Associates (1990) *Cognitive Therapy of Personality Disorders.* New York: Guilford Press.

Beck, A.T., Epstein, M., Brown, G. and Steer, R.A. (1988) 'An inventory for measuring clinical anxiety: psychometric properties', *Journal of Consulting and Clinical Psychology,* 56: 893–97.

Beck, A.T., Rush, A.J., Shaw, B.F. and Emery, G. (1979) *Cognitive Therapy of Depression.* New York: Guilford Press.

Beck, A.T., Weissman, A., Lester, D. and Trexler, L. (1974) 'The measurement of pessimism: the hopelessness scale', *Journal of Consulting and Clinical Psychology,* 42 (16): 861–5.

Beck, A.T., Sokol, L., Clark, D.A., Berchick, B. and Wright, F. (1992) 'Focused cognitive therapy for panic disorder: a crossover design and one year follow up', *American Journal of Psychiatry,* 147: 778–83.

Beck, J. (1995) *Cognitive Therapy: Basics and Beyond.* New York: Guilford Press.

Bedi, N., Chilvers, C., Churchill, R., Dewey, M., Duggan, C., Fielding, K., Gretton, V., Miller, P., Harrison, G. and Williams, I. (2000) 'Assessing effectiveness of treatment of depression in primary care', *British Journal of Psychiatry,* 177: 312–18.

Bögels, S.M., Mulkens, S. and de Jong, P.J. (1997) 'Task concentration training and fear of blushing', *Clinical Psychology and Psychotherapy,* 4: 251–8.

Bor, R., Parker, J. and Papadopoulos, L. (2000) 'Psychological treatment of a fear of flying', *Counselling Psychology Review,* 15 (2): 13–17.

Bor, R., Parker, J. and Papadopoulos, L. (2001) 'Brief solution-focused initial treatment sessions for clients with a fear of flying', *Counselling Psychology Review,* 16 (4): 32–40.

Borkovec, T.D. and Inz, J. (1990) 'The nature of worry in generalised anxiety disorder: a predominance of thought activity', *Behaviour Research and Therapy,* 28: 153–8.

Borkovec, T.D., Abel, J.L. and Newman, H. (1995) 'Effects of psychotherapy on co-morbid conditions in generalised anxiety disorder', *Journal of Consulting and Clinical Psychology,* 63: 479–83.

Botella, C. and García-Palacios, A. (1999) 'The possibility of reducing therapist contact and total length of therapy in the treatment of panic disorder', *Behavioural and Cognitive Psychotherapy,* 27 (3): 231–47.

Boulenger, J., Fournier, M., Rosales, D. and Lavallée, Y. (1997) 'Mixed anxiety and depression: from theory to practice', *Journal of Clinical Psychiatry,* 58: 27–34.

Bouman, T.K. and Visser, S. (1998) 'Cognitive and behavioural treatment of hypochondriasis', *Psychotherapy and Psychosomatics,* 67: 214–221.

Bourne, E.J. (1990) *The Anxiety and Phobia Workbook.* Oakland, CA: New Harbinger.

Bower, P., Byford, S., Sibbald, B., Ward, E., King, M., Lloyd, M. and Gabbay, M. (2000) 'Randomised controlled trial of non-directive counselling, cognitive behaviour therapy, and usual general practitioner care for patients with depression. II. Cost effectiveness', *British Medical Journal,* 321: 1389–92.

Bowlby, J. (1969) *Attachment and Loss,* Vol. 1: *Attachment.* New York: Basic Books.

Brewin, C.R. (1996) 'Theoretical foundations of cognitive-behavioural therapy for anxiety and depression', *Annual Review of Psychology,* 47: 33–57.

Brown, J.S.L., Cochrane, R. and Hancox, T. (2000) 'Large-scale health promotion stress workshops for the general public: a controlled evaluation', *Behavioural and Cognitive Psychotherapy*, 28 (2): 139–51.

Brown, T.A. and Barlow, D.H. (1992) 'Co-morbidity amongst anxiety disorders: implications for treatment and DSM-IV', *Journal of Consulting and Clinical Psychology*, 60: 835–44.

Burns, D. (1999) *The Feeling Good Handbook*, rev. edn. London: Penguin.

Burns, D. and Auerbach, A. (1996) 'Therapeutic empathy in cognitive-behavioural therapy: does it really make a difference?' in P. Salkovskis (ed.), *Frontiers of Cognitive Therapy*. New York: Guilford Press, pp. 135–64.

Burns, D.D. and Spangler, D.L. (2000) 'Does psychotherapy homework lead to improvements in depression in cognitive-behavioural therapy or does improvement lead to increased homework compliance?' *Journal of Consulting and Clinical Psychology*, 68 (1): 46–56.

Butler, G. (1994) 'Treatment of worry in generalised anxiety disorder', in G. Davey and F. Tallis (eds), *Worrying: Perspectives on Theory, Assessment and Treatment*. Chichester: Wiley.

Butler, G. (1998) 'Clinical formulation', in A.S. Bellack and M. Hersen (eds), *Comprehensive Clinical Psychology*, vol. 6. Oxford: Pergamon, pp. 1–24.

Butler, G. (1999) *Overcoming Social Anxiety and Shyness*. London: Robinson Publishing.

Butler, G. and Hope, T. (1995) *Manage Your Mind: The Mental Fitness Guide*. Oxford: Oxford University Press.

Butler, G., Wells, A. and Dewick, H. (1995) 'Differential effects of worry and imagery after exposure to a stressful stimulus: a pilot study', *Behavioural and Cognitive Psychotherapy*, 23: 45–56.

Cartledge, P. (2001) *The Greeks*. London: BBC Worldwide.

Casement, P. (1985) *On Learning from the Patient*. London: Tavistock.

Chambless, D.L. and Hope, D.A. (1996) 'Cognitive approaches to the psychopathology and treatment of social phobia', in P. Salkovskis (ed.), *Frontiers of Cognitive Therapy*. New York: Guilford, pp. 345–82.

Chambless, D.L., Caputo, G.C., Bright, P. and Gallagher, R. (1984) 'Assessment of fear of fear in agoraphobics: the Body Sensations Questionnaire and the Agoraphobic Cognitions Questionnaire', *Journal of Consulting and Clinical Psychology*, 52: 1090–7.

Chapman, H.R. and Kirby-Turner, N.C. (1999) 'Dental fear in children. A proposed model', *British Dental Journal*, 187: 408–12.

Clark, D.M. (1986) 'A cognitive approach to panic', *Behaviour Research and Therapy*, 24: 461–70.

Clark, D.M. (1988) 'A cognitive model of panic', in. S. Rachman and J. Maser (eds), *Panic: Psychological Perspectives*. Hillsdale, NJ: Erlbaum.

Clark, D.M. (1996) 'Panic disorder: from theory to therapy', in P. Salkovskis (ed.), *Frontiers of Cognitive Therapy*. New York: Guilford, pp. 318–44.

Clark, D.M. (1997) 'Panic disorder and social phobia', in D.M. Clark and C.G. Fairburn (eds), *Science and Practice of Cognitive Behaviour Therapy*. Oxford: Oxford University Press, pp. 119–54.

Clark, D.M. (1999a) 'Anxiety disorders: why they persist and how to treat them', *Behaviour Research and Therapy*, 37: S5–S27.

Clark, D.M. (1999b) 'Implementing a new cognitive treatment for social phobia'. Paper presented at the Annual Conference of the British Association for Behavioural and Cognitive Psychotherapies, Bristol.

Clark, D.M. and Fairburn, C.G. (eds) (1997) *Science and Practice of Cognitive Behaviour Therapy*. Oxford: Oxford University Press.

Clark, D.M. and Wells, A. (1995) 'A cognitive model of social phobia', in R. Heimberg, M. Liebowitz, D.A. Hope and F.R. Schneier (eds), *Social Phobia: Diagnosis, Assessment and Treatment*. New York: Guilford Press.

Clark, D.M., Salkovskis, P.M., Hackmann, A., Wells, A. and Gelder, M. (1999) 'Brief cognitive therapy for panic disorder: a randomised controlled trial', *Journal of Consulting and Clinical Psychology*, 67: 583–9.

Clark, D.M, Salkovskis, P.M., Hackmann, A., Middleton, H., Anastasiades, P. and Gelder, M. (1994) 'A comparison of cognitive therapy, applied relaxation and imipramine in the treatment of panic disorder', *British Journal of Psychiatry*, 164: 759–69.

Clark, D.M, Salkovskis, P.M., Hackmann, A., Wells, A., Fennell, M., Ludgate, J., Ahmad, S., Richards, H.C. and Gelder, M. (1998) 'Two psychological treatments for hypochondriasis: a randomised controlled trial', *British Journal of Psychiatry*, 173: 218–25.

Corrie, S. (2002) 'The role of the therapeutic relationship in promoting psychological change: a cognitive-behavioural perspective', *Counselling Psychology Review*, 17 (2): 23–31.

Cottraux, J., Note, I., Albuisson, E., Yao, S.N., Note, B., Mollard, E., Bonasse, F., Jalenques, I., Guerin, J. and Coudert, A.J. (2000) 'Cognitive behaviour therapy versus supportive therapy in social phobia: a randomised controlled trial', *Psychotherapy and Psychosomatics*, 69 (3): 137–46.

Craske, M.G. and Rowe, M.K. (1997) 'A comparison of behavioural and cognitive treatments of phobias', in G.C.L. Davey (ed.), *Phobias: A Handbook of Theory, Research and Treatment*. Chichester: Wiley, pp. 247–80.

Curtis, G.C., Magee, W.J., Eaton, W.W., Wittchen, H.-U. and Kessler, L.G. (1998) 'Specific fears and phobias: epidemiology and classification', *British Journal of Psychiatry*, 173: 212–17.

Davey, G.C.L. (1997) *Phobias: A Handbook of Theory, Research and Treatment*. Chichester: Wiley.

Davidson, K.M. (2000) *Cognitive Therapy for Personality Disorders: A Guide for Therapists*. New York: Butterworth-Heinemann.

Department of Health (2001) *Treatment Choice in Psychological Therapies and Counselling. Evidence Based Clinical Practice Guideline*. London: Department of Health.

DeRubeis, R.J. and Crits-Christoph, P. (1998) 'Empirically supported individual and group psychological treatments for adult mental disorders', *Journal of Consulting and Clinical Psychology*, 66 (1): 37–52.

Dryden, W. (1987) *Counselling Individuals: A Rational Emotive Approach*. London: Whurr.

Dryden, W. (1998) *Developing Self Acceptance. A Brief, Educational, Small Group Approach*. Chichester: Wiley.

Dryden, W. and Feltham, C. (1994) *Developing the Practice of Counselling*. London: Sage.

Dugas, M.J., Letarte, H., Rhéaume, J., Freeston, M.H. and Ladouceur, R. (1995) 'Worry and problem solving: evidence of a special relationship', *Cognitive Therapy and Research*, 19: 109–20.

Durham, R.C., Fisher, P.L., Trevling, L.R., Hau, C.M., Richard, K. and Stewart, J.B. (1999) 'One year follow-up of cognitive therapy, analytic psychotherapy and anxiety management training for generalised anxiety disorder: symptom change, medication usage and attitudes in treatment', *Behavioural and Cognitive Psychotherapy*, 27 (1): 19–36.

Edelmann, R.J. (1990) 'Chronic blushing, self-consciousness and social anxiety', *Journal of Psychopathology and Behavioural Assessment*, 12: 119–27.

Edwards, D.J.A. (1990) 'Cognitive therapy and the restructuring of early memories through guided imagery', *Journal of Cognitive Psychotherapy: An International Quarterly*, 4 (1): 33–50.

Egan, G. (2002) *The Skilled Helper*, 7th edn. Pacific Grove, CA: Brookes/Cole.

Ehlers, A. (1995) 'A one year prospective study of panic attacks: clinical course and factors associated with maintenance', *Behaviour Research and Therapy*, 31: 269–78.

Ehlers, A. and Breuer, P. (1992) 'Increased cardiac awareness in panic disorder', *Journal of Abnormal Psychology*, 101: 371–82.

Emmelkamp, P.M.G. and Beens, I. (1991) 'Cognitive therapy with obsessive compulsive disorder: a comparative evaluation', *Behavior Research and Therapy*, 29: 292–300.

Emmelkamp, P.M.G., Bouman, T.K. and Blaauw, E. (1994) 'Individualized versus standardised therapy: a comparative evaluation with obsessive compulsive patients', *Clinical Psychology and Psychotherapy*, 1: 95–100.

Epstein, S. (1994) 'The integration of the cognitive and psychodynamic unconscious', *American Psychologist*, 49 (8): 709–24.

Epstein, S. (1998) *Constructive Thinking: The Key to Emotional Intelligence*. Westport, CT: Praeger Publishing.

Eysenck, M. (1997) *Anxiety and Emotion: A Unified Theory*. Hove: Psychology Press.

Fennell, M.J.V. (1989) 'Depression', in K. Hawton, P.M. Salkovskis, J. Kirk and D.M. Clark (eds), *Cognitive Behaviour Therapy for Psychiatric Problems*. Oxford: Oxford University Press, pp. 169–234.

Fennell, M.J.V. (1998) 'Low self-esteem', in N. Tarrier, A. Wells and G. Haddock (eds), *Treating Complex Cases*. Chichester: Wiley, pp. 217–40.

Fennell, M.J.V. (1999) *Overcoming Low Self-Esteem*. London: Robinson Books.

Fisher, P.L. and Durham, R.C. (1999) 'Recovering rates in generalized anxiety disorder following psychological therapy', *Psychological Medicine*, 29: 1425–34.

Foa, E.B. and Kozak, M.J. (1991) 'Emotional processing: theory, research and clinical implications', in J.D. Safran and L.S. Greenberg (eds), *Emotion, Psychotherapy and Change*. New York: Guilford Press, pp. 21–49.

Freeston, M.H. and Ladouceur, R. (1999) 'Exposure and response prevention for obsessive thoughts', *Cognitive Behavioural Practice*, 6 (4): 362–82.

Freeston, M.H., Rhéaume, J., Letarte, H., Dugas, M.J. and Ladouceur, R. (1994) 'Why do people worry?' *Personality and Individual Differences*, 17 (6): 791–802.

Freeston, M.H., Ladouceur, R., Gagnon, F., Thibodeau, N., Letarte, H. and Bujold, A. (1997) 'Cognitive-behavioural treatment of obsessive thoughts: a controlled study', *Journal of Consulting and Clinical Psychology*, 65 (3): 405–13.

Gendlin, E. (1981) *Focusing*. New York: Everest House.

Goldstein, A.J. and Stainback, B. (1991) *Overcoming Agoraphobia: Conquering Fear of the Outside World*. New York: Viking Penguin.

Gould, R.A. and Clum, G.A. (1993) 'A meta-analysis of self help treatment approaches', *Clinical Psychology Review*, 13: 169–86.

Greenberger, D. and Padesky, C. (1995) *Mind over Mood*. New York: Guilford Press.

Guidano, V.F. and Liotti, G. (1983) *Cognitive Processes and Emotional Disorders*. New York: Guilford Press.

Guthrie, E. (1995) 'Treatment of functional somatic symptoms: psychodynamic treatment', in R. Mayou, C. Bass, and M. Sharpe (eds), *The Treatment of Functional Somatic Symptoms*. Oxford: Oxford University Press, pp. 144–60.

Hackmann, A. (1997) 'The transformation of meaning in cognitive therapy', in M. Power and C.R. Brewin (eds), *Transformation of Meaning in Psychological Therapies*. Chichester: Wiley, pp. 125–40.

Hackmann, A. (1998) 'Cognitive therapy with panic and agoraphobia: working with complex cases', in N. Tarrier, A. Wells and G. Haddock (eds), *Treating Complex Cases*. Chichester: Wiley, pp. 27–45.

Hackmann, A., Clark, D. and McManus, F. (2000) 'Recurrent images and early memories in social phobia', *Behaviour Research and Therapy*, 38: 601–10.

Hackmann, A., Surawy, C. and Clark, D. (1998) 'Seeing yourself through others' eyes: a study of spontaneously occurring images in social phobia', *Behavioural and Cognitive Psychotherapy*, 26 (1): 3–12.

Hailstorm, C. and McClure, N. (1998) *Anxiety and Depression: Your Questions Answered*. London: Churchill Livingstone.

Hammersley, D. (1995) *Counselling People on Prescribed Drugs*. London: Sage.

Harvey, H.I., Nelson, S.J., Lyons, R.A., Unwin, C., Monaghan, S. and Peters, T.J. (1998) 'A randomised controlled trial and economic evaluation of counselling in primary care', *British Journal of General Practice*, 48: 1043–8.

Harvey, J.M., Richards, J.C., Dziadoz, T. and Swindell, A. (1993) 'Misinterpretation of ambiguous stimuli in panic disorder', *Cognitive Therapy and Research*, 17: 235–48.

Hollon, S.D., DeRubeis, R.J. and Evans, M.D. (1996) 'Cognitive therapy in the treatment and prevention of depression', in P. Salkovskis (ed.), *Frontiers of Cognitive Therapy*. New York: Guilford Press, pp. 293–317.

Inskipp, F. and Proctor, B. (1999) 'Post-tribalism: a millennium gift for clients?' Keynote address given at the Annual Conference of the British Association for Counselling, University of Warwick, September.

Ivey, A.E., Ivey, M.B. and Simek-Downing, L. (1987) *Counselling and Psychotherapy: Integrating Skills, Theory and Practice*. Englewood Cliffs, NJ: Prentice Hall International.

James, I.A. (2001) 'Schema therapy: the next generation but should it carry a health warning?' *Behavioural and Cognitive Psychotherapy*, 29: 401–7.

Jenkins, J.R., Bebbington, P., Brugha, T.S., Farrell, M., Lewis, G. and Meltzer, H. (1998) 'The British psychiatric morbidity survey', *British Journal of Psychiatry*, 173: 4–7.

Kabat-Zinn, J. (1990) *Full Catastrophe Living*. New York: Bantam Doubleday Dell.

Kabat-Zinn, J. (1994) *Mindfulness Meditation for Everyday Life*. London: Piatkus.

Kabat-Zinn, J. (1995) *Wherever You Go, There You Are: Mindfulness Meditation in Everyday Life*. New York: Hypericon Books.

Kabat-Zinn, J., Massion, A.O., Kristeller, J., Peterson, L.G., Fletcher, K.E., Pbert, L., Lenderking, W.R. and Santorelli, S.F. (1992) 'Effectiveness of a mediation-based stress reduction program in the treatment of anxiety disorders', *American Journal of Psychiatry*, 149 (7): 936–43.

Kahan, M., Tanzer, J., Darvin, D. and Borer, F. (2000) 'Virtual reality-assisted cognitive behavioural treatment for fear of flying: acute treatment and follow up', *CyberPsychology and Behaviour*, 3 (3): 387–92.

Kendall, P.C. and Hammen, C. (1998) *Abnormal Psychology: Understanding Human Problems*, 2nd edn. Boston: Houghton Mifflin.

Kennerley, H. (1995) *Managing Anxiety: a Training Manual*, 2nd edn. Oxford: Oxford University Press.

Kennerley, H. (1997) *Overcoming Anxiety: a Self Help Guide using Cognitive Behavioural Techniques*. London: Robinson.

Layden, M.A., Newman, C.F., Freeman, A. and Morse, S.B. (1993) *Cognitive Therapy of Borderline Personality Disorder*. Boston: Allyn & Bacon.

Leahy, R.L. and Holland, S.J. (2000) *Treatment Plans and Interventions for Depression and Anxiety Disorders*. New York: Guilford Press.

Linehan, M. (1993a) *Cognitive Behavioural Treatment for Borderline Personality Disorder*. New York: Guilford Press.

Linehann, M. (1993b) *Skills Training Manual for Treating Borderline Personality Disorder*. New York: Guilford Press.

Liotti, G. (1991) 'Insecure attachment and agoraphobia', in C. Murray-Parkes, J. Stevenson-Hinde and P. Marris (eds), *Attachment across the Life Cycle*. London: Tavistock, pp. 216–33.

Marks, I.M. and Mathews, A.M. (1979) 'Brief standard self-rating for phobic patients', *Behaviour Research and Therapy*, 17: 263–7.

McManus, F., Clark, D.M. and Hackmann, A. (2000) 'Specificity of cognitive biases in social phobia and their role in recovery', *Behavioural and Cognitive Psychotherapy*, 28 (3): 201–10.

McNally, R.J. and Foa, E.B. (1987) 'Cognition and agoraphobia: bias in interpretation of threat', *Cognitive Therapy and Research*, 11: 567–81.

Mechanic, D. (1986) 'The concept of illness behaviour: culture, situation and personal predisposition', *Psychological Medicine*, 16: 1–7.

Mellings, T.M.B. and Alden, L.E. (2000) 'Cognitive processes in social anxiety: the effects of self focus, rumination and anticipatory processing', *Behaviour Research and Therapy*, 38: 243–57.

Mellor-Clark, J. (2000) *Counselling in primary care in the context of NHS quality agenda: the facts*. Rugby: British Association for Counselling and Psychotherapy.

Meyer, V. (1966) 'Modification of expectations in cases with obsessional rituals', *Behaviour Research and Therapy*, 4: 273–80.

Morrison, N. (2001) 'Group cognitive therapy: treatment of choice or sub-optimal option?' *Behavioural and Cognitive Psychotherapy*, 29 (3): 311–32.

Mulkens, S., Bögels, S.M. and de Jong, P.J. (1999) 'Attentional focus and fear of blushing: a case study', *Behavioural and Cognitive Psychotherapy*, 27: 153–64.

Murray, E. and Foote, F. (1979) 'The origins of fear of snakes', *Behaviour Research and Therapy*, 17: 489–93.

Noyes, R. (2000) 'Epidemiology of hypochondriasis', in D. Lipsitt and J. Starcevic (eds), *Hypochondriasis: Theory and Clinical Practice*. New York: Oxford University Press.

O'Brien, M. and Houston, G. (2000) *Integrative Therapy: A Practitioners' Guide*. London: Sage.

Obsessive Compulsive Cognitions Working Group (1997) 'Cognitive assessment of obsessive-compulsive disorder', *Behaviour Research and Therapy*, 35: 667–81.

Öst, L.G. (1997) 'Rapid treatment of specific phobias', in G.C.L. Davey (ed.), *Phobias: a Handbook of Theory, Research and Treatment*. Chichester: Wiley, pp. 228–46.

Öst, L.G. and Hellström, K. (1997) 'Blood-injury-injection phobia', in G.C.L. Davey (ed.), *Phobias: a Handbook of Theory, Research and Treatment*. Chichester: Wiley, pp. 63–80.

Öst, L.G. and Sterner, U. (1987) 'Applied tension: a specific behavioural treatment of blood phobia', *Behaviour Research and Therapy*, 25: 25–9.

Öst, L.G., Salkovskis, P. and Hellström, K. (1991) 'One session therapist-directed exposure versus self-exposure in the treatment of a spider phobia', *Behaviour Therapy*, 22: 407–22.

Öst, L.G, Alm, T., Brandberg, M. and Breitholtz, E. (2001) 'One versus five sessions of exposure and five sessions of cognitive therapy in the treatment of claustrophobia', *Behaviour Research and Therapy*, 39 (2): 167–83.

Padesky, C.A. (1993) 'Socratic questioning: changing minds or guiding discovery?' Keynote address to European Congress of Behavioural and Cognitive Therapies, London.

Padesky, C.A. (1994) 'Schema change processes in cognitive therapy', *Clinical Psychology and Psychotherapy*, 1 (5): 267–78.

Padesky, C.A. (1995) 'Cognitive therapy of anxiety: key treatment principles and methods'. Audiotape published by the Center for Cognitive Therapy, Newport Beach, CA.

Padesky, C.A. and Greenberger, D. (1995) *Clinicians Guide to Mind over Mood*. New York: Guilford Press.

Padesky, C.A. and Mooney, K. (1990) 'Clinical tip. Presenting the cognitive model to clients', *International Cognitive Therapy Newsletter*, 6: 13–14.

Padesky, C.A. and Mooney, K.A. (1998) 'Between two minds: the transformational power of underlying assumptions'. Workshop given at 28th Congress of the European Association for Behavioural and Cognitive Therapies, Cork, Eire, 8th September.

Padesky, C.A. and Mooney, K. (2000) 'Applying client creativity to recurrent problems'. Workshop, Centre for Cognitive Therapy.

Palmer, S. and Dryden, W. (1995) *Counselling for Stress Problems*. London: Sage.

Palmer, S., Bor, R. and Josse, J. (2000) 'A self help toolkit for conquering fears and anxieties about flying', *Counselling Psychology Review*, 15 (2): 18–29.

Papageorgiou, C. and Wells, A. (1998) 'Effects of attention training on hypochondriasis. A brief case series', *Psychological Medicine*, 28 (1): 193–200.

Perczel-Forintos, D. and Hackmann, A. (1999) 'Transformation of meaning and its effects on cognitive behavioural treatment of an injection phobia', *Behavioural and Cognitive Psychotherapy*, 27 (4): 369–75.

Persons, J.B. (1989) *Cognitive Therapy in Practice. A Case Formulation Approach*. New York: W.W. Norton & Co.

Pilgrim, D. (2000) 'Psychiatric diagnosis: more questions than answers', *The Psychologist*, 13: 302–5.

Poulton, R., Davies, S., Menzies, R.G., Langley, J.D. and de Silva, P.A. (1998) 'Evidence for a non-associative model of the acquisition of a fear of heights', *Behaviour Research and Therapy*, 36 (5): 537–44.

Rachman, S. (1997) *Anxiety*. Hove: Taylor & Francis.

Rachman, S. and de Silva, P. (1978) 'Abnormal and normal obsessions', *Behaviour Research and Therapy*, 16: 233–48.

Rachman, S.J. and Lopatka, C. (1986) 'A simple method for determining the functional independence of two or more fears', *Behaviour Research and Therapy*, 24: 661–4.

Ricketts, T. and Donohoe, G. (2000) 'Anxiety and panic', in C. Feltham and I. Horton (eds), *Handbook of Counselling and Psychotherapy*. London: Sage, pp. 431–9.

Robson, P. (1989) 'Development of a new self-report questionnaire to measure self esteem', *Psychological Medicine*, 19: 513–18.

Roth, A. and Fonagy, P. (1996) *What Works for Whom? A Critical Review of Psychotherapy*. New York: Guilford Press.

Rowan, J. (2000) 'Back to basics: two kinds of therapy', *Counselling*, 12 (2): 76–8.

Safran, J.D. and Segal Z.V. (1990) *Interpersonal Processes in Cognitive Therapy*. New York: Basic Books.

Salkovskis, P.M. (1989) 'Cognitive-behavioural factors and the persistence of intrusive thoughts in obsessive problems', *Behaviour Research and Therapy*, 23: 571–83.

Salkovskis, P.M. (1991) 'The importance of behaviour in the maintenance of panic and anxiety: a cognitive account', *Behavioural Psychotherapy*, 19: 6–19.

Salkovskis, P. (1996a) 'The cognitive approach to anxiety: threat beliefs, safety-seeking behaviour, and the special case of health anxiety and obsessions', in:P. Salkovskis (ed.), *Frontiers of Cognitive Therapy*. New York: Guildford, pp. 48–74.

Salkovskis, P.M. (1996b) 'Avoidance behaviour is motivated by threat beliefs: a possible resolution of the cognition–behaviour debate', in P.M. Salkovskis (ed.), *Trends in Cognitive and Behavioural Therapies*. New York: Wiley, pp. 25–41.

Salkovskis, P.M. (1999) 'Understanding and treating obsessive-compulsive disorder', *Behaviour Research and Therapy*, 37: S29–S52.

Salkovskis, P. and Bass, C. (1997) 'Hypochondriasis', in D.M. Clark and C.G. Fairburn (eds), *Science and Practice of Cognitive Behaviour Therapy*. Oxford: Oxford University Press, pp. 313–39.

Salkovskis, P.M. and Harrison, J. (1984) 'Abnormal and normal obsessions: a replication', *Behaviour Research and Therapy*, 22: 549–52.

Salkovskis, P.M. and Kirk, J. (1997) 'Obsessive compulsive disorder', in D.M. Clark and C. Fairburn (eds), *Science and Practice of Cognitive Behaviour Therapy*. Oxford: Oxford University Press.

Salkovskis, P., Forrester, E., Richards, H.C. and Morrison, N. (1998) 'The devil is in the detail: conceptualizing and treating obsessional problems', in N. Tarrier, A. Wells and G. Haddock (eds), *Treating Complex Cases*. Chichester: Wiley, pp. 46–80.

Salkovskis, P.M., Shafran, R., Rachman, S. and Freeston, M.H. (1999) 'Multiple pathways to inflated responsibility beliefs in obsessional problems: possible origins and implications', *Behaviour Research and Therapy*, 37: 1055–72.

Salkovskis, P.M., Clark, D.M., Hackmann, A., Wells, A. and Gelder, M. (1997) 'An experimental investigation of the role of safety-seeking behaviours in the maintenance of panic disorder with agoraphobia', *Behaviour Research and Therapy*, 37: 559–74.

Sanders, D. (1996) *Counselling for Psychosomatic Problems*. London: Sage.

Sanders, D. (2000) 'Psychosomatic problems', in C. Feltham and I. Horton (eds), *Textbook of Counselling and Psychotherapy*. London: Sage.

Sanders, D. and Wills, F. (1999) 'The relationship in cognitive therapy', in Colin Feltham (ed.), *Understanding the Counselling Relationship*. London: Sage, pp. 120–38.

Saul, H. (2001) *Phobias: Fighting the Fear*. London: HarperCollins.

Schulte, D. (1997) 'Behavioural analysis: does it matter?' *Behavioural and Cognitive Psychotherapy*, 25: 231–49.

Schulte, D., Künzel, R., Pepping, G. and Schulte-Bahrenberg, T. (1992) 'Tailor made versus standardized therapy of phobic patients', *Behaviour Research and Therapy*, 14: 67–92.

Scott, M.J. and Stradling, S.G. (1998) *Brief Group Psychotherapy. Integrating Individual and Group Cognitive Behavioural Approaches.* Chichester: Wiley.

Scott, M.J. and Stradling, S.G. (2000) *Counselling for Post-Traumatic Stress Disorder*, 2nd edn. London: Sage.

Segal, Z.V., Williams, J.M.G. and Teasdale, J.D. (2001) *Mindfulness-Based Cognitive Therapy for Depression.* New York: Guilford Press.

Sequeira, H. and van Scoyoc, S. (2001) 'Should counselling psychologists oppose the use of DSM-IV and testing?' *Counselling Psychology Review*, 16 (4): 44–8.

Slee, P.T. (1994) 'Situational and interpersonal correlates of anxiety associated with peer victimisation', *Child Psychiatry and Human Development*, 25 (2): 97–107.

Spielberger, C.D., Gorsuch, R.L., Lushene, R., Vagg, P.R. and Jacobs, G.A. (1983) *Manual for the State Trait Anxiety Inventory.* Palo Alto, CA: Consulting Psychology Press.

Steketee, G. (1999a) *Overcoming Obsessive Compulsive Disorder: Therapist Protocol.* Oakland, CA: New Harbinger.

Steketee, G. (1999b) *Overcoming Obsessive Compulsive Disorder: Client Protocol.* Oakland, CA: New Harbinger.

Stern, R. and Fernandez, M. (1991) 'Group cognitive and behavioural treatment of hypochondriasis', *British Medical Journal*, 303: 1229–30.

Stopa, L. and Clark, D.M (1993) 'Cognitive processes in social phobia', *Behaviour Research and Therapy*, 31: 255–67.

Stopa, L. and Clark, D. (2000) 'Social phobia and interpretation of social events', *Behaviour Research and Therapy*, 38: 273–83.

Strawbridge, S. and James, P. (2001) 'Issues relating to the use of psychiatric diagnostic categories in counselling psychology, counselling and psychotherapy: what do you think?' *Counselling Psychology Review*, 16: 4–6.

Stuart, S. and Noyes, R. (1999) 'Attachment and interpersonal relationships in somatisation', *Psychosomatics*, 40: 34–43.

Tallis, F. (1995) *Obsessive Compulsive Disorder: a Cognitive and Neurophysical Perspective.* Chichester: Wiley.

Tarrier, N. and Calam, R. (2002) 'New developments in cognitive behavioural case formulation: epidemiological, systematic and social context: an integrative approach', *Behavioural and Cognitive Psychotherapy*, 30 (3): 311–28.

Teasdale, J. (1999) 'Metacognition, mindfulness and the modification of mood disorders', *Clinical Psychology and Psychotherapy*, 6: 146–56.

Thorpe, S. and Salkovskis, P. (1995) 'Phobic beliefs: do cognitive factors play a role in specific phobias?' *Behaviour Research and Therapy*, 33: 805–16.

van Balkom, A.J.M., van Oppen, P., Vermeulen, A.W.A., van Dyck, R., Nauta, M.C.E. and Vorst, H.C.M. (1994) 'A meta-analysis of the treatment of obsessive compulsive disorder: a comparison of antidepressants, behaviour and cognitive therapy', *Clinical Psychology Review*, 14: 359–81.

Walk, R.D. and Gibson, E.J. (1961) 'A comparative and analytical study of visual depth perception', *Psychological Monographs*, 75 (519): 1–44.

Ward, E., King, M., Lloyd, M., Bower, P., Sibbald, B., Farrelly, S., Gabbay, M., Tarrier, N. and Addington-Hall, J. (2000) 'Randomised controlled trial of non-directive counselling, cognitive behaviour therapy, and usual general practitioner care for patients with depression. I. Clinical effectiveness', *British Medical Journal*, 321: 1383–8.

Warwick, H.M.C. (1992) 'Provision of appropriate and effective reassurance', *International Review of Psychiatry*, 4: 76–80.

Warwick, H.M.C. and Marks, I.M. (1988) 'Behavioural treatment of illness phobia and hypochondriasis: a pilot study of 17 cases', *British Journal of Psychiatry*, 152: 239–41.

Warwick, H.M.C. and Salkovskis, P.M. (1985) 'Reassurance', *British Medical Journal*, 290: 1028.

Warwick, H.M.C. and Salkovskis, P.M. (1989) 'Hypochondriasis', in J. Scott, J.M.C. Williams and A.T. Beck (eds), *Cognitive Therapy in Clinical Practice*. London: Croom Helm, pp. 78–102.

Warwick, H.M.C., Clark, D.M., Cobb, A.M. and Salkovskis, P.M. (1996) 'A controlled trial of cognitive behavioural treatment of hypochondriasis', *British Journal of Psychiatry*, 169: 189–95.

Watson, J.B. and Rayner, R. (1920) 'Conditioned emotional responses', *Journal of Experimental Psychology*, 3: 1–14.

Wegner, D.M. (1989) *White Bears and Other Unwanted Thoughts: Suppression, Obsession, and the Psychology of Mental Control*. New York: Guilford Press.

Wegner, D.M., Schneider, D.J., Carter, S.R. and White, T.L. (1987) 'Paradoxical effects of thought suppression', *Journal of Personality and Social Psychology*, 5: 5–13.

Weissman, M.M., Markowitz, J.C. and Klerman, G.L. (2000) *Comprehensive Guide to Interpersonal Psychotherapy*. New York: Basic Books.

Wells, A. (1995) 'Meta-cognition and worry: a cognitive model of generalised anxiety disorder', *Behavioural and Cognitive Psychotherapy*, 23: 301–20.

Wells, A. (1997) *Cognitive Therapy of Anxiety Disorders. A Practice Manual and Conceptual Guide*. Chichester: Wiley.

Wells, A. (1998) 'Cognitive therapy of social phobia', in N. Tarrier, A. Wells and G. Haddock (eds), *Treating Complex Cases*. Chichester: Wiley, pp. 1–26.

Wells, A. (2000) *Emotional Disorders and Metacognition*. Chichester: Wiley.

Wells, A. and Butler, G. (1997) 'Generalised anxiety disorder', in D.M. Clark and C.G. Fairburn (eds), *Science and Practice of Cognitive Behaviour Therapy*. Oxford: Oxford University Press, pp. 155–78.

Wells, A. and Hackmann, A. (1993) 'Imagery and core beliefs in health anxiety: content and origins', *Behavioural and Cognitive Psychotherapy*, 21 (3): 265–74.

Wells, A. and Matthews, G. (1994) *Attention and Emotion: A Clinical Perspective*. Hove: Lawrence Erlbaum.

Wells, A. and Morrison, T. (1994) 'Qualitative dimensions of normal worry and normal intrusive thoughts: a comparative study', *Behaviour Research and Therapy*, 32: 867–70.

Wells, A. and Papageorgiou, C. (1995) 'Worry and the incubation of intrusive images following stress', *Behaviour Research and Therapy*, 33: 579–83.

Wells, A. and Papageorgiou, C. (1998) 'Social phobia: effects of external attention on anxiety, negative beliefs and perspective taking', *Behaviour Therapy*, 29: 357–70.

Wells, A. and Papageorgiou, C. (1999) 'The observer perspective: biased imagery in social phobia, agoraphobia and blood/injury phobia', *Behaviour Research and Therapy*, 37: 653–8.

Wells, A. and Papageorgiou, C. (2001) 'Brief cognitive therapy for social phobia: a case series', *Behaviour Research and Therapy*, 39: 713–20.

Wells, A., Clark, D.M. and Ahmad, S. (1998) 'How do I look with my mind's eye?

Perspective taking in social phobic imagery', *Behaviour Research and Therapy*, 36: 631–4.

Wells, A., White, J. and Carter, K. (1997) 'Attention training: effects on anxiety and beliefs in panic and social phobia', *Clinical Psychology and Psychotherapy*, 4: 226–32.

White, J. (1998a) '"Stress control" large group therapy for generalised anxiety disorder: two year follow up', *Behavioural and Cognitive Psychotherapy*, 26 (3): 237–46.

White, J. (1998b) '"Stresspac": three year follow up of a controlled trial of a self help package for the anxiety disorders', *Behavioural and Cognitive Psychotherapy*, 26 (2): 133–41.

White, J. (2000) *Treating Anxiety and Stress. A Group Psycho-Educational Approach Using Brief CBT*. Chichester: Wiley.

White, J., Keenan, M. and Brooks, N. (1992) '"Stress Control": a controlled comparative investigation of large group therapy for generalised anxiety disorder', *Behavioural and Cognitive Psychotherapy*, 20: 97–114.

Whittal, M.L. and McLean, P.D. (1999) 'CBT for OCD: the rationale, protocol and challenges', *Cognitive and Behavioural Practice*, 6 (4): 383–96.

Williams, S.L. and Farbo, J. (1996) 'Cognitive and performance-based treatments for panic attacks in people with varying degrees of agoraphobic disability', *Behaviour Research and Therapy*, 34: 253–64.

Wills, F. (1997) 'Cognitive counselling: a down to earth and accessible therapy', in C. Sills (ed.), *Contracts in Counselling*. London: Sage.

Wills, F. (2002) *Accentuate the Positive: Putting Positive Data into Case Conceptualisations*. Departmental Research Paper, Social Studies, University of Wales College Newport.

Wills, F. and Sanders, D. (1997) *Cognitive Therapy: Transforming the Image*. London: Sage.

Wilson, G.T. (1996) 'Manual based treatments: the clinical application of research findings', *Behaviour Research and Therapy*, 34: 295–314.

Yalom, I.D. (1995) *Theory and Practice of Group Psychotherapy*, 4th edn. New York: Basic Books.

Young, J. and Behary, W.T. (1998) 'Schema-focused therapy for personality disorders', in N. Tarrier (ed.), *Cognitive Behaviour Therapy for Complex Cases*. Chichester: John Wiley & Sons, pp. 340–76.

Young, J.E. and Klosko, J.S. (1993) *Reinventing your Life*. New York: Dutton.

Zuercher-White, E. (1999) *Overcoming Panic Disorder and Agoraphobia: Therapist Protocol*. Oakland, CA: New Harbinger.

Index